GETTING IT RIGHT

GETTING IT
RIGHT

• • •

How

Working Mothers

Successfully

Take Up the

Challenge of Life,

Family, and Career

Laraine T. Zappert, Ph.D.

POCKET BOOKS
New York   London   Toronto   Sydney   Singapore

POCKET BOOKS, a division of Simon & Schuster, Inc.
1230 Avenue of the Americas, New York, NY 10020

ISBN: 0-671-04180-0

First Pocket Books hardcover printing February 2001

10   9   8   7   6   5   4   3   2   1

To my family

ACKNOWLEDGMENTS

The great use of life is to spend it for something that outlasts it.

—William James

No book can ever be considered the work of one author. Were it not for the hundreds of women whose experience has been distilled into the pages of this book, I would never have been able to accomplish my task. To all of them, I am extremely grateful. In addition, there are a number of people who have contributed very directly to this work, and I would like to thank them for the time and energy that they dedicated to ensuring its success.

Let me begin by saying that I would not be where I am today were it not for four faculty members who supported my work many years ago, and enabled me to accomplish what I set out to do in my life. Professors Lawrence K. Williams, Donald P. Hayes and William Foote Whyte of Cornell University and Dr. Mervin Freedman of the Wright Institute were and remain my mentors, and I am most grateful for their intelligent guidance and support.

My friends and my colleagues at Stanford, particularly and alphabetically, Dr. Orit Atzmon, Barbara Babcock, Dr. Martel Bryant, Ginger Case, Mary Cunha, Kelly Denton-Borhaug, Sally Dickson, Carole Dressler, Dr. Jean Eagleston, Marge Fellman, Jean Fetter, Dr. Cia Forman, Dr. Ivan Gendzel, Dr. Carlos Greaves, Dr. Katherine

Hellmuth, Gerri Hendrickson, Deborah Hindery, Susan Hoerger, Marilyn Hoskins, Sandra Hunter, Leah Kaplan, Dr. Gloria Kardong, Mark Kelman, Steve King, Maria Lopez, Dr. Elizabeth Mahler, Dr. Alejandro Martinez, George and Buffy Miller, Nicki Moffat, Dr. Celia Moreno, Dr. Mary Ann Norfleet, Virginia Pollard, Dr. Gail Prichard, Ann Richman, Dr. Alan Ringold, Linda Rosenblum, Inger Sagatun-Edwards, Elsa Salaverry, Terry Shepard, Myra Strober, Debra Thomas, Jessica Troy, Dr. Rick Van Rheenan and all the others who read, provided comments or just plain supported me in my work, to all of you, I am enormously grateful.

Special thanks to the past and current Deans of the Stanford University Graduate School of Business, Michael Spence and Robert Joss, respectively, for their support and encouragement of this project. Thanks particularly to Abbey Homans Wilder and Geri Gould of the GSB Alumni organization for allowing me the opportunity to survey their graduates, to Karen Melchior and Jo Conover for their help in designing the MBA questionnaire, and Tom Cooper and his colleagues at the Pacific Consulting Group for their help with the data analysis.

This book would not have been possible without the extraordinary efforts of my agent, Jillian Manus, who believed in this project from its inception and who had the vision to ensure its success. Similarly, I am deeply indebted to my editor, Emily Bestler, and her assistant, Kip Hakala, who championed this project and brought it to life.

As in every other aspect of my life, I could not have accomplished anything that I have without the love and extraordinary support of my family. This book was truly a family effort. From my daughter, came thoughtful insights and intelligent editing, along with an unwavering support and encouragement for my efforts. From my son, who with his good friend, Dan Shearn, spent many long summer afternoons doing my data processing and design, came the strong belief that this project would work, and the willingness to do everything he could to ensure its success. Finally, from my husband, who began helping me with data design thirty years ago, came all the traits that made him "the right partner" for this professional woman. This book is dedicated with love and gratitude to you all.

CONTENTS

Introduction

"I've always been pretty much able to accomplish whatever I've set my sights on. I did well in school, got an MBA from a top program, and I got the job I wanted when I graduated. I've done well since, and I made partner at my firm in record time. I even managed to find a husband along the way.

"But lately, I don't know. I can't seem to make it work anymore."

Silently, tears started to stream down Rebecca's face. This woman, a business school graduate who had been referred to me by a friend, went on to explain:

"Since I had the boys, I just don't have the drive or determination I used to have. I was doing okay with one child, even two was workable, but three kids has pushed me over the edge.

"Even with a nanny, and even with not traveling as much as I used to, I'm exhausted all the time. I'm feeling completely unmotivated at work and I'm not being a good mom. I have a supportive husband, but even he's losing patience with me.

"I don't know what's wrong with me. I'm just not coping."

Not coping? Three kids under 6 years of age and a full-time job, and you're not coping?

Although I was sorely tempted to challenge this young woman's definition of *coping*, clinical experience had taught me the virtue of just letting her talk. What unfolded was a tale too often told: the tale of a young, bright, successful professional woman who had done all the right things. A woman who had worked hard in school, who was successful in the professional world, and who managed to have a relationship and a family along the way. The proverbial "woman who had it all." And yet by her own admission, she felt like nothing so much as an abject failure. She described herself as mediocre at everything she was trying to do—she felt like a lousy manager, a second-rate wife, and an inadequate mother:

"I don't care about my job the way I should or the way I used to. Others say I do good work, but I know I'm coasting, and I'm disappointed in myself. A lot of the time I feel like I'm putting in a token effort. I just go in, do what I have to do, and leave.

"I don't know what's wrong with me. I'm stressed out and irritable all the time. I'm short tempered with the kids. I can't sleep, and I've gained weight. I'm a mess.

"My husband says he loves me, but I don't see how he can. We never spend time together anymore. We haven't had sex in six months.

"This isn't the way I envisioned my life. This isn't what I want. Sometimes I find myself wondering if life is even worth living. That scares me."

Sadly, the concerns that brought this women to my office were all too familiar. In the two-plus decades that I have been in clinical practice at Stanford University, I have heard this theme in countless variations: highly talented, ambitious and dedicated women who want to do all that they are capable of doing, and who succeed on many fronts, but who pay an extraordinary emotional price for that success.

As more women are shattering the professional and technical barriers that previously denied us access to the most challenging and gratifying careers, many of us are finding that *concerns about competence*: "Can I make it as a business executive or as an entrepreneur?"—or the analogous choices in other professions—*are being replaced by concerns about process*: "How do I do the things I have been trained to do, and still have a life?" *For most professional women today, how to fully engage in our careers and still maintain some semblance of balance in our lives is the critical issue.*

Answers to these questions do exist, although they are not always easy to come by. Although legions of us struggle with the stresses associated with being a professional woman on a daily basis, many of us find this struggle to be a rather singular pursuit. With our time fully committed to the demands of work and/or family, we often find ourselves isolated from friends and others who are attempting to do the same things that we are doing. Because previous generations of women often did not pursue the same professional avenues as those being chosen today, the absence of relevant role models is all too apparent.

The illusion that often exists is that other women are doing it better: Other women are getting it right. They are managing to have it all, with energy and spirit to spare. Yet the very fact that such an illusion exists does a great disservice to those of us who are striving to achieve the kind of life that we had hoped for when we embarked on our professional careers.

A terrible irony exists in the fact that for many of us, the very characteristics responsible for our professional success can often serve us poorly when we attempt to construct an integrated life. The same striving for perfection—consistently making the good effort, working harder in the face of unrealistic expectations (our own and others'), all the traits that serve us well professionally—can sow the seeds of profound psychological distress when we add new dimensions to our lives. Lacking insight from others, the expectations we may set for ourselves can predictably fall short of the mark.

Much like the young woman in the example above—who went on to describe that, in addition to being the mother of three children under the age of six, she was also the lead person on a multimillion-dollar project at work, and had recently embarked on an ambitious home-renovation project with her husband—many of us feel we should be able to sustain levels of commitment and activity that defy both logic and human capacity. Even for women who are used to accomplishing the impossible, the toll for such accomplishments is not without its attendant costs.

It is to address the issues of excellence, balance, and basic sanity for professional women that this book is dedicated. Having devoted so much of my academic and clinical career to developing strategies for women in dealing with the stresses associated with professional life—not to mention my own attempts as a working mother to find the right balance of professional and personal life—I believed that a book of strategies on this topic was long overdue.

When presented with the opportunity to study a large number of women who had graduated from the Stanford Graduate School of Business between 1931 and 1995, I recognized a unique opportunity to draw on the experiences of hundreds of professional women who were among the best and the brightest of their generations. From them would come information critical to validating the insights gained from over two decades of clinical work with professional women. Although obviously the experience of a woman graduating in the 1930s from the Stanford Business School would vary tremendously from those graduating in the 1990s, I firmly believed, and continue to do so even more strongly now, that there is something very important to be learned from women who have accepted the challenge to do difficult things, and to do them well.

Clearly, the women of the Stanford Business School are not exactly your average team. When I first suggested to a colleague that I planned to write a book on my experiences with professional women at Stanford, she remarked, "That's an interesting idea, but what do I, or anyone else for that matter, have in common with those women? They live life on a different level." This came from a highly successful attorney, herself an Ivy League graduate.

Although I was somewhat dismayed by her comment, it did cause me to reexamine my assumption that there was something truly valuable for all professional women that could be filtered or translated from the experience of the Stanford women. Although it is indeed true that the Stanford women occupy a rather exceptional place in the society of working women, it is equally true that despite rather extraordinary talents, ambition, and dedication, these women struggle with the same issues common to all of us:

- Can I be successful at work?
- How do I compete in a man's world?
- How do I handle the stresses of my job?
- How can it get all done?
- Where does my partner fit in and/or how do I find one?

- What is best for my kids—how does my work affect them?
- Is this really what I want for my life?

Although this book neither purports to answer all the questions facing working women nor addresses the very real and often intractable concerns of women working in nonprofessional jobs, it does attempt to address some of the questions most consistently posed by professional women.

Many of these issues have been addressed quite effectively by the Stanford women we studied, and the insight and advice they offer are presented in the text. The solution to other issues, however, has eluded even the best and brightest.

It is important for us as women to not have to reinvent the wheel as every generation enters the workplace. Rather, we can and should profitably build on the experience of other female professionals in confronting the challenges of the workplace.

Moreover, it is equally important for us to identify the issues for which no viable solutions have as yet emerged. Knowing that we are not alone when we cannot seem to get a handle on a particularly intractable situation will go a long way to helping us avoid self-recrimination. Knowing when our expectations are unrealistic will also help us to avoid the temptation to work harder in the face of a problem that may require a very different approach. Being able to differentiate the "merely" difficult from the "truly" impossible will enable us to recognize and appreciate the fact that sometimes there are no perfect solutions, and sometimes "good enough" has just got to do.

My hope is that insights gathered from the professional women in my clinical practice, supported by the experience of the women in our Stanford sample, will benefit the thousands of us who struggle with the same concerns day in and day out. Many of us are too exhausted at the end of the day to find the time and energy to share our experiences with other women, and many of us lack the opportunity to learn from one another's efforts. My experience in developing the Professional Women's Group Program in the Schools of Law, Medicine, Engineering, and Business at Stanford has demonstrated how powerful and therapeutic such sharing of information and insight can be.

"Knowing that you're not alone is a very healing experience," one recent graduate of the Stanford MBA program wrote of her women's group experience. "Instead of asking the question 'Why can't I make this work,' I now focus on what can I realistically do. It's much more productive, and it makes me feel like I'm a part of something larger than myself."

Much of what is effective about the Women's Group Program is the opportunity to learn from others confronting the same or similar challenges. It is hoped that this book will serve as a comparable resource for women in a variety of professional situations.

One does not have to be an MBA to benefit from the guidance provided in this book. Any woman who sees her work as a professional commitment and treats it accordingly is, by definition, a professional woman. All occupational groups have professionals who involve themselves with their work in ways that reflect some measure of training, expertise, and dedication beyond that ordinarily associated with "just a job."

The women cited in this book come from a variety of professional and occupational backgrounds, and each offers a distinct perspective on the issues of balancing personal and professional commitments. The symmetry of the concerns expressed by these women is remarkable for its consistency. Although each profession has its own unique stresses, this and other research has demonstrated that the issues we confront as women professionals are remarkably similar—women are more like other women than we are like men, regardless of our professional affiliations.

Clearly, there are no universal solutions to the stresses confronting all professional women, and attempting a one-size-fits-all model would obviously be simplistic and ultimately prove unsatisfying. We can, however, share the lessons we've learned along the way. In doing so, we can help each other immeasurably in our efforts to create a life worth living.

CHAPTER 1

The Stanford Survey

A common assumption among psychologists is that we all research our own neuroses, and I clearly am no exception. Since the 1980s at Stanford, the primary focus of both my clinical and research work has been the stresses inherent in the lives of working women. No big surprise—I knew those stresses intimately. It was apparent to me early in my professional training that integrating a successful career with a successful family life was going to be a significant challenge— one at which I was seriously disadvantaged by the lack of relevant advice and counsel available to those of us contemplating this particular course in life.

A WINDOW ON MY FUTURE

My first experience with the difficulties inherent in venturing down my chosen professional/personal path came as a freshman in college. Having been felled by a bout of flu during finals, I was permitted to take a make-up on, ironically, my first psychology exam. My instructor for the course, a young assistant professor, and the rare woman on the psychology faculty at the time, invited me to her home to take the exam.

Showing up at her door, I was greeted by a woman in obvious distress; a woman whom I had previously seen only as the consummate professional in the classroom. In one arm she held a screaming baby; with the other, she blocked the exit of a tear-streaked toddler. She apologized for the chaotic scene, pushed aside a pile of unfolded laundry so that I could work on my exam, and went off to attend to her two children. Her husband (now ex-husband), also a faculty member, was nowhere in sight.

I do not remember anything about the exam, but I will never forget the image of this woman, who, despite extraordinary talent and ambition, was so valiantly and painfully struggling to cope with all the demands competing for her attention. It was one of those apocryphal moments in life, and one that was indelibly etched in my mind. Clearly, it influenced my thinking about having children for more than a decade.

It was not until several years later, during time spent in Latin America working on doctoral research, that I was able to observe a different way of integrating personal and professional priorities.

As an American woman who had experienced the pre-1970s, pre–women's movement biases in our own country that excluded women from most professional positions, I was pleasantly surprised, indeed fairly shocked, to find so many Latin American women holding professional degrees and working at highly respected posts in government and private industry. Not only were these professional women (and the authority they wielded) accepted in the workplace—a surprising circumstance given the infamous "machismo" ethic—but these women were also able to adroitly manage a fully involved, highly satisfying family life. How did they do that?

The answer was as simple as it was unfortunate. Their success in doing both was predicated on the existence of a servant class that freed women professionals from the usual household responsibilities. These women were able to spend all of their nonwork time with their children and their families and still maintain highly engaged professional careers.

Obviously there were problems with a servant class—not the least of which were the devastating consequences for the migrant women who often had to abandon the care of their own children to secure work—but the idea of a support system that allowed professional women to fully accomplish their personal and professional ideals was an intriguing notion. Clearly, only if women could secure the necessary support would they be in a position to do both things. So, short of inventing a servant class, how does one go about accomplishing this end?

Answering that question is the task of this book. Let us begin by taking a look at the women in our Stanford survey.

WHO ARE THE STANFORD WOMEN?

In the late 1990s, I was invited to address a conference for alumnae of the Stanford University Graduate School of Business. My bargain with the business school was that I would address their alumni if I could do for that group of female alums what had been done for other reunion groups—namely, survey them on a variety of issues of importance in their lives. It was an extraordinary stroke of luck to have access to an exceptional sample of women professionals going back over 60 years. I would only hope that the business school would be equally pleased with the outcome of our bargain.

To survey the women of the Stanford Business School, a questionnaire was designed by myself and two recent women MBA graduates. We sent the questionnaire to all women graduating before 1975 and a random sample of women from the graduating classes of 1976 through 1995. In all, over 300 women responded to our survey.

DEVELOPING THE QUESTIONNAIRE

Much like the women we set out to study, from its inception our questionnaire suffered from hyperambition. Our committee of three came up with an endless stream of interesting questions that we wanted to pursue. It took incredible discipline to keep the questionnaire under 10 pages, but the concern that too lengthy an instrument would discourage participation was a relatively compelling deterrent.

One of my worst fears in creating the questionnaire was that we would learn a whole lot about very few women, that the amount of information we were asking of our sample was simply too great. What actually occurred, however, could not have been further removed from that concern.

Although we had estimated that it would take between 1.5 and 2 hours to complete the questionnaire, many of those responding went well beyond that estimated time to tell us about their experiences. In many instances, the survey evoked far more information than the simple 5-point scales had requested. Letters and other documents often accompanied the data contained in the surveys returned to us. We were literally besieged with information.

In designing the layout of the questionnaire, we thought that we had left ample room for comments. More than a few women, however, admonished us for not providing enough space to elaborate on their experiences and thoughts. Often, the questionnaires were annotated with scores of helpful comments and insights, and quite regularly, they arrived with all available space covered in writing, including the margins.

On several occasions, the questionnaires were accompanied by drawings made by children who drew along with (and sometimes on top of) their mother's work. Several women apologized for stains on the survey, reflecting the fact that they had completed the questionnaire while balancing a sandwich at their desks or preparing a meal at home. Others apologized for water marks caused by children or grandchildren splashing in a nearby pool. Illegible handwriting was often explained by the fact that the questionnaires were filled out in cars, trains, and planes. Clearly, multitasking was the operant mode.

These were busy women, and many precious minutes were dedicated to providing insightful answers to the questions posed. For that, we were extremely grateful. It was equally clear that the issues raised in the questionnaire touched a nerve for these women, and the generosity in their thoughtful replies forms the basis for much of what follows.

Even in the way they filled out their questionnaire, these women were demonstrating their remarkable capacity to get things done. As one woman, a busy executive described her life:

> Generally I manage pretty well with sixteen balls in the air at work and absolute chaos at home. Imagine how dangerous I'd be if I ever got a full night's sleep!

THE SURVEY

The questionnaire we designed covered a broad range of topics. We asked the women about their experiences at business school, as well as about their personal and professional experiences since graduation:

- How had they handled the challenges they confronted in their careers?
- What kinds of choices had they needed to make?
- How had those choices affected other parts of their lives?

In a section on careers and families,

- We asked about the problems that arise when a professional woman decides to start a family.
- We solicited their insights on the impact of children on a professional career.
- We solicited their opinions on the right time to start a family.
- We asked about what things helped or hindered when children were introduced into the equation.
- We sought advice and strategies on how to manage the conflicts that exist for working parents.

In the final section of the questionnaire,

- We examined the values these women found sustaining in their attempts to create an integrated life.
- We asked about what was important in their lives.
- We solicited whatever advice they might have for professional women just beginning the journey.

In our sample, we found that most of our respondents were very enthusiastic about filling out the questionnaire, and more than a few indicated that the questionnaire helped them to think about issues of importance to them in very different ways than they had previously done.

THE WOMEN WE STUDIED

Far exceeding our wildest expectations, the sample of women responding to our survey was truly astonishing. Of the more than 300 women who returned completed questionnaires, our oldest respondent was 86 years old and our youngest was 26. Our earliest respondent graduated from the Stanford Business School in 1931 during Herbert Hoover's presidency, whereas our last group of respondents graduated in the postmodern world of 1995. All told, their educational experiences spanned over 60 years, and they accounted for fully three generations of professional women.

The women we studied did just about everything in terms of work, from CEOs and corporate executives to small-business owners and sales managers. Our women worked in engineering and high tech, sales and marketing, education, accounting, investment banking, consulting, law, medicine, and a variety of other fields. Some had worked on oil rigs; others had managed lumber plants, produced films, had run large and small family businesses or were among the earliest players in the then-emerging online fields. One of the women in our survey had more than 15,000 employees working for her, whereas another managed to work as a physician throughout her time at business school. Our women counted among their number business executives, engineers, physicians, attorneys, teachers, authors, entrepreneurs, and homemakers.

Most of the women in our sample worked full time, and nearly half of them worked more than 60 hours per week. For their efforts, they earned, on average, about $100,000 a year. Over two thirds of them were married, and nearly 40 percent of them had children.

Although the ages of the children ranged anywhere from under 1 year old to 56 years old, the majority of the women with children in our survey had children under the age of 2.

Pioneers, Settlers, and Successors

Women who graduated from the Stanford Business School at different points in its history have obviously had significantly different work and life experiences. To better appreciate these differences, we divided the women we studied into three groups: Those women who *graduated before 1976* we called the *Pioneers.* The women who *graduated between 1976 and 1985* we called the *Settlers,* and those women who *graduated between 1986 and 1995* we called the *Successors.*

AT A GLANCE:
DEMOGRAPHICS

	PIONEERS	SETTLERS	SUCCESSORS
Predominant job type	Pre–1976	1976–85	1986–95
	Various	Self-employed	Large corporation
Income	$51K–$100K	$101K–$200K	$51K–$100K
Work 40+ hr/wk	52%	60%	80%
Married	61%	80%	59%
Have children	67%	54%	31%

Pioneers (Pre–1976)

Prior to the late 1970s, each graduating class at highly selective business and professional schools like Stanford included less than a handful of women. One of the women who graduated in the early 1970s recalled her admissions interview:

> When I appeared for my admissions interview with the dean, he looked over my application and inquired, "You're from Rochester? And what part of the Eastman family are you from?"

Although the applicant was not related to the Eastman family of Kodak fame, the dean was simply acknowledging a reality of the time. Most women who applied for admission to the elite business schools in those days were principally the female heirs to family fortunes—family fortunes for which no male heirs were available to run the business.

The Pioneers who graduated before 1976 were clearly unique in many other ways. Often they were the only woman, or one of very few women, pursuing professional degrees at a time when such an educational opportunity was principally the purview of men. For example, between 1960 and 1970, only 24 women earned MBA degrees from Stanford Business School.

The Pioneers who graduated in the 1930s, 1940s, or 1950s often were the only women in many of their classes, and as a result, they were highly visible. Wrote one 1950s Pioneer:

> With only one other woman in my MBA class, it was clearly hard to blend in. Because we stood out, it was necessary to be better and smarter. There really was a feeling of being a pioneer and setting an example for other women.

For many Pioneers, their rarity as professional women in the halls of academia guaranteed what one woman described as "a benign neglect." Other pioneers questioned whether neglect could ever be described as truly benign. Wrote another 1950s Pioneer:

> I objected to being called Mr. X over and over again in classes. I knew the dean was none too happy to have women in the school. I tried very hard to scholastically prove myself.

In general, the women of the Pioneer group reported that they were treated well in business school, despite the fact that the opportunities open to, or envisioned, for them were often quite limited. An early 1960s graduate sent us a copy of a letter of recommendation she received from a faculty member when she was applying for a job after receiving her MBA. It read:

> To whom it may concern:
> Mrs. X was a student in my business policy course given at Stanford during 19__.
> In this rather intensive course each student was required to prepare twelve written reports analyzing in detail the present position of a firm in its industry, and recommending a future course of action for the firm.
> Among 20 students, Mrs. X's work was outstanding, and received one of the two A's given in the course. . . .

Mrs. X is a very capable, personable young lady who would be an excellent addition to the staff of any firm.

Were I a business executive who needed an administrative assistant, I would hire her like a shot.

Sincerely,

Dr. ———

Professor of Business

Quite an outstanding piece of American cultural history!

In general, Pioneer women found employment in occupations and industries that traditionally had been more accessible to women—that is, government, nonprofit, and educational organizations and family-owned businesses. Despite their lack of widespread integration into the workforce, the Pioneers blazed a path through uncharted professional waters and laid the foundation for those who came after them. *For the Pioneers, the defining issue appears to have been "let me do it."*

Today, this group finds itself the most satisfied overall. The majority of the Pioneers either are retired and managing their investments or have comfortably worked themselves into the executive positions that had been their goal all along. Sixty-one percent of these women are married, and nearly 70 percent of them have children.

Settlers (Between 1976 and 1985)

The Settlers, who graduated from the business school between 1976 and 1985, were among the first women in business and professional schools who represented a sizable minority of their graduating classes, approximately 25 percent. Following on the heels of the Pioneers, the Settlers were among the first women in a variety of previously all-male occupations—investment banking, management consulting, venture capital, and so on. Like their sisters in medicine, law, and engineering, in most instances these women had few, if any, role models and mentors to guide them in their professional development.

Interestingly, in many instances, the women in the Settler group reported having to fight even more battles for acceptance into occupations and work organizations than did the Pioneers. Because there were so few Pioneers, by and large they were seen as less threatening to the all-male professional workforce. Although clearly the Pioneers fought their share of the battles, Pioneers, for the most part, report being treated more like odd ducks than genuine threats.

As greater numbers of women began graduating from business and professional schools, however, these Settlers began to challenge their male peers for professional ascendancy. The hostility and resistance confronted by the Settlers in attempting to open corporate doors frequently left an indelible mark on their experience of the workplace.

Aspiring to a range of business and professional opportunities previously unavailable to women, the defining question for the Settler group was "Can I make it?" One Settler, an early 1980s graduate who worked in sales and trading on Wall Street, recounted:

> It was hard not having female role models and always feeling like I had to be "one of the guys"—but that's what it took to be accepted. As a woman I was seriously disadvantaged by not being part of the inner circle of male managers. No matter how good I was, being a woman changed things.

Most of the Settlers in our survey currently work full time, and over 60 percent of them work more than 40 hours a week. Over 80 percent of these women are married, and more than half of them have children. Given these statistics, it is no surprise that, as a group, the Settlers report the greatest stress between work and family demands. They are the highest wage earners but also the most likely to be self-employed, a fact that may account for some of the twinges of dissatisfaction these women report. As one Settler wrote:

> When your income is based solely on what you can produce, there is no slack. You always have to keep your eye on the bottom line.

Most of our Settlers are right in the early and middle stages of their child-rearing years. Many of these women see independent employment as the most viable way of remaining in the workforce while coping with the challenges of career and motherhood. For many, self-employment allows them to fulfill both professional and personal goals. As we shall see in later chapters, although this option is not without its attendant stresses, by and large these women report that they are very satisfied with this arrangement. As one Settler describes her choice:

> I love working at home on my own as a freelance consultant, analyst, and business writer. I make less than I did in industry, but the balance and freedom working on my own affords is great. I'll never again take a "real job" . . . (never is a long time . . . !).

Because the Settlers are the ones who are in the midst of creating some semblance of balance in their lives, what they have to say about their current experiences in combining work and motherhood is particularly relevant to the theme of this book.

Successors (Between 1986 and 1995)

The Successors, the women who graduated from the business school between 1986 and 1995, often benefited from the experience of the women who went before them. Although the novelty of women attending professional schools clearly had diminished by the time these women entered business school, prior to the fall of the year 2000 the number of women at Stanford, as at the other elite business schools, had never risen above 30 percent of a graduating class.

Although often not the first or only woman in traditionally male occupations, the Successors still encounter few role models ahead of them to provide relevant professional guidance and advice. Although they have the advantage of knowing that women can and do succeed in high-profile jobs in such traditionally male fields as finance and high tech, the fact that few, if any, of their role models have risen to the most senior levels of management is not lost on them.

For the Successors, the question of whether women could be investment bankers or venture capitalists is essentially moot. For the most part, few question their ability to do the job. These women know that they are competent because they had worked as investment bankers, technical specialists, engineers, and managers before they went to business school.

Unlike their earlier counterparts, the critical issue for many of the Successors is "Do I want to do it?" Many of them question the viability and soundness of trying to combine a high-profile career with the compelling demands of a balanced life, particularly one involving children. Even those who are not currently contemplating families of their own, question the wisdom of dedicating so much time to their jobs at the cost of their own well-being.

One investment banker who regularly spent more than 80 hours a week at work wrote:

> Work has taken over—I like to go to the theater with my fiancé, but we never get to do that. I have no balance in my life; I survive on stamina and drive. It's been OK up until now, but I really can't take much more of this. It's a dumb way to live.

The intrusion of career on personal life is of particular concern for this group, as over 80 percent of the Successors spend more than 40 hours a week working, and for nearly half of these women, a 60- to 80-hour work week is typical.

These women tended to be the youngest respondents to our survey. Most of them do not yet have children, and slightly more than half of them are married.

Although it has become far more acceptable for professional women today to want to have children, the concern these women share is whether they can successfully integrate all the things they want to do in life—and at what cost. Although few, if any, of the Successors would give up the range of opportunities available to them, many legitimately question how their careers will fare once they begin to have families of their own. *Whether one can have a truly successful career without sacrificing the well-being of one's self and family is the great unanswered question of the day.*

A WORD ABOUT THE IDENTITIES
OF THE WOMEN IN THIS STUDY

Before we move on to what we learned from all of this, a word about the identities of the women cited in this book. As you will see as we proceed, the examples in this book draw on the women in our Stanford survey as well as the women professionals I have seen in clinical practice. As a clinician, I have an ethical responsibility not to reveal the identity of any of my patients. This is a responsibility that is central to the work I do, and it requires that anything I say about patients must be sufficiently disguised so as to avoid personal identification. In conducting this research, we made a similar pledge to our subjects: that we would do nothing to reveal their identities. As a result, certain identifying and/or demographic characteristics of the women cited in this book have been altered to protect their privacy. I have attempted to do so in a way that does not significantly alter the substance of the material under consideration. Similarly, certain quotes had to be modified for confidentiality and/or editorial purposes.

A WORD ON HOW THIS BOOK IS ORGANIZED

Because many of us are too busy to read books from cover to cover, I have tried to organize the material of this volume in a way that is most useful and accessible to us as we go about our demanding lives. Even though as an author I feel strongly connected to all the material in this book, I have italicized what I believe are particularly important findings for the speed-read at midnight. I have also organized each of the chapters in the following way:

- **Experience:** In this section, the question or problem of the chapter is defined, discussed, and illustrated with examples drawn from the Stanford Business School research, clinical experience, and other sources.
- **Lessons Learned:** This section focuses on the lessons that can be derived from the research and clinical experience.
- **Action Plan:** This is the how-to part of the book—how do we apply the lessons that we have learned? The Action Plan contains strategies and advice as well as worksheets and checklists that can be effective in dealing with the issues raised in the chapter.

PART I

Professional Women and Children

CHAPTER 2

Is Having Children the Right Decision for Professional Women?

My husband and I are either going to buy a dog or have a child.
We can't decide whether to ruin our carpet or ruin our lives.

—Rita Rudner

EXPERIENCE: WHAT PROFESSIONAL WOMEN SAY ABOUT *THE DECISION*

I Might Want Kids

If there is one issue that induces sleepless nights and angst-filled discussion among young professional couples, it is the topic of having children. Although many professional women say they want children, once the topic is broached, a whole host of compelling questions emerges: Do I want kids? Should I have them? What do I know about them? Will I be a good parent? Will we? Not to mention: What will happen to my career? And even further: What will happen to the rest of my life?

One of my patients, a pharmaceutical researcher in her late thirties, recently described her thinking on the issue of having kids:

> I wish I had some kind of a sign that it was the right thing for me to do. My husband really wants them, but I'm not so sure. I think I do—and certainly that's what all my friends are doing—but somehow I never really had a clear sense that I definitely wanted children.

I mean, I like kids okay, but I haven't spent a lot of time around them, and I don't feel all that comfortable with other people's children. I think other women just have more of an instinct about this sort of thing. I wonder if that means that I shouldn't have them.

Certainly not every woman wants to become a mother, nor should every woman feel compelled to be a mother. Many of us question our suitability for assuming the motherhood role, particularly if career and professional interests figure prominently in our lives. However, not having a clear and convincing sense of how we would be as mothers often evokes serious doubts about our parenting capabilities. Somehow our uncertainty about becoming a parent translates into an indication that we are unsuited for motherhood. From both the clinical and research perspective, however, I can say that there is little, if any, evidence to support this notion, and we do ourselves a great disservice by falling prey to the faulty logic that often underlies this assumption.

From the clinical perspective, it is absolutely a fact that women approach the issue of having children with varying degrees of certainty. There are definitely women who have known since childhood that they wanted to have children, and some of these women were fortunate enough to have had the opportunity to test out their parental talents on younger siblings and neighborhood children. For many professional women, however, the issue is far less clear.

Most professional women today have had few opportunities to test their parenting readiness, and even fewer of us have had the opportunity to truly become familiar with caring for young children. Families have gotten smaller at the same time that we, as women, have concentrated on our studies (and sports) rather than engage in more traditional female activities, like baby-sitting. As a result, large numbers of us find ourselves completely bereft of relevant experience. For women who are used to organization and planning, the thought of doing something for which we have limited, if any, preparation, and for which no good manuals exist, can be exceedingly daunting.

The issue is further complicated by the fact that the decision to have children is rather irreversible—one cannot simply decide to return them if things don't work out—and the time horizon of a woman's fertility further limits our options if we wish to conceive our own children. Add to this quandary the lack of relevant information about the effects of having children on one's career, as well as the effect that children have on the other important relationships in our lives, and the cause of the anxiety plaguing so many of us is readily apparent.

What If I Don't Think I Want Kids?

A different but equally anxiety-provoking set of issues exists at the other end of the spectrum. *For those professional women who are fairly certain that they do not want to have children, the significant biases toward a maternal role for women in our society represent an inescapable pressure.* The feelings evoked by a decision to not have children surprise many women, not unlike my patient, a graphic designer approaching her fortieth birthday:

> I can't believe the pressure that exists to have kids today. Everywhere you go, people are having two, three kids. It's become the expectation. If you say you're not sure you want them, people look at you like you're some kind of social miscreant. My mother-in-law has all but accused me of ruining her son's life because I won't acquiesce. I spent most of my life working, and I'm at a point in my career where I can kick back and enjoy it. I don't really want to start in with diapers and all that.

It appears that no matter which way we lean on the decision about having children, anxiety figures prominently into the process. Because the stakes in this decision process are so high, this is not a decision to be made from the perspective of anxiety and fear.

How Do I Go About Making Such a Profound Decision?

The first step in any good decision-making process is to take a look at what is known. What do professional women who have been there and have made the decision say about their choices? Here, the data from our Stanford study is particularly instructive:

- What do the women say about their decision to have children?
- How have children affected their careers?
- What effects have their children had on their relationships with their partners?

After reviewing the data from our Stanford study, we will take a look at strategies for sorting out concerns and identifying ways of making more informed choices on this issue.

◆ ◆ ◆

LESSONS LEARNED

"The Hours Stink and the Pay Is Lousy, but It's the Best Job You'll Ever Have!"—1980s Settler
Nearly every mother in our Stanford survey agreed with this respondent that motherhood is tough but wonderful.

When we asked our Stanford mothers if having children had been the right decision for them, "Yes, definitely" was the response that came back from over 98 percent of the women we surveyed. No other question earned such unilaterally positive responses. Our questionnaires came back annotated with comments like these:

> Children were the very best decision in my life.
> —1990s Successor, two children ages 2 and 5

> Every career experience pales in comparison to being a mother.
> —1970s Pioneer, one child age 23

> My children represent the only successful venture in my life.
> —1980s Settler, two children ages 7 and 21

> I am so fortunate to have three children who have given me the most wisdom of all the life choices I have ever made.
> —1980s Settler, three children ages 4, 7, and 10

> I love my kids and learn from them and enjoy them every day, even though they sure can be difficult! I can't imagine a life without them. I would probably be a miserable workaholic!
> —1980s Successor, two children age 4

The enthusiastic endorsements of the joys of motherhood went on for pages. It was truly an impressive set of unequivocal responses.

And even though one would perhaps expect such positive responses from women who had chosen to become mothers, such an overwhelming endorsement of the motherhood experience from as career-committed a group of women as this one was both notable and unexpected.

For the few mothers who expressed some ambivalence about their decision to have children, their doubts tended to be based on their ambivalence at the time, as one 1970s Pioneer with two children recalled:

> In retrospect, it was the right decision for me. At the time, I thought children were an imposition on my career! I had adapted to corporate life so well that I didn't know there would be a conflict between having children and my career. I had to give up certain career options, like turning down a corporate vice presidency when I discovered that my daughter was having learning problems. But it's been definitely worth it to me. My experience is that a child is a joy forever, while corporations come and go.

It is important to note that although the mothers in our sample were overwhelmingly positive about their experience, it is also true that those women who chose not to have children did not, for the most part, report belated regrets at their decision. Many indicated that having a child was something they simply never wanted for themselves, and they were quite happy with their decision. Sadly, we did have several women who indicated that they had missed out on the opportunity to have children because they waited too long and were subsequently unable to conceive.

There Is a Career Upside to Having Children

> Dealing with my two-year-old is not unlike the experience of dealing with my boss. Neither has any patience, and they both think they own me.
>
> —1980s Settler

This woman's experience may not be exactly what comes to mind as a career upside to having children, but there definitely appear to be some notable advantages to be gained from our experience as parents. Asking the women in our survey about how their children had affected their careers prompted some very interesting—and somewhat unanticipated—responses.

As expected, a fair number of women (42 percent) reported that their careers had been compromised in some way by the arrival of children in their lives. What we did not expect to find, however, was that nearly half of the women in our sample (48 percent) felt that their careers had been enhanced by their decision to have a family.

For many women, the benefits of having children centered on reordered priorities and a healthier perspective on life. Several echoed the feelings of this 1980s Settler, a corporate vice president and mother of three young children:

> I have more self-awareness and more inner security about who I am as a person. I know what my limits are, and what I value. Having children creates a strength and perspective at work, and I find myself less threatened, but I'm also less tolerant of inflated egos.

Others reported that they had redefined their priorities in ways that made more sense to them. A senior manager with two young children wrote:

> I'm a more balanced and happier person. It makes it easier to ride through the ups and downs of a career when you have a family to go home to. Children have a great way of minimizing work crises.

Many women found that having a family forced them to be less absorbed and defined by their work, with a greater ability to "multitask, set priorities, and stick to the essentials." For some, having a family literally demanded that they exercise more creativity in thinking about their career options, as another 1980s Settler and mother of three found:

I might not have taken the risks I did if others weren't driving my actions. In the process, I discovered that I never want a full-time career again, if I can avoid it financially.

Some women gained valuable people skills and found that they became better managers. "If I can deal with a screaming toddler, the other stuff is small potatoes," wrote one. Several others remarked on finding themselves both humbled and more compassionate as a result of being a parent. This 1980s Successor, a stay-at-home mother of two young children, explained:

I expect that when I return to the workforce I will bring many new skills with me. My patience, my ability to deal with the unexpected, and my sheer capacity for work have all been enhanced by motherhood.

Though the women in our survey left little doubt that the experience of motherhood, particularly when combined with a career, was challenging, it is also true that for many of them, the parenting experience offered some significant career upsides.

"Pick a Good Guy Who Supports Your Career"—*1970s Settler*

The advice to choose a mate supportive of one's career surfaced more than once in the responses we received to our questions about deciding on children. "Easier said than done," reported many, but if there is one issue that our respondents agreed on, it was the idea that if you are thinking about having both a family and a career, you should choose your partner carefully. So critical was the partner issue to the well-being of professional women that Chapter 10 is devoted specifically to the topic of the right partner.

It comes as no surprise to any working mother that how well things work out as we attempt to integrate our personal and professional lives is directly related to the quality of the support we receive at home. Wrote one 1970s Settler with two teenagers:

Having a successful career and raising a family is very much influenced by the kind of support you get from your spouse. Find a husband who shares your views of equal responsibility and build your own model of motherhood. Don't imitate your mother.

Even if one is fortunate enough to have a "good guy" for a partner, an appreciable array of stresses are inevitably associated with introducing children into a relationship. What is frequently underappreciated, however, is the fact that for many women, having children actually exerts a positive influence on their relationship with their partner. Several of our Stanford women echoed the feeling of this 1970s Pioneer with two grown children:

Of course there are strains, but there is also an extraordinary sense of completeness. I don't think my husband and I would be nearly as close if we hadn't had to work through the rough spots—often for the sake of the kids. We had to learn how to be a family, not just a couple. You can't just do whatever suits you best.

Having to "become an adult," as one mother put it, "because there was room for [only] one baby in the family" was often the unanticipated and enjoyably maturing consequence of being a parent.

More Advice from Those Who Have Been There

Because the mothers in our study were so overwhelmingly positive in their assessment of motherhood, it is helpful to hear from them directly. Below is a sampling of the advice they offered on the subject of deciding to have a family:

Just do it. Analysis doesn't work here.
—1980s Settler, finance, three children ages 25, 28, and 30

Go for it—it's great. You may screw up your career, but you will find other stuff to do.
—1980s Settler, corporate vice president, three children
ages 2, 6, and 9

There is no greater, lasting joy than raising and nurturing a family if a woman is prepared to grow from the changes required. The adjustments need to be lifelong.

> —1980s Settler, product manager, two children ages 8 and 12

If a family is important to you, make it a high priority. Your family will always stay with you, but you can get laid off or fired from work. I've known so many women who've worked to climb the corporate ladder only to find themselves hugely disappointed at their relative infertility later in life.

> —1980s Settler, corporate director, two children ages 5 and 8

Kids are a lot of work, both physical and emotional. Make sure you really want them—it is a one-way decision.

> —1970s Settler, CFO, no children

Do it. Screw work.

> —1970s Settler, analyst, two children ages 13 and 16

If your self-esteem requires a high-pressure/high-profile job, consider not having children. Contrary to all the media hype, it is a perfectly acceptable decision: You can contribute a hell of a lot more to society as a whole if you don't have the lifetime responsibility of kids. It's not so bad.

> —1980s Settler, parent, two children ages 5 and 8

Make sure you and your spouse agree on time commitments and expectations within the family. If possible, choose a more flexible career path or enlightened organization.

> —1980s Settler, venture capitalist, no children

Raising a family is wonderful. Don't deny yourself this happiness in order to appease the jerks in suits!

> —1990s Successor, CEO, no children

Do you want kids? Do you and your husband have a great relationship? Are you in agreement about a future family? If all are yes—go!

—1990s Successor, consultant, four children
ages 2, 4, 5, and 7

Don't sacrifice your children for the organization or career—the organization will never care about your life; your family will.

—1990s Successor, senior business analyst, no children

Think seriously about what makes you happy. Are you willing to make big compromises?

—1980s Settler, stay-at-home mother, two children
ages 1 and 3

My experience is that a child is a joy forever . . . . Corporations may come and go! Do not lose out on the opportunity to have a family!

—1970s Pioneer, stay-at-home mother, two children
ages 16 and 21

Do it anyway. Work is only one part of a successful life.

—1980s Settler, director of marketing, no children

If you want a family, do it. It's a very important part of your life. You shouldn't have to choose one or the other. Don't ever feel guilty. You don't have to be a stay-at-home mom to be a good mom.

—1970s Pioneer, consulting, two children ages 14 and 16

If the woman likes babies/children/teenagers, then I would wholeheartedly endorse parenthood—our children are the highlights of our lives. I know that my husband who has had to work [full time] outside the home would say that our children are more important than any job or company. When our children have gone off to college, then I'll return to the workforce.

—1970s Settler, volunteer, two children ages 12 and 15

Go ahead! It's the greatest "success" life can offer. But be prepared for the management challenge of it all.

—1970s Settler, technician, two children ages 7 and 10

Would you really prefer to work 60 hours a week and not have a
life?

—1980s Settler, finance, two children ages 5 and 8

◆　◆　◆

ACTION PLAN: FIVE STEPS TO MAKING
THE DECISION

Our research leaves little doubt as to the how the women in our survey felt about their decision to have children. For most of them,
choosing to become a mother was a profoundly positive experience
in their lives. If you are in the process of deciding on children, the
question that emerges is, of course, *How do I decide whether having
children is the right choice for me?*

From this basic question, all sorts of other questions emerge:

- What if I'm not sure I want kids?
- How do I know if I have what it takes?
- Will I be a good parent?
- What do I know about having kids?
- How will becoming a parent affect my career?
- Is my relationship strong enough to sustain the pressures of par-
  enthood?
- Most important of all, what about me? How am I going to feel as
  a mother?

Because these are difficult questions, the answers are often complicated. Below is a series of five steps that I have found helpful in
working with my patients, both individual women and couples, who
are going through the process of deciding about children.

Step 1: Accept the Inevitable—at Some Point, You're Going to Have to Make a Decision

Is there a professional woman alive today who has not heard about the biological clock? Perhaps no other issue inspires as much anxiety among us as the concern that, as one patient described it, "I can hear my eggs drying up as we speak." Panic, angst, and cursing the lack of cryogenic egg banks are all part of the inevitable fertility time horizon for women.

We all know that at some point the option of having our own biological child is close-ended. Yet for many of us, making a decision about having children, particularly when we are actively engaged in our careers, is extremely anxiety provoking. We often will do everything we can to forestall the decision, even to the point of denying ourselves the opportunity to become mothers.

Although obviously the biological clock does not preclude our becoming parents by other means, like adoption, *too often our anxiety about not being able to make a decision can cause us to make one by default—that is, to make a decision by not making a decision.*

The women in my practice who have chosen this default option of "deciding by not deciding" are generally less satisfied with the way things turn out than are those women who have made a choice, one way or the other, about having kids. The underlying principle appears to be that if we have to make a decision, it's better to make an active one and get on with our life, than to always wonder what might have been.

Step 2: When Up Against the Wall, Check Out the Writing

If we accept that, as women, we are going to have to make a decision one way or another on the issue of having children, we need to spend some time figuring out what is written on that wall that we are up against.

The first step in making an active decision is to take a good look at the issues involved in the decision process:

- What are your concerns regarding the decision to have children?
- What options exist for resolving these concerns?
- What are the sticking points in your decision process? Where does your decision process get bogged down?

Because neither the questions nor the answers that arise are intuitively obvious, the Deciding on Children Worksheet at the end of this chapter provides a template for working through this process.

Step 3: Do the Worksheet—It Clarifies Your Feelings

The Deciding on Children Worksheet (page 38) is very useful as a way of organizing one's thoughts on the subject of having children.

Some words of advice in doing the worksheet:

- Think expansively. This is something that I recommend repeatedly when one engages in problem solving. Don't just write down the first and only option that comes to mind.
- Think of several options, no matter how implausible.
- Think creatively and write down all options before eliminating any as unrealistic. Sometimes the most inventive solutions arise out of the least probable suggestions.

Step 4: The Talking Cure Works

There is no easy way to make a decision as singularly important as whether to have children, but the Deciding on Children Worksheet offers a way of sorting through the issues and identifying some of the stumbling blocks along the way.

I have found that once the sticking points are identified, the next step is to talk about them. Oddly, this is the step that seems to get overlooked, or just plain avoided, with troubling regularity. For most people, the notion of talking about things that are emotionally laden understandably creates anxiety. Using your answers on the worksheet as talking points can eliminate much of the emotional confusion and anxiety that often accompanies a "big talk," as this one is likely to be.

If discussing the issues with your partner reaches a stalemate, it may be time to call in the professionals. There are times in most relationships when a little bit of help can go a long way toward moving a couple along in their decision process.

By way of example, let's look at the experience of a couple I worked with recently, whom I shall call Katie and Russell. For them, protracted and often futile discussions on the topic of children had brought them to my office. They were at the point in their relationship where frustration and a lack of progress on the issue had led them to seriously contemplate ending their marriage.

KATIE AND RUSSELL'S STORY

Katie, a 33-year-old graphics manager at a high-tech firm, wanted to make a decision about children right away, but her husband, Russell, clearly did not feel the same sense of urgency.

Katie and Russell had been married for 6 years, and Katie felt like it was time for them to "fish or cut bait" on the issue. She was tired of living with the uncertainty of not having a plan for her life and felt that being unable to make a decision on children had serious implications for her career.

She, like many other women in their thirties, was concerned about fertility issues, and she felt caught between not being able to fully invest in her career and not being able to contemplate becoming a mother. She felt Russell's unwillingness to commit to a decision on kids was literally tearing her, and their relationship, apart.

After some discussion (and completing the worksheet), it became clear that Russell had really heard only part of his wife's concerns—namely, the issues about fertility. He was focusing his decision on the fact that at 33, Katie really didn't have to be overly concerned about fertility. From his perspective, why the rush?

In our discussions, it became clear that it was not just fertility issues that were concerning Katie but also the uncertainty of her life and her inability to make important career and life decisions. Understanding this, Russell became much more cooperative in the decision-making process. I suspect that our discussions did as much to help Russell understand the communication issues involved as it did to allow him to become aware of his own ambivalence about becoming a father.

Step 5: Embrace the Unpredictable—It's Part of the Process

It is important to recognize that even once you have done your homework and sorted through your options, some measure of ambivalence about an undertaking as life altering as having children is, quite naturally, to be expected. In fact, if it were not present, one might suspect that the decision was being taken a little too lightly.

More often than not, however, as women and as professionals, we expend an inordinate amount of psychological energy attempting to analyze a decision from every angle. Although some analysis may be a positive first step, eventually we run up against the unknown and the unpredictable, and that is a problem for us. If there is one thing that we, as high-achieving types, hate, it is to confront something that we can neither predict nor control. Before we engage in a course of action, we insist on knowing its outcome as well as how it is going to feel. That is where we can run into trouble.

Recently, I came across an interesting piece of psychological research that spoke eloquently to the dilemma we often find ourselves in when we try to predict our feelings about the future. The article described how remarkably bad we are (both men and women) at predicting how we are going to feel about the outcome of some future event.

One of the examples cited in the article was that of lottery winners who were interviewed several times after they won big jackpots. Invariably, these big winners reported that their initial euphoria, which they had anticipated would last a long while, disappeared relatively quickly. Nearly to the person, the respondents reported that despite their good fortune, they soon found themselves settling back to their prejackpot level of happiness, whatever that happened to be.

The psychologists also cited a Harvard study of 100 college professors interviewed before and after they found out whether they had been granted tenure. This study demonstrated that regardless of the outcome the professors were less intensely happy (or unhappy) than they had originally anticipated that they would be.

The moral of this, and similar research, appears to be this: Good or bad, it's hard, if not impossible, to predict how you're going to feel. Extrapolating from this research, one might argue that every major decision in life at some point requires a leap of faith. Clearly, deciding on children is no exception.

What we have learned from our research is that the decision to have children was overwhelmingly positive for the professional women we studied. Even though many women acknowledged that having a family had altered their career ambitions or progress, most agreed that one could figure out "the career thing" around children. Many suggested that new career options often emerged from the need to integrate one's family interests with one's work. The mothers in our survey left little doubt that despite the difficulties of having both children and a career, having children was the single most transcendent experience of life.

Despite what the research says, a decision about having children is exclusively the province of the couple making that decision. It is important to know it is possible to have a career *and* successfully raise a family. Everyone will undoubtedly weigh in with an opinion, but ultimately, only you and your partner can decide what is best for your lives. Chances are, no one else will be around for the 3 A.M. feedings.

DECIDING ON CHILDREN WORKSHEET

Instructions: Make a copy of the Deciding on Children Worksheet *for each partner. After each partner completes an individual worksheet, discuss the findings.*

To clarify the issues that play a role in the decision to have children, please answer the following questions:

1.   Am I concerned about how children will affect my career?

If yes, list the concerns
(e.g., *Fear career slowdown*)

List of things I can do about them
(e.g., *Do a reality check: talk to women in field*)

_____   _____
_____   _____
_____   _____
_____   _____
_____   _____

2.   Am I concerned about how children will affect my relationship?

If yes, list the concerns
(e.g., *No time as couple*)

List of things I can do about them
(e.g., *Establish regular date night*)

_____   _____
_____   _____
_____   _____

_____   _____

_____   _____

3. Am I concerned how children will affect my well-being?

If yes, list the concerns
(e.g., *Concerned about lifestyle
changes*)

List of things I can do about
them (e.g., *Identify things that
would change*)

_____   _____

_____   _____

_____   _____

_____   _____

_____   _____

4. Am I concerned about parenting issues?

If yes, list the concerns
(e.g., *Poor parenting models*)

List of things I can do about
them (e.g., *Take parenting
classes*)

_____   _____

_____   _____

_____   _____

_____   _____

_____   _____

5. Am I concerned about other issues?

If yes, list the concerns
(e.g., *Financial concerns*)

List of things I can do about
them (e.g., *See financial planner*)

_____   _____

_____   _____

_____   _____

_____   _____

_____   _____

6. If I do not have children, what are my concerns?

List the concerns
(e.g., *I might not feel complete*)

List of things I can do about
them (e.g., *Talk to other women
who have not had children*)

_____   _____

_____   _____

_____   _____

_____   _____

_____   _____

_____   _____

CHAPTER 3

Are Professional Women Good Mothers?

EXPERIENCE: WHAT ARE THE PRIORITIES OF PROFESSIONAL WOMEN?

"That's a no-brainer," declared a male colleague as he peeked over my shoulder at the title of the chapter I was working on: "Are Professional Women Good Mothers?" Anticipating from his tone some flippant observation about "absentee moms and latch-key children," I was pleasantly surprised by what he had to say: "My patients who are working professionals are very good mothers—no, in fact, most of them are rather extraordinary mothers. I've often been struck by how dedicated they are to their children."

My surprise at my colleague's response was very telling—I really did not know what to expect. Even though his observations clearly resonated with my own clinical experience, the fact that professional women *are* good mothers is an observation that is all too infrequently validated.

For most of us, external positive assessments of our accomplishments as mothers are generally absent from our experience. Those of us who work while raising children are caught in the crucible of an American cultural war aimed squarely at working mothers.

One of my patients, a physician with three small children, recently recounted her own take on this issue:

There's not a lot of support for working mothers, even though there are more of us now than ever. It's particularly hard when you don't "have to" work. Others see your continuing to work as an expression of vanity or selfishness—that you choose to work when you could be home with your children. It's viewed as an "either—or" thing, and often a working mother is seen as someone who puts her children's interests second to her career aspirations. I don't know about other women, but I'm working in order to ensure that my children have the things my husband and I think are important for them—things like a good education, a nice home to live in—things like that. And I work really hard to make sure that my working does not interfere with their happiness.

From my experience with literally thousands of professional women, I would have to agree with this woman's assessment. *In fact, I would be hard pressed to recall a professional woman who did not set her children as a primary priority in her life.* Further, I have yet to meet a professional woman whom I would describe as a "bad mother." Clearly different women take different paths with respect to their children and their careers. Although I obviously have seen professional women in the throes of difficult marriages or personal crises behave in ways that may not have been in the best interests of their children, *never* have I met a woman professional who willfully ignored the needs of her children for the sake of her career. *Our research on MBA women supports my clinical experience on this issue.*

♦ ♦ ♦

LESSONS LEARNED

As Professional Women, Our Children Are Our Number One Priority
One issue that virtually all the women in our sample agreed on was that if a woman had children, her children were her number one priority—regardless of her career aspirations. Although not every

woman in our sample desired to become a mother, nor were all women pleased with the types of trade-offs necessitated by being a working mother, the women we studied indicated that children would be, and should be, the first priority of a working mother.

Our study was replete with comments like "Families come first," "Children are the most important priority in a women's life," "A family is infinitely more important than a career," and "You can get laid off tomorrow, but you'll always be a mother"—all coming from some of the most high-powered women professionals in the country.

One woman, a 1980s Successor with two small children, wrote poignantly of her experience:

> Having children has been the hardest thing I have ever done. I realized that no one could ever love them as much as I do, and I felt that they deserved to be raised by me. Once I had them, my career became a secondary consideration. It wasn't easy for me to leave a successful position as a management consultant with a big firm. I'll always wonder what level of success I could have achieved if I had not left. But I have absolutely no regrets. My children have given much more meaning and joy to my life than any job I've ever had. Life is short, childhood is short, and money and power don't create happiness. Rocking my baby to sleep is what gives me the greatest pleasure. My family is really what matters in my life.

As Professional Women, We Do Not Make Trade-offs That Harm Our Children

As professional women, it is notable how much we are willing to sacrifice of ourselves to integrate the needs of our families with those demanded by our jobs. When making trade-offs, professional women assiduously work at avoiding compromises that have negative consequences for the well-being of their children. It is often the case that the children of professional women want for nothing, including true quality time with their mothers.

In our research, numerous women wrote of giving up very successful and lucrative career options when they conflicted with what they felt was best for their children, as this 1980s Successor explained:

> I had to give up my position as director of marketing once I had kids. It was a great job with great people and lots of future earning potential. But the "dual career" thing didn't work in our house. Both of our jobs were too demanding in terms of time and travel. The kids would have been orphans, because my husband could never be there to back me up at home. I really hated giving up my job, but if I hadn't quit, I'd be divorced and a single parent. I couldn't do that to my kids or my husband—over a job!

It was not uncommon for the women in our study to report that they would refuse to take positions requiring overnight travel or weekend work in order to be at home with their children. Many indicated that they refused promotions or lucrative opportunities in order to maintain some semblance of a family life. Even those who worked long hours reported making special efforts to ensure that their time at home was devoted specifically to their children, as this pediatric surgeon and mother of three recounted:

> I have an entire army of people working for me—a housekeeper, someone to cook, a nanny. It seems ridiculous, but with my call schedule and three children, this is the only way I could make it happen. Whenever I'm home I have someone else do errands, cooking, etc., so I can be with the children for uninterrupted time. It takes some organization but works out really well. My husband's schedule is just as crazy as mine, so he's not able to help a whole lot. It costs a bloody fortune, but it is the only way that neither my career nor my family would suffer.

As Professional Women, We Are Willing to Make Tremendous Sacrifices to Be Good Mothers

Many of the women I see in my practice work "executive hours," or, as one attorney explained it, "any eighty hours a week I choose." Working in a professional capacity in most instances necessitates a level of responsibility and responsiveness that far exceeds the demands of a 9-to-5 job. For many professional women, working full time means spending, on average, 60 hours per week at work. When this level of commitment is coupled with the responsibilities of a home and family, the sacrifices required to make it all work are indeed considerable.

For some, the sacrifice amounts to a second shift of responsibilities at home that extends the work week to well beyond 100 hours. One 1990s Successor, the mother of a teenage daughter, who reported that she typically works 60 hours a week as a management consultant, described her experience trying to balance the competing demands on her time and energy:

> I have to sacrifice sleep often, but I'm usually home for dinner and homework with my daughter. It's hard to have it all: a wife's career, a husband's career and a family. It's easy to say that family is most important, but it is hard to live it.

The experience of this woman is not unlike that of many other professional women with children. Many women in our study reported making special accommodations in their schedules to ensure that they could drop their children at school and/or could be home in the afternoons to pick them up. Even mothers whose schedules did not accord them this much flexibility reported dedicating evenings and weekends almost exclusively to being with their children.

It is clear that the sacrifices we make for the sake of our families require extraordinary dedication and a willingness to forgo, or postpone, our own needs to accommodate the needs of our families. For many of us, this means writing our reports between 10 P.M. and 1 A.M. because that is when the children are finally asleep. For others it means putting exercise and grooming rituals on hold until after the homework's been corrected, the pets have been fed, and the backpacks are ready. And is there a working mother alive who has not had the experience of desperately struggling to stay awake the next day after being up all night with a sick child? Obviously an involved partner makes a lot of difference in shouldering these responsibilities, but not every professional woman has one, and even those who do have one, find it difficult to get a good night's sleep with a sick child in the next room.

Taken to the extreme, this dedication to the needs of our families can have significant consequences for our own health and well-being. Striking the right balance between the needs of one's family and one's own needs is a critical piece of the puzzle we need to solve.

As Professional Women, We Make a Priority of Our Children's Needs and We Participate Actively in Their Lives

Regardless of whether we are working or not, as professional women we make it a priority to participate in our children's activities. Regardless of how we must rearrange our schedules, we stay involved in our children's lives. We are passionate about their educations, and we make a priority of their physical and emotional well-being. The women in our Stanford study often reflected on the importance of staying involved in their children's lives. One mother, a 1980s Settler with two preteen daughters described: "becoming her daughter's basketball coach despite a lack of previous experience just to ensure that the sport would be available to girls at the school."

As this woman demonstrated, when we sign up to do something—to chair a committee, to raise money for a new gym, to teach an art class, or to coach a soccer team—we get the job done, and we do it very well. The efficiency and organizational skills that serve us well professionally are applied to our children's activities with the same diligence as they are in the workplace, and the end result is impressive indeed.

Recently, one of my patients, an engineer with an MBA from Stanford, completed a stint as head of her daughter's school's multi-million-dollar capital campaign, a successful venture that resulted in the completion of a new junior high facility. Applying many of the same skills that she had learned as a management consultant to analyzing and spearheading the school project, she was able to cap a highly successful volunteer team effort with an outstanding accomplishment.

In a similar, although less considerable way, several years ago I cochaired a committee for the annual father–son night at my son's school. After reviewing the usual options—casino night, basketball games, and so on—the committee of working mothers, in a moment of certifiable lunacy, decided it would be fun to do something completely "new and different." One of the other cochairs was a mother of two and a business executive whose firm was based on the East Coast. She spent four days a week working in Boston and was home with her family in California from Thursday through Sunday.

Given our schedules, we planned everything by fax, phone, and e-mail and met only when necessary, on Saturday mornings. Despite serious challenges to our sanity, we did, in fact, manage to produce a "new and different" event. It took time and organization, but most importantly, it took my cochair, who, in addition to being a model of efficiency, possessed an engaging can-do spirit that kept us all going when things got stressful. This sense of determination and optimism in the face of rather formidable odds helped us sail through the rough spots and allowed us to stage the first (and perhaps last) father–son go-cart construction challenge in the school's history.

Working or Not, as Mothers We Make a Priority of Spending Time with Our Children

Although those of us who work outside the home may not be around all day, when we *are* there we tend to *be* there. Our sample was replete with anecdotes of time happily spent with children. From these women emerged a picture that is familiar to most, if not all, of us. As mothers, we genuinely enjoy our children and we enjoy spending time with them—reading to them, playing with them, going places with them, and just hanging out and being with them. As many of the women in our Stanford survey indicated, relying on outside services (restaurants, take-out meals, cleaning help, and so forth) is a strategy that allows us to spend more of our time directly with our families.

We enjoy getting to know our children, and we talk with them a lot. We are interested in what they think, and we communicate on a wide range of topics. Because we are well-informed and engaged in the world, we encourage our children to do the same. As a result, many professional women report that their relationships with their children are far better than the relationships they enjoyed with their own mothers. It is clear that the kinds of discussions we have with our children effectively set the stage for closer interactions with our children once they reach adolescence.

As Mothers and as Professionals, We Are Acutely Attuned to and Concerned About the Well-Being of Our Children

Given our professional backgrounds and the availability of information on children's health and well-being, we know enough about children to be appropriately concerned. As professionals, we stay up to date on issues of importance in our children's lives, and we act on that knowledge as needed. We think about what is right for our children, we worry about it (sometimes to an extreme), and do our best to ensure that our children flourish. We read, we research, we consult professionals—we leave no stone left unturned—when our children's well-being is at stake. One need look no further for proof of this dedication than the extraordinary efforts professional women make with respect to the selection of prenatal care, pediatric attention, playgroups, preschools, and so on, for our children.

Outside of Work, Our Lives Often Revolve Around Our Children and Their Activities

It is not the children who suffer in the families of professional women. If anything, many of us tend to be so "childcentric" that our lives outside of work revolve around our children and their activities. Anyone who has eaten in a restaurant lately can attest to the fact that most professional families take their children with them nearly everywhere they go. As one young couple recently recounted:

> We had 10 years of quiet, intimate dinners before we had kids. We only have our children for such a short time; we want to be with them. The time we have with them is too precious to let them stay at home with a sitter when we're around. We'll have plenty of time to be alone again when they are teenagers and they won't want to be seen with us.

For many professional women the idea of spending time with our children is truly a welcomed experience. In fact, most of the Stan-

ford women we studied cited "more time with family" as their principal reason for shortening their work schedules. Additionally, family
vacations have become the norm for many professional families, and
although occasionally this focus on children can be detrimental to
the couple relationship, the principal outcome is that children spend
more time with both of their parents.

Time for "Nonessential" Activities—Friends, Hobbies, or Ourselves—Is Often Seriously Curtailed

This 1980s Settler, the mother of two children, who worked full time
in finance, described her experience:

> It used to be that I would keep up with friends and family. I
> wrote letters, talked on the phone, and kept in touch, even when
> I was working full time. Once I had children, though, I didn't
> have the time for anything other than the family and my job.
> Now, my exercise gets squeezed in, if at all, at the most ridicu-
> lous times, and I barely have time to e-mail someone for a birth-
> day. I feel out of touch with a lot of my friends—I don't have a lot
> of time to do things with them—and sometimes the isolation can
> be pretty stressful.

For many of us, life can become pretty intensely focused on work
and family, and this singular focus on the "critical issues" can lead to
sacrificing other important relationships in one's life. Many professional women lament how hard it is to maintain, or even make
friends:

> When everyone is working and you have kids, you either see
> someone for lunch or it doesn't happen. There's no time for hang-
> ing out, going shopping with a friend, whatever. Maybe you can
> get in a bike ride on rare occasions, but that's it. I miss the "girl
> time" to hang out and talk.

Conflicting Roles and Multiple Obligations Often Do Not Allow Us to Feel Good About Our Accomplishments as Both Mothers and Professionals

Assuming multiple roles is part of the psychological terrain for any
professional woman—we may be mothers, partners, providers,

workers, daughters, sisters, friends, and so on, and we take each of these roles seriously. *In trying to fill our multiple roles, we often hold ourselves to a standard of excellence that does not allow us to appreciate how well we are doing in any one of them.* One patient, a high-tech product manager, recently described her predicament:

> Sometimes I'm so stretched that I feel like I'm not doing anything very well. Last week my boss started complaining about my not spending enough "face time" in the office—that I'm not seen as being really committed to my job. I was furious that she picked that day to call me on my dedication. I had gone into work even though my two-year-old was home with the flu. I was feeling awful about leaving him, and this was all I needed. I was so upset, it was all I could do to keep from walking out right there and then.

As for this young mother, consistently trying to meet conflicting expectations over a period of time can seriously compromise our sense of efficacy and self-esteem. Even though this woman had had excellent performance reviews and completed her projects on time, the fact that she was not able—or rather, was unwilling—to spend the desired "face time" in the office had consequences for her work evaluation.

Many working mothers report similar concerns about being judged poorly for not spending extra time "hanging around the proverbial water cooler," or its more recent equivalent, the fax machine. One woman, an executive vice president, recounted her experience with "face time":

> As a single parent, I never have time to hang out. I want to get my work done and go home. Early in my career, when I was the only woman on the management team, the men in my group would often schedule "meetings" in the evening. They liked to meet after work for drinks and sometimes for dinner. I never participated in these events, as I had a baby-sitter to worry about, and I wanted to see my kids. But I soon learned that these meetings were far from optional. Not being available on

an informal basis worked to my detriment. I was labeled as "not committed and not a team player." I had to work doubly hard to live down that reputation. It really made me angry, because I often worked much harder and more efficiently than the men in my group. Somehow that didn't count. I discovered much later on that it's not what you do—it's what others think you do— that matters.

As this woman unfortunately learned, "optional activities" in the workplace often can have multiple and covert meanings.

For Professional Women, Efficiency Can Be a Double-Edged Sword

Multitasking is a critical skill for all professional women, especially those of us with children. We multitask better than most, and we are called on to do it more often. It is our ability to be efficient, to multitask and maximize our limited time, that allows us to spend more nonwork hours with our families.

As we saw in the example above, however, this efficiency can work to our detriment if we are not available to participate in informal work processes. Although the opportunities for telecommuting are significantly altering the professional landscape, there are obviously still work situations and employers who require a consistent physical presence in the office.

As the corporate vice president above indicated, it's often not *what we do* but *how we do it* that affects the evaluation of our efforts. "Pay attention to how one is perceived" and "participate in the appropriate amount of office 'face time' " were suggestions offered by several of our most seasoned corporate veterans.

Interestingly, a few of the female managers in our Stanford survey reported feeling empathetic toward, but quite frustrated with, some working mothers who they felt were "short-timers." Principally, their complaints centered on mothers who were absent from the workplace on a regular basis because of child-related issues. Similarly, some professionals in our study who were not parents expressed resentments about having to back up coworkers who left early to pick up a child when there was still work to be done.

As Professional Women, We Often Have Difficulty Accepting Anything Less Than Perfection

Clinical experience suggests that as professional women, we tend to be rather conscientious about our work and set very high standards for ourselves. We do what we commit to do, and we do it well. As an example, many working mothers in my practice have opted to cut back on their official hours and receive a reduced paycheck rather than to spend less time (and effort) at work while accepting a full-time salary. Similarly, many women in our Stanford study reported that once they had children, they could no longer put in the hours they used to on the "big projects." Few, however, reported feeling comfortable about allowing the quality of their work to diminish as a result of having children. Even though they might limit the scope of the projects they assumed, the work they did had to meet their own standards of excellence.

A serious problem may arise for many of us, however, when we translate our notion of excellence into a demand for perfection in all areas of our lives. Because we tend to be exacting in our standards, many of us feel we should be able to attain some fictionalized norm of perfection—if we just tried harder, we could do it better. Dealing with unrealistic expectations is explored in the next chapter, but perfection is so much a part of the experience of professional women that it warrants some mention here.

Most of us do very well in the various roles we assume, but that reality is sometimes hard for us to recognize. As professionals, we thrive on control, and for many of us, the fact that order and neatness are on permanent holiday in our homes offends our compulsive natures. We tend to ignore the fact that, by and large, what our closets lack in organization, we make up for in our dedication to our children. We may be tired when we're reading *Goodnight Moon* for the fourth time before getting our toddler to turn out the light, and indeed we may be worried about how we are going to get through all the paperwork before tomorrow's meeting, but somehow, it all gets done. And more often than not, it gets done exceedingly well.

We need to accept that excellence and perfection in all we do may simply be out of reach—it is the cost of doing so much. Sometimes "good enough" has got to do. That is the essential trade-off that the women in our Stanford study consistently addressed. "Don't try to be all things to all people," advised one 1980s Settler. "Men don't, and they do OK for themselves."

We have to accept that all of our careful planning, organization, and efficiency evaporates the instant a child gets sick, a baby-sitter fails to show up, or an unplanned work crisis enters the picture. All it takes is for one of these things to happen, and our efficient lockstep grinds to an agonizing halt. On those days when nothing seems to be going right—when the children are a disaster and work is in abject free fall—the question "And I'm doing this why?" understandably springs to mind.

Our Parental Instincts Are Our Best Barometers

In working with parents of young children, I find that very often the answer to the question "What would be different if I were around more?" (and perhaps, "if I were in a better mood") focuses more on what parents would get to enjoy as a consequence of being home more, not what additional benefits their children would gain. This is a very telling response in itself and not one to be ignored. It suggests that our children's needs are most likely being well met and high-lights the fact that in many ways, our needs as mothers may not be as well addressed.

Parents with older children often see other ways in which their presence would make a significant difference in their children's lives, as one mother, a 1980s Settler with teenagers observed:

> Once my kids became teenagers, they needed a parent who was there and who could talk with them in ways that a nanny couldn't. It's more parental guidance and advice that they need now, not just someone who is loving and kind. I chose to cut back on my hours because I wanted to spend more time with the children while they were still at home.

In this case, the choices made by this mother were clearly dictated by a recognition of what was right for her family. For another family, the solution might be quite different. Our sample included several families in which the husband stayed home or seriously curtailed his career involvement to spend more time with the children. Obviously, there is no one solution for all. Our parental instincts, however, are probably our best barometer for recognizing when something does not feel right with our children. That is the first step to figuring out what to do about the situation. The answers are almost always there, but we may have to ask a lot of questions before the right ones emerge.

◆　◆　◆

ACTION PLAN: TAKING A PARENTING REALITY CHECK

Getting Perspective

I have yet to meet a working mother who did not, at some point, question whether she was doing a good enough job as a parent. *The first step in answering that question is the recognition that both clinical and research evidence suggests that the person who pays the price for managing the balancing act is us.* As professional woman and mothers, we are the ones who assume major responsibility for most aspects of family life, and we do so in ways that do not compromise the well-being of our children. As our research has demonstrated, our children are our first priority, and as such, we dedicate ourselves to ensuring their well-being. It is vitally important for professional women to understand this fact. Although most of us know we are doing a very credible job as mothers, we all confront a great deal of doubt about whether what we are attempting to do is in the best interest of our children. Clearly there are lots of variables that enter into the well-being of children, but our research suggests that our children's needs do not go unaddressed because of our careers. Rather, even though we may choose different avenues for integrating career and family, our priorities and attention remain singularly focused on the well-being of our children.

Because this fact is so difficult for so many of us to hold on to, I suggest the following exercise, the Parenting Reality Check Worksheet. I have used this exercise successfully in my practice to help women professionals assess their efficacy as parents.

With respect to our children, every mother, in her heart of hearts, knows the answer to the question "Are my kids doing all right?" Essentially, the Parenting Reality Check Worksheet evolves from this very simple question. In doing the Parenting Reality Check, the question to consider is *not* "Is everything perfect?" but rather "Are things generally okay?" In filling out the form, do not focus on the day-to-day things that can often be attributed to changing moods and circumstances but rather think about the big picture.

PARENTING REALITY CHECK WORKSHEET

Instructions: *Ask and answer the following questions.*

1. **As a parent, what do I sense about how my children are doing—are my kids doing all right?**

    Why I feel this way

    _____ Yes   _____

                         _____

    _____ Not sure   _____

                         _____

    _____ No   _____

                         _____

2. **What do the children tell me about how they are doing on a regular basis?**

    _____

    _____

    _____

    _____

3. **What do the people who know them best tell me about them? Is there some consensus?**

    _____

    _____

_____

_____

4. Looking over my answers to questions 1 through 3, what do I conclude about whether my children are doing all right?

_____

_____

_____

_____

5. What would be different if I were around all the time?

_____

_____

_____

_____

6. What would be different if I were around more?

_____

_____

_____

_____

7. What would be different if I were less stressed?

_____

_____

_____

_____

8. How is this stress related to my job?

_____

_____

_____

_____

9. **What ideas do I have for doing things differently?** *(Here, outline your thinking about possible solutions to the stress you may experience as a parent.)*

_____

_____

_____

_____

CHAPTER 4

Is Guilt the Cost of Doing (or Not Doing) Business?

EXPERIENCE: PROFESSIONAL WOMEN AND GUILT

It happens every morning. I make it out the door just fine, but as soon as I turn around and look at the window, I fall apart. I see my Katie standing there waving to me . . . and I think, "What the hell am I doing? Why am I leaving my beautiful little girl with the baby-sitter? Why am I doing this . . . to meet with a client? It doesn't make sense . . . and then the tears start.

Just as this young mother described, my guess is that some version of "driveway remorse" is replayed in millions of homes across America on a daily basis. I can hardly imagine a working mother with young children who has not at some point asked herself, "Why am I doing this? Am I doing the right thing? Is it okay to work while my children are young? How young is young?"

For some, the answer to the question "Why am I doing this?" is pretty straightforward: "I wouldn't eat if I didn't work." For others, however, the answer is a bit more complicated. As professionals, we work for a variety of reasons: economic, personal, and professional. Attached to each of these reasons is some measure of psychological cost, not the least of which is guilt. But is it all about guilt? Do we, as professional women, feel anxiety and remorse about our children solely because we feel guilty about the choices that we have made? Obviously not. Surely guilt is a part of it, but our feelings are also about separation and change, about the sadness of having to deny ourselves a real pleasure in our lives, and about our desire to work.

That those women who have no choice but to go off to work every morning feel every bit as conflicted, if not more so, than those of us who could chose to stay home is undeniably true. Yet no professional woman is immune to the anxiety and guilt we feel when the interests of our families collide with those of our careers. What is curious, however, is the fact that, for professional women, it appears that whatever choice we make—whether we choose to work or to not work when we have young children—the end result appears to be some measure of guilt.

One patient of mine, an attorney, and now the stay-at-home mother of a two-year-old daughter, described the powerful guilt she felt at not fulfilling the expectations that she and others had set out for herself:

> I spent $100,000 on law school and all I really want to do is sit at Gymboree with my daughter. I feel an enormous burden of guilt at not putting my education to good use. I worry about how my daughter is going to feel if I'm still at home once she grows up.

At the other end of the spectrum is the experience of one of the 1990s Successors in our Stanford study who returned to work while her children were young:

> No matter what I do, I can't avoid feeling guilty. Either I'm short-changing my kids or I'm not giving 150% to my job. I was on the East Coast calling on a customer when my daughter took her first steps.

Perhaps the most stressful psychological liability for professional women today is the extent to which guilt and uncertainty consume inordinate amounts of our time, energy, and emotional well-being. Under the best of circumstances, tremendous sacrifices are required of us and our partners just to stay afloat when children enter the equation. That guilt should further compromise our limited time and energy speaks persuasively to the need for us to learn how to counteract its deleterious effects.

* * *

LESSONS LEARNED

For Professional Women, Guilt Is a Cost of Doing (or Not Doing) Business

As we saw in the examples above, as women and as professionals, no matter what choice we make, we can wind up feeling guilty. If we focus on our children and families, we (and others) may fault us for our inability or unwillingness to be wholeheartedly dedicated to our careers. On the other hand, if we feel some measure of dedication to our professional lives, then profound concerns arise as to our willingness, or our ability, to be there for our families. As women who are both unequivocally devoted to our families as well as dedicated professionals, how do we win at this one? First, perhaps we need to recognize a few simple truths.

Not Every Professional Woman Wants to Work Once She Has Had Children

As we saw in the previous chapter, and as my clinical experience has consistently demonstrated, it is difficult, if not impossible, for anyone to predict how one will react to motherhood. Becoming a mother is such a life-altering experience that our reactions to that event are uniquely personal. Even women who are initially ambivalent about having children may find themselves completely captivated by the experience.

As a consequence, how we feel about the important issues in our lives, including our work, is reevaluated once children enter the picture. Some women find the demands of a new child, coupled with the attendant lack of adult interaction, overwhelming. For them, returning to the workplace can spell psychological relief.

For others, integrating work and a new family member is just natural progression in their lives. Even though they have some regrets when their maternity leaves end, they are equally pleased to be back at work.

For still others—and this includes some of the most driven, career-focused women I know—once they have children, their desire to return to work all but evaporates.

In my clinical practice, questions often arise as to whether a woman can, or more important, truly *wants* to maximize her career interests once she has had children. For many professional women, the idea of downshifting off the career path is not a wholly unpalatable idea. A lot of young professionals, both men and women, are quite surprised to find themselves less enamored of the intensity of a professional career once they have had children.

The women in our Stanford study were no exceptions, as this 1980s Settler and mother of three children under 6 describes:

> I was really surprised to find that my career focus changed so completely once I had kids. Work no longer gets 100 percent of my attention, and emotionally I don't care about killing myself for the company anymore. I know that I have to be positive and involved with three kids the minute I walk in the door. Raising a successful family is my primary concern right now.

Although such reevaluations of career commitment are a common occurrence among professional women, they can also be a source of shame, guilt, and self-recrimination. In my practice, many women have described "not giving a damn about my work or my boss the way I used to" and "not having the patience to put up with a lot of the b.s. in the office." Often, these concerns are guiltily expressed in the context of asking, "What is wrong with me?"

The answer is clear: "Nothing's wrong with you." How you feel is just that—how you feel. What is right for one person may be absolutely not right for someone else. Where work may have been the central focus of one's life before children, a new center may emerge once you become a mother. How much of that central ground you will be willing to cede to work once you have children is essentially an important personal choice. Feelings about whether you wish to return to work after having a child—immediately, soon, later, or never—are neither discernible beforehand nor derivable from a simple analysis of pros and cons.

Just like the myriad of other unknowns that go with being a parent, a certain measure of uncertainty is an unavoidable part of the life process. With respect to our uncertainty about our professional lives once we have children, the best strategy for us may involve building into our career plans a flexibility that will accommodate the unpredictability of our feelings.

Not Every Professional Woman Wants to Stop Working Once She Has Had Children

Many professional women find themselves feeling guilty about not being active in their careers once they become mothers, but those who return to work after having children can find themselves feeling guilty for exactly the opposite reason. Their guilt centers principally around uncertainty about how work affects the well-being of families. "Am I causing my children harm by continuing to work?" is the key question.

Even if we feel confident that we have made the right choice for our family, we often find ourselves questioned or second-guessed by those who simply do not understand why one would choose to return to work if it is not a financial necessity. One patient, an executive recruiter, recently recounted her experience with this issue:

> I had my own doubts about continuing to work once we had children, but I know myself. I would be bored to death being at home all the time. I didn't think it would be good for my kids or for me. I've worked hard to get where I am, and I don't want to throw it all away. I think I'm doing the right thing. My husband understands, but my parents certainly don't. They let me know in no uncertain terms that they think I'm making a big mistake. It concerns me a lot, because I really don't know what the long-term consequences of my choice are.

Another woman, a marketing manager, recounted how she was berated by other professional women for her decision to continue working after her third child was born:

At first, I was really incredulous. Here was my boss, herself a working mom, telling me that now that I had three kids, wasn't it time to focus my energies on my family? I couldn't believe it coming from her. Then my obstetrician weighed in—asking whether I had considered what my "obsession to have a career" was doing to my family? I about lost it! Fortunately, my husband is supportive, and I see no evidence that my work has had a negative impact on my kids.

For many of us, as professionals, the idea of giving up a career once children arrive on the scene is antithetical to why we chose professional careers in the first place. Despite changing gender demographics, attaining a measure of professional stature is still a hard-fought battle for most women. Not only have we spent years in educational preparation, but our work experience has allowed us to attain a level of professional competence and advancement that would not be easily jettisoned either personally or economically.

Like this publishing executive with four children, many professional women view continuing to work after having children as a kind of psychological insurance:

I see my career as a way of balancing things in my marriage. It ensures that I have a more equal share of the power in our relationship. I pay for all things associated with the children: education, childcare, clothing, toys, etc. It allows me to have an unequivocal say in important areas of my marriage.

Other women, like this mother of three, employed in retail merchandising, view their work as a kind of insurance against unanticipated misfortune:

I grew up in a family in which my mother didn't work after getting married. My father left us when I was 8, and it was a disaster. My entire childhood was consumed by financial crises. Our lifestyle slipped over the edge of poverty on more than a few occasions. The bitterness my mother felt towards her circumstances left an indelible image in my mind. I know what it feels like to have creditors hounding you. I would never subject my children or myself to that kind of circumstance.

For women who have weathered difficult financial circumstances occasioned by single parenthood, spousal unemployment, or illness, the assurance that one can provide for one's family in an emergency is critically important.

Yet as compelling as these reasons are, choosing to work is not only about guarding against untoward circumstances. For many of us, work is, as one patient recently described, "like breathing," as this 1980s Settler reported:

It's simply something that I do. It is an integral part of who I am. I couldn't imagine my life if I didn't have my work. I think seeing both me and my husband as dedicated, hard-working professionals is very good role modeling for our children.

No One Can Make Us Feel Guilty Without Our Permission

Eleanor Roosevelt once reminded her audience that "No one can make you feel inferior without your consent." As working mothers, we need to remember that similarly, *no one can makes us feel guilty without our consent.*

This point was driven home to me quite personally and effectively in the course of writing this book. When I informed an acquaintance that the publishing deadline for completing this work coincided almost exactly with the departure of my youngest child for college, she cheerily informed me, "That's great—now he'll never get to see you during his last six months at home."

She scored a direct hit. I felt the full measure of maternal guilt.

So what does a practicing psychologist do in that situation? Well, I did momentarily consider a behavioral approach—like severing her offending tongue—but in reality, I just felt awful. I mumbled a sarcastic rejoinder about appreciating her support and raced home to discuss the matter with my perplexed son. He, being a sweet and supportive kid, immediately informed me that I was "nuts" and that I should "stop worrying about stupid stuff." That said, the guilt evaporated—proof positive of the efficacy of the cognitive strategies suggested below.

On a more serious note, however, that we as professional women feel guilty about the choices we make may be somewhat inevitable. The danger, as I see it, exists when we make career- and life-altering decisions because we are unclear about how to deal with our guilt. I would suggest that as women and as professionals, we accept some measure of guilt as a "sunk cost" and focus our energies on modulating its impact.

To that end, I suggest the following 8-step action plan.

◆　◆　◆

ACTION PLAN: EIGHT-STEP PLAN FOR DEALING WITH GUILT

Step 1: When Dealing with Guilt, Adopt a Cognitive Approach

There is impressive evidence to support the efficacy of adopting cognitive strategies for dealing with a range of negative emotions, including guilt. Although recent research supports the use of such strategies, often in combination with medication, for alleviating the most serious forms of depression and anxiety, cognitive strategies are equally effective for dealing with less intense forms of negative emotions.

Basically, a cognitive approach seeks to apply rational thought to the resolution of emotional conflicts. Cognitive strategies are particularly effective in modulating intrusive negative thoughts and feelings by engaging the thinking side of the brain. Breaking problems down into manageable parts and recognizing the thought choices made along the way can help a person to become "unstuck" and to resolve the issues at hand.

Take for example, the situation in which many working parents find themselves: that of being late picking up their child from day care. One standard strategy for many of us is to not leave the office until the very last minute, then to drive like the proverbial bat out of hell to get to the day-care center before the "dollar a minute" fee goes into effect. The whole time, we're swearing at everyone on the road, slamming our hands into the steering wheel, and admonishing ourselves for being "really lousy parents."

A cognitive approach would suggest that we start by accepting the inevitable—sometimes we will be late to pick up our child. Instead of berating ourselves mercilessly, one part of a long-range cognitive strategy would be examining what we could do to set better limits to prevent work slipover.

Another more immediate and important piece of such a strategy, however, would be to replace the negative and damaging self-talk of "what a terrible parent I am" with more effective reminders that our children will not be waiting in the street and that everyone occasionally miscalculates time. Obviously, we cannot ignore our responsibilities, and we (and our partners) may need to reexamine and readjust our commitments, but what is done is done, and no amount of self-recrimination is going to get us there any faster. Instead of focusing on what we did not do right, we would be better off focusing on how to not make the same mistake again.

Making the choice to label a behavior in a psychologically benign fashion flies in the face of more Freudian interpretations, but it allows us to focus on the issue at hand, that of being a calm and responsive parent when we finally arrive to pick up our children. Facing an angry day-care provider may temper some of our resolve, but we might as well approach the situation with everything going for us.

Such strategies cannot be adapted for all occasions—there are times when we really "ought to feel guilty"—but in many circumstances, a variety of cognitive techniques have demonstrated utility in diminishing pointless guilt.

Step 2: When Dealing with Guilt, Get the Facts

One fundamental cognitive strategy for dealing with stressful situations is to get information. As professionals, we owe it to ourselves to do just that: When in doubt, we need to do what we do best—engage the intellect and get the facts.

Guilt can result when we feel ill informed about the factual basis of our fears. For professional woman, doing research, gathering information, and mobilizing resources is our stock-in-trade. If we are not sure how our work affects our families, then we owe it to ourselves to be as informed about this issue as possible. If we worry about what type of child care has the most beneficial effects on a child's development, then we must engage our compulsivity wisely and obtain the information we need.

A recent research study provides an interesting case in point. The study looked at the effects of maternal employment on behavior and cognitive development of children. After reviewing the data from a longitudinal study of children between the ages of 3 and 12, psychologist Elizabeth Harvey found evidence that "early parental employment has a positive effect on children's development by increasing family income." As Dr. Harvey explained it, "This positive pathway seemed to affect children's behavior problems and academic achievement but not children's compliance, self-esteem, or language-cognitive development." This study supported the findings of previous research that indicated that "if the quality of parenting at home is good, having a working mother does not hurt children."

This study created an enormous stir in the media when it was released, primarily because of the intense feelings on both sides of this issue. As the headlines heralded MOTHERS' EMPLOYMENT WORKS FOR CHILDREN, a collective sigh of relief went up from working mothers everywhere. "At last, evidence that our work is not damaging to our children!"

Obviously, the findings of this particular research were not uniformly positive, but the existence of this type of scientifically informed data is an enormous help to all of us. As in this case, getting the facts allows us to understand the consequences of our work and also goes a long way toward allaying the self-doubts and recrimination that so often plague us.

Step 3: When Dealing with Guilt, Take the Long View

If there is one thing that the respondents in our Stanford study affirmed repeatedly, it was the fact that the competing demands of career and family change over the course of one's lifetime. Just as our career success may be redefined once children enter the equation, many of the most experienced women in our study, the Pioneers and Settlers, observed that one's emotional availability for work changes with the circumstances of our lives. A 1970s Pioneer with two grown children explained:

> The guilt you feel about working when you first have a baby is really different [from] how you feel once your child goes to school. Absolutely, you feel torn when the child is young and at home all the time—every minute at work feels like time stolen from your child—but once a child is in school, things get a lot easier. They're busy and so are you. The time crunch is still there, but the guilt lessens.

Another woman, a 1980s Settler, formerly in sales and now a stay-at-home mother of three teenagers, said:

> I found that my children needed me more as they got older. I didn't feel right about leaving them with someone else. I wanted to be there, and I was surprised about how strongly I felt about this. My career was very important to me, but the type of work I did didn't allow me to work part time. I think I made the right decision, but I don't know what the ultimate effect will be on my career, if I should decide to restart it.

As the experience of these women illustrates, restricting our vantage point to the immediate may cause us to miss the larger and more complete picture.

Obviously, the needs of children change over time, just like those of a career. Creating the flexibility to deal with whatever changes the future holds is important to our sense of confidence in the choices that we are making now.

Step 4: Invite Participation—a Family Is a Team Effort

> I have yet to hear a man ask for advice on how to combine marriage and a career.
>
> —Gloria Steinem

I was reminded of that line recently while having lunch with a friend from college. He was asking me about my research and, more particularly, why it was that women seemed to struggle so much with the issue of combining career and family. Was it something in the nature of women, he asked, or was it something about where we were as a society? "Men" he observed, "don't seem to have the same issue."

The answer that rolled off my tongue was as immediate as it was dismissive "That's because men have wives!" However, the earnest intent of his question warranted closer consideration. Clearly, the fact that traditionally men have had wives to manage child care and family responsibilities is the principal reason why most men, like my friend, do not find their professional lives to be in conflict with their family commitments. Still, I was left wondering whether there was something about us as women and the way we viewed our roles that caused us to feel the personal–professional conflict so acutely.

From both the clinical and the research perspectives, it is clear that most professional women assume a measure of managerial responsibility for things related to their families and home life. Perhaps we do not do the work directly—for example, someone else may cook, clean, or baby-sit—but most often, it is the woman who "manages" family life. A recent interview with pro golfer Julie Inkster illustrated this point. When asked what was the hardest part of being on the professional tour, this dedicated mother of two daughters and LPGA Grand Slam winner reported:

> If my family's not with me, it's organizing them all before I go— making sure everybody can get where they're supposed to be when they're supposed to be.

Similarly, a patient of mine, a travel writer whose work often took her away from home for periods of time, described an experience much like that of Julie Inkster:

> Yes, my husband takes care of our daughter, too. For instance, he's the one who usually takes Laura to her pediatrician appointments, but I'm the one who usually notices that she is sick in the

first place. I call to schedule the appointment. I remind him in the morning to leave work on time to take her there, and I check with him on follow up. Sometimes it seems like it would be easier to just do it myself.

Certainly, many of us can identify with that feeling, and for most working mothers, the "second shift" phenomenon is a reality, but why?

This 1990s Successor with a young child and a full-time career in retail merchandising offers some clues:

When a child is sick and you feel you have to go to work, it is the worst conflict imaginable. No matter how much things change, no matter how much men actually participate in family life, a woman in this society is still held responsible for the actual child rearing.

To try to better understand this issue, we looked at the data from our Stanford study. In our survey, we asked the respondents, "Who does most of the *non–work hours* child care in your home?"

In over 58 percent of cases, the women answered, "I do it all." In the majority of the cases, when the women in our study were not working, they assumed all of the child-care responsibilities for their families. This finding almost exactly replicated the results of a previous study we had conducted 10 years earlier with a sample of male and female graduates of the Stanford Business School. In 1985, we asked both male and female MBAs with children who was doing all, or most, of the child care and household tasks in their homes. We found that in the vast majority of the cases, it was the women who assumed primary responsibility for these activities.

Interestingly, when we asked these women how they felt about this allocation of family responsibilities, fully 89 percent indicated that they were satisfied with this arrangement. The question that remained unanswered was, of course, why the women were happy with this arrangement, and unfortunately our research did not provide that answer.

Moving forward to the present day, among the professionals in my practice, more women are reporting that their partners are playing an increasingly significant role in family life—taking on major responsibilities in caring for the children and assuming a variety of domestic/familial chores. It is not at all uncommon for professional women to report that they themselves do little or none of the cooking or household chores and that their husbands are doing the daily drop-off at or pickup from school. Fathers are far more consistently present at school events, even during working hours, and the sight of a father caring for children in stores, restaurants, or even sporting events has ceased to be unusual.

However, even in those families where fathers contribute significantly to family life, as we have seen, it is most often the woman who assumes the psychological responsibility for the well-being of the children. It is from this psychological responsibility that the seeds of guilt and self-doubt emerge. Too often, we all are quick to blame a mother if something goes wrong with her children. One patient, a research scientist with two children, aged 6 and 9, described her experience:

> When a child has a problem in school, it's immediately seen as a failing on the part of the mother. When my son had some reading difficulties in third grade, his teacher suggested that perhaps if I were home more, he wouldn't have this problem. She never suggested to my husband that he stay home and work with him, or that his schedule was somehow adversely affecting our child.

As responsible and accomplished professionals, we can sometimes find it hard to remember that not everything that happens to our children, good or bad, is something that we can encourage or prevent. Although we clearly have a responsibility to ensure our children's well-being, we are not alone in that responsibility. We share that obligation with the child's other parent, and we must allow our partners to take on, both physically and psychologically, equal responsibility for the welfare of our families.

If we conceive of our child-rearing and household responsibilities as truly shared, then we must truly share whatever guilt arises from those situations. But what if "He isn't bothered by the house being a mess" or "He doesn't worry about the kids' grades the way I do"—frequently repeated complaints of the working mothers I see in my practice. Therein lies the crux of the issue: Our partners don't have to worry—that's what they have us for. As long as we're doing it for them, why should they duplicate our efforts? We worry too much, and many times, we allow them to worry too little.

For example, take the issue of a child's academic performance. This is obviously a complicated mix of many factors in which emotional maturation and biology play often underappreciated roles. It is rarely just parental career involvement, or the lack thereof, that contributes to the difficulties a child may be experiencing in school. Worrying about academic progress, particularly in isolation, does little to address the root of the problem. Academic performance is a shared concern, and the resolution to problems associated with it requires a shared response. In short, we would do well to worry less and invite more participatory responses.

One patient of mine, a former teacher, found that asking for help held several surprising and unanticipated benefits:

> I was completely obsessed with the issue of nursery school. I knew I was being ridiculous, but I am very concerned about Melissa's education. I know John is, too, but he just doesn't get as agitated about it as I do. Whenever I'd talk to him, he'd just say, "Let's see what happens when we get closer to the decision." It was making me crazy. After discussing it in here, I promised myself I would tell him straight out that I needed some help. I was shocked by how that request changed our interaction. He suggested that maybe we should observe a few classes together and compare notes. While I had already visited the schools, somehow going with him allowed me to see things from a different perspective. We talked about it afterwards and the right choice was obvious to both of us. I feel so much more relaxed about it now, because we made the decision together. And John enjoyed being there so much, he arranged to share the co-op time.

PROFESSIONAL WOMEN AND CHILDREN

Not all efforts at joint ownership of familial responsibility result in such positive outcomes, but it appears that we, as professional women, might be doing our families a favor if we borrowed a page from our partner's game plan:

- Assume less psychological ownership of things that are rightfully joint responsibilities.
- Invite full participation in decision making and execution of child-care and household responsibilities.
- Let the responsible person be accountable for outcomes.

These are all things that we do in the business world every day, and we might benefit from adopting similar strategies in our personal life.

Step 5: When Dealing with Guilt, Examine Expectations

One of the things that make us successful as professional women is our compulsivity and our drive. All high-achieving people tend to be fairly compulsive, as it takes a fair measure of dedication to accept the challenges that we routinely undertake. This drive and determination that serves us well on the job, however, may be—as they say in the computer industry—"both the bug and the feature" when it comes to integrating our personal and professional lives.

Take, for example, the fact that for many professional women, household disorganization is a chronic source of frustration, anger, and guilt. Again, a lot of things enter into the house's being a "mess"—not the least of which are differences in tolerance levels and who assumes ultimate responsibility for its orderliness. As best we can determine, neatness and orderliness are not sex-linked characteristics, yet responsibility for life's orderliness appears, in many couples, to be the purview of women more so than of men—even though a man may like living an ordered life, it is often seen as the woman's responsibility to accomplish that orderliness. In many families, the psychological responsibility for household organization belongs to, or is claimed by, the woman.

Illustrative of this point is the surprising frequency with which Martha Stewart's name surfaces in discussions with professional women. We seem to have a complicated relationship with the arbitrator of domestic style. It is clear that no one with both a family and a fully engaged career could personally partake of the elegant, gracious, but highly labor-intensive Martha lifestyle, but all too often we are troubled by the illusion that we should be able to do so. Maybe not exactly Martha, but something close. Obviously, if cooking, entertaining, and so on are relaxing activities that we enjoy, we should include them in our lives, but if we cannot quite manage that right now, do we really need to own the guilt? Clearly, our partners do not. As one columnist for the *New York Times* recently observed, "We all *watch* Martha Stewart, but nobody really *does* Martha Stewart!" For many of us, watching Martha is a "virtual" substitute for doing the things that time does not permit.

A healthy examination of our expectations for our families and ourselves is an important part of excising unnecessary guilt from our lives. Perfectionism in all aspects of our lives is an infallible prescription for psychological disaster. That drive and determination can be good is indubitable, but unrealistic expectations can take us to places that we do not need to go.

Step 6: In Dealing with Guilt, Surround Yourself with People Who Share Your Enthusiasm

Recently, when several entrepreneurs were asked to name the factors most instrumental in their success, topping their list was the idea of "surrounding yourself with people who share your dream." Certainly, the importance of a proximate group of enthusiastic supporters during a time of growth, change, or transition is not a novel concept. At Stanford, the Professional Women's Group Program has succeeded mainly because it allows women to discuss issues of personal importance during a transitional period of their lives.

Although one would expect that professional women with children would seek out a similarly supportive group process, most working mothers do not. All too often, limited time resources seriously hamper our ability to do anything other than work or be with our families. The opportunity to meet other people and talk about the things that matter to us simply does not happen, and our isolation directly affects our ability to modulate guilt. *But there is perhaps no better way of exculpating unnecessary guilt than by finding others who truly share the same concerns.* Everyone wants to know what is "normal." "Is what I'm feeling okay? Is what I'm doing normal? What do others do in similar circumstances?" Most of us have not a clue about what other professional women do with respect to their families.

This point was underscored most recently when I met with a group of editors to discuss the publication of this book. Given the topic of the manuscript, not surprisingly, most of the editors were women, and interestingly, women who collectively spanned several generations—not unlike the women in our survey. At every meeting, inevitably the discussion turned to the variety of strategies that we had adopted to cope with the incessant demands of active careers and growing families.

"Guilty" secrets were shared—like one mother who described how she had once paid someone to color Easter eggs with her children because she hated coloring eggs but did not want to deprive her children of the experience. Or another mother who admitted that she often resorted to bribes to encourage her children's cooperation when a time crunch did not lend itself to protracted negotiations—something every one of us there could identify with.

We left the meetings agreeing that in addition to having participated in highly productive sessions, we had enjoyed the companionship and the opportunity to talk about things that were important in our lives. The younger childless women in the groups remarked on how encouraging the meetings had been, as they, like the Successors in our study, were actively engaged in trying to see into their own futures. Even in as brief and unlikely a circumstance as a business meeting, the simple act of collectively sharing our concerns, not to mention a few good laughs, went a long way toward alleviating our maternal angst.

As women, talking is something we tend to like to do, and we can use that skill to our benefit. In fact, when we asked the women in our Stanford study which activity they engaged in most often to enhance the quality of their lives, fully 83 percent of them cited talking with family and friends. *This pleasure is something that too often gets neglected in our overcommitted lives, and we may deny ourselves the opportunity to be surrounded by people who share our enthusiasm.*

Step 7: When Dealing with Guilt, Consider the Source

As any working mother knows, even in those instances when we feel we have made the appropriate choices regarding our families and our careers, guilt can be evoked by external sources. For some of us, support for our choices, even from those closest to us, may be surprisingly hard to find. One patient of mine, an executive at a major airline, recently described with great sadness her inability to convince her husband of the appropriateness of her desire to stay at home with her two daughters while they were still in preschool. She was quite shocked and more than a little dismayed by her husband's adamant assertion that, "for the good of the family," she "needed to return to work full time."

The guilt and frustration that this executive felt for wanting to step away from her career, or at least slow it down, was a significant source of stress in her life. In this case, the request, or rather demand, that she remain in the workforce was not based on financial necessity. Rather, her husband's concerns appeared to be motivated by the significant alteration of the family's lifestyle that would be occasioned by the wife's exit from the workplace. Such overt lack of support is rare in most relationships between professionals, it can show up in subtle and often unconscious ways. The familial anxiety and attendant guilt evoked by the prospect of reverting to a single paycheck is not to be ignored.

Problems of guilt and self-doubt arise also when we find ourselves surrounded by people who either don't "get" our choices or who, worse yet, have their own agendas. To understand how to deal with the guilt provoked in either case, one must recognize agendas for what they are. It is a clinical fact that most often the things people say about someone else reflect a lot more about themselves than about the person being addressed.

Take for example, the unintentional guilt provocateur. This may be the well-intentioned parent who advises us to not abandon our career to be a stay-at-home mom. This person may be truly concerned with our well-being and wish to spare us some of the pain that she has experienced in her own life. She may also be unable to comprehend the extent to which the conflicting demands of our lives make staying in the workforce at the present time antithetical to our (and our family's) well-being.

The provacateur's anxiety, however, is just that—*that person's* anxiety. It does not take into account the circumstances relevant to our decision process, nor does it look at the options that are available to us that were not a part of that person's experience. Before taking such advice to heart, we might do well to consider the source of the comments made and recognize the feelings that often underlie the concerns expressed.

The not-so-well intentioned guilt provocateur is another story. Most people, if called on their "guilt tripping," would probably object to having it characterized as intentional, but there are clearly people who have conscious or unconscious agendas that get acted out on professional women.

One recent example was a situation recounted by a patient of mine, a journalist, who received an e-mail of congratulations from her sister-in-law on accepting a major promotion that would place her in the national spotlight. Attached to the e-mail was a copy of a news article describing the drug problems of children of some famous (working) mothers. "FYI" read the subject header. One would be hard pressed to interpret that message benignly. Quite naturally, it provoked a response of guilt and concern about the future well-being of the reporter's children, which was, not surprisingly, accompanied by some significant anger and bewilderment as to the note's intent.

In discussing the matter, it became clear that the sister-in-law, having just recently abandoned her own plans to return to law school, felt threatened by the success of the journalist's career. Although it was difficult for my patient to comprehend the competitiveness and anxiety underlying her sister-in-law's response, it was helpful for her to gain some perspective on the issue and to prepare herself for any future assaults.

In sum, because as professional women and mothers we are often at the center of a high-stakes controversy, we can be the target of misguided anxieties that play into our own concerns. *Although it would be foolhardy to reject out of hand all criticisms that may be lobbed our way; we might carefully examine expressions of concern for their credible content and extract from them whatever benefits there are.*

Step 8: When Dealing with Guilt, Focus on the Positive

In thinking about the issue of a positive focus, I am reminded of the story of a clergyman who, when asked why he believed in the existence of God, responded that, while he obviously lacked proof, it simply made him feel better to believe. For professional women, the proof of the "rightness" of our particular choices will not be apparent until our children are grown into adulthood—and then some. Given that we lack absolute proof on which to base our decisions, we do have a choice. We can choose to focus on the negative—we can worry and obsess incessantly about whether we have done the wrong thing—or alternatively we can decide to make the most informed choices we can, on the basis of the best information available.

For many professionals, the idea of simply "choosing to focus on the positive" flies in the face of everything that we have been taught. Critical thinking is an essential part of our life experience, and it defies our mind-set to resist protracted analysis. We find it difficult to accept that which we cannot intellectually control. Yet much in life falls into the category of the uncontrollable, and we must live with that reality whether we like it or not. Given that, focusing on those things that we can control—for example, how we choose to expend our mental energies—is often our best, and most productive, strategy.

A rather simple exercise can often be quite effective in this regard. With patients who are concerned about their mothering, I ask them to make a list of the 10 things they are doing *right* with respect to their families and children. I instruct them to keep the list with them at all times and to refer to it whenever they find themselves concerned about their parenting efficacy. This concrete exercise turns out to be amazingly effective in helping women maintain a focus on the positive aspects of their efforts.

A Final Word on Guilt

Before concluding this chapter, I want to touch on a very real concern raised earlier when we addressed the issue of the "driveway remorse" that so many of us experience. It is a given that most working mothers must leave their children to go to work. Even though we all know that sometimes children can play the guilt card as well as, if not better than, most adults, this does not deny the very real concern that is evoked by a child's plaintive pleas for us not to leave them. Who could fail to be touched by a child's laments of "I never get to play with you, Mommy"? It is not at all surprising how often we, as mothers, feel that we would be better mothers if we devoted ourselves singularly to the needs of our children. It goes without saying that we would probably qualify for sainthood if we did indeed do that. However, in reality, no one spends her entire day every day with her children. Even mothers whose days are not delimited by meetings and deadlines do not spend every waking minute with their children. Nor do our partners, and that is as it should be. Most women recognize that devoting 24 hours a day to one's children is neither a necessary nor healthy focus of maternal energy.

The most effective mother is going to be one who maintains a sense of balance in her life, whether she is working outside the home or not. Focusing attention on a range of intellectual, social, and physical activities creates a sense of personal and familial well-being—not an easy thing to do when one is busy, but certainly something worth aspiring to. As one patient of mine, a former music executive, reminded me recently:

> If Mom's not happy, no one is happy. When I got depressed, everyone in the family suffered. I couldn't cope with the guilt I felt at being on a plane so much and missing the important things that were going on in my kids' lives. The turning point was when I overheard my seven-year-old daughter explain to her little brother that "Mommy had another family" that I would visit on my trips.

When we are trying to make the right personal and professional choices, it is critically important to take into account the impact of maternal well-being on the entire family. For this particular patient, reducing her travel schedule was an effective and appropriate strategy. For her, like for so many of us, time was a guilt-inducing variable in her life. "If only there were more hours in the day," she lamented, "then perhaps I wouldn't feel like I was always shortchanging someone."

Because time is such an important variable for all professional women, I've included below a Family Time Worksheet, which I have found helpful in creating truly workable solutions.

FAMILY TIME WORKSHEET

Instructions: For the best results, copy the worksheet, have each partner fill out a copy independently, and then discuss your answers.

1. **Over the course of an average day, about how much time do you spend with your children?** _____
   About how much time does your partner spend with them? _____

2. **When does family time happen?** _____
   Does that feel right?

   Yes _____ No _____ Maybe _____

   If not, what can be done about that? _____
   _____
   _____

3. **Do your kids enjoy family time?**

   Yes _____ No _____ Maybe _____

   If not, why is that? _____
   _____

   What needs to change? _____
   _____
   _____

4. **Do you and your partner enjoy family time?**

   Yes _____ No _____ Maybe _____

   If not, why not? _____
   _____

   What can you each do about that? _____
   _____
   _____

5. Are each of you truly present (100%) when you spend time with your family?

Yes _____ No _____ Maybe _____

If not, why not? _____

_____

What can you each do about that? _____

_____

_____

6. If you can't spend all the time you'd like with your family each day, do you make the effort to do so on weekends, vacations, etc.?

Yes _____ No _____ Maybe _____

If not, why not? _____

_____

What can you each do about that? _____

_____

_____

7. Is there something you feel you need to do to refocus your priorities?

Yes _____ No _____ Maybe _____

What commitments can be jettisoned for the time being to accommodate your priorities?

_____

_____

_____

_____

PART II

• • •

Children and Careers

CHAPTER 5

Do Professional Women Have to Choose Between Career Success and Having a Family?

EXPERIENCE: HOW PROFESSIONAL WOMEN VIEW THEIR OPTIONS

Can a woman have it all? Can she have a high-powered professional career and still have kids? Sure—just as long as she doesn't plan on ever seeing them!

—1980s Settler, venture capitalist

Are things really as bad as this woman suggests? Is it truly impossible for a professional woman to pursue a successful career and still raise a strong and healthy family? Should a woman who is dedicated to a professional career forgo the pleasure of having children? Or can she make it work somehow? There is no doubt that the question of whether a woman can truly do a credible job of having both a career and a family is the most critical concern for professional women today. As one patient of mine, a physician with two small children, recently observed:

I know the idea of "having it all"—of having a perfect job and a perfect family—is a lot of b.s., but I want to do both, and I want to do them both well. I refuse to believe that I can't do it. I am determined not to give in to those who have something invested in proving me wrong. There has to be some way to make it work. The problem is, you don't know how well you're doing until your kids are older and you get to see how things turn out. It's very anxiety provoking not knowing if you'll be able to pull it off.

Every professional woman with children, no matter how competent or self-assured, has at some point in time come face-to-face with the reality of whether it is truly possible to "have it all"—whether she should, or must, choose between career success and having a family. For the thousands of professional women engaged in the daily battle to balance the demands of work and family, the answer to the question "Can it be done?" is neither simple nor straightforward.

From both the clinical and research perspective, there is good news and bad: Can a woman have a satisfying career and a healthy family life? Absolutely! Is it easy to do? Absolutely not! The critical question appears to be not so much whether it can be done (as thousands of us are already committed to doing it) but rather "What is the best way of going about it?" Here, the data from our Stanford survey can inform our choices.

◆　◆　◆

LESSONS LEARNED

First, the bad news:

There Is a Cost to Doing It All
As a young mother and former corporate attorney recently recounted the psychological costs that accompany attempts to "do it all" are often unanticipated:

> I can't believe how disillusioning this all is. I was raised as a feminist. I was raised to believe that I could do anything and be anything I wanted. And I did. I wanted to become an attorney, and I did it. I loved my life. I worked crazy hours, spent two days a

week on a plane, and still I loved it. Then I had my daughter, and suddenly my whole world shifted. Nobody ever told me I would feel the way I did. I was totally in love with her. For the first time in my life, I didn't want to go to work. I wanted to stay home with my child, and I resented every moment I spent away from her. It was my awful secret. I no longer cared about work. I didn't care a whit about the whole career thing. I couldn't believe it myself. I felt like I was betraying the whole women's movement. I felt like a fraud. How come other women could do it but I couldn't or, worse yet, I didn't want to?

For women like this attorney, who are raised with a sense that one can do and be anything one wants, the idea of combining a family life with an absorbing professional career seemed rather straightforward. Problems arise, however, because the desire (or the need) to accelerate one's career most often coincides with the optimal physical and psychological time to have and raise children.

Most of us manage to cobble together some semblance of a workable solution, but the toll such demands can take on our psychological health are well documented. According to our earlier study of Stanford MBAs, just two years after graduation, the women reported significantly higher levels of stress in their lives. They experienced significant difficulties maintaining boundaries between their work and family demands and were four times more likely than the men to seek psychological counseling for stress-related problems.

The results of our current MBA research, although not a comparison of male and female respondents, demonstrated a similar degree of role stress among the women we studied. When we asked our female MBAs how much conflict they experienced between their family responsibilities and their career demands, we found that over half of them (54 percent) indicated that they experienced a great deal of stress associated with juggling these conflicting demands. Not uncommon were comments about the toll taken by trying to do all things well, as this 1990s Successor explained:

Children require an amazing amount of attention. That's something that I definitely want to provide, and it's meant that my career has had to take a backseat. That's hard because it conflicts with my desire to do well in my job. And the conflict is a day-to-day thing: having to reschedule meetings to stay home with a sick child, having to travel when you'd rather be home. It creates significant stress for me, but it has not had a tremendously negative effect on my family, I hope, and certainly has had no discernible effect on my career.

Any working professional with children knows that the cost of managing the balancing act is very real. Both careers and families are capable of absorbing all our time, as this 1980s Settler describes:

> I think about it every day when I'm sorting out our schedules. I try to suppress the stress, but I'm sure it's still there. It creates a lot of ambivalence for me because I am not quite doing what I'd really like to do, but rather I have stayed in my job because it's the only way to make it all work. Every now and then I actually find myself wishing my husband made tons of money, I wouldn't have to work like many of my friends, and I could just be at home with the kids, and volunteer.

Given how difficult it is to integrate the demands of careers and family, it is a wonder that so many of us are attempting to do it.

To Professional Women, Both Children and Careers Matter

Part of the tension that we experience in trying to create balance in our lives is a direct result of the fact that *both* our children and our careers are important to us. As we saw in Chapter 3, as professional women and mothers, we make a priority of our children. Family life is important to us, and there is little doubt that for most of us, our families are the most important aspects of our lives. For those of us who have devoted large portions of our lives to developing professional careers, opting out of that career is no small matter. As one 1980s Settler with three young children explained it:

> I didn't want to be an absentee mom. It wasn't so much my concern about whether the kids would be all right with a nanny—

they were doing fine. It was me. I didn't want to miss out on the day-to-day stuff with my kids. I liked being able to pick them up after school and being able to go to their basketball games in the afternoon. Those were the things I didn't want to miss. But it meant turning down a promotion to vice president and not advancing as much as I could have at work. It was my choice, but it was a hard one. I will always wonder what I left on the table.

One could argue that as professional women we occupy a rather enviable status among working mothers, yet for many of us a two-income family is a necessity rather than an option today. In some areas of the country, even two professional incomes do not keep pace with housing costs, and both the professional woman and her family have come to depend on two incomes. Deciding to leave the workforce or cut back on the work commitments often necessitates significant changes in a family's lifestyle. As we have seen in the previous chapter, these changes are not necessarily greeted with enthusiastic support. One attorney with two teenage children describes her family's reaction to her thoughts about staying home:

> My kids don't want me to quit my job. Whenever I broach the topic with them or their dad, they reassure me that they would rather have me "bringing home the bucks" than have to give up some of the benefits they enjoy. It's rather disconcerting, but at least I don't feel guilty about being at work.

For Women Professionals, It's a Career, Not a Job

The situation is further complicated for most of us by the fact that work is an important and defining aspect of our lives. Many professional women are clear about the need and desire to maintain a professional life and identity. After years of education and training for a professional career, having to leave or deviate from a career path is a painful and soul-searching decision for us to make. It is a decision made all the more difficult by the limited amount of information available about the options that exist for professional women to balance work and family responsibilities. A young surgeon headed for a career in academic medicine spoke to this issue:

> I have spent so many grueling years perfecting my skills that it would be an incredible waste to throw it all away. I've suffered a lot to get to where I am and I've overcome enormous hardships. I know I want to have a life that includes kids, but there were so few women ahead of me in my specialty, and none of them have children, so it's tough to figure out.

Because most professional women have few role models who have successfully integrated personal and professional responsibilities, it is often difficult to gauge the future impact of our current career choices.

At the Highest Levels, Most Professional Careers Are Not Compatible with Involved Parenting

It is no surprise that for professional women the kind of work that would be attractive to us, and compatible to our skill sets, is not easily fashioned into work compatible with parenting responsibilities. Because of the extensive time commitments of professional work, it is often difficult for us to tailor a schedule that readily accommodates active parental involvement. Stepping down from full-time engagement in fields like law, finance, or consulting, for example, often results in work that is less central to the organization and may result in slowed or lost advancement. One mother, previously employed in venture capital, recently recounted her experience:

> Once I had kids, I couldn't put in a lot of extra time for the big projects that impressed the partners at my old firm. Working as a consultant has been better for my family, but I'm not in the mainstream or working on the cutting edge. It's been my choice, but not one I'm entirely happy with. Having forgone a partnership track has definitely limited my future options, not to mention my present financial compensation.

A stay-at-home mom, a 1980s Successor who had previously worked in marketing, shared a somewhat different perspective on the issue:

I went from a high-profile powerful job to a part-time job to no job. I couldn't continue to function at the level my job demanded and still be the kind of parent I wanted to be. I honestly don't believe that I will "suffer" for having changed my career path and for delaying a traditional career. Who knows what path will come next? For me, having a family has been the most satisfying thing in my life—no other job could offer these rewards.

Now, the good news:

The Most Seasoned Veterans in Our Study Are the Most Optimistic About Successfully Combining Work and Family Life

Overall, the women in our Stanford sample who had worked as professionals for the longest time were the ones who felt the most optimistic about the chances of a woman successfully integrating career and family interests. These women, the Pioneers, were clear about the fact that although combining career and family might not be easy, attempting to do so was not a prelude to personal or professional disaster.

This finding was unexpected and somewhat counterintuitive. Common sense would suggest that if any group of women would have had to struggle with the demands of managing a career and raising a family, the Pioneers in our study would have had to do so. One would expect that these early MBA graduates would have had more difficulty than later graduates in meeting the challenge of balancing career and family and would have had no support in doing so from the larger society. If, as many of our respondents reported, quality child care is difficult to come by now, one can only assume that it was harder to find in the 1970s and earlier. If workplaces currently do not provide support for working parents, could it possibly have been better earlier on? Yet interestingly enough, it is the Pioneers, the women who presumably would have confronted the most difficult challenges in combining work and family, who felt the most optimistic about it. How could that be?

One answer may lie in the typical personality characteristics of the women who make up the Pioneer group. Our study did not include measures of personality traits, but personal experience may shed some light on the subject. In the early 1980s, I was invited to present a paper on women in science and engineering at a university conference. One of the other speakers was a highly regarded female physician who, in discussing her own experiences as a medical pioneer, launched into a tirade about all the "women's issues bull." From her perspective, there were only medical issues and gender played no part in any of them. For her, being a woman made absolutely no difference in medicine. To survive, you had to be "one of the guys" and you had "to give as good as you got." This woman, like many others of her generation, was determined, perhaps of necessity, to be just as macho as her male counterpart. (Nearly 20 years later, her take on the subject had altered considerably).

Similarly, many of the Pioneers in our survey, like other first-generation groups, may have been more determined than later groups of women to succeed at the goals they set for themselves regardless of the personal costs involved. They clearly were nontraditional by the standards of their day, and they needed to prove that they could do whatever it took to accomplish their goals. For the Pioneers, playing by the existing rules and denying the roadblocks that stood in their way were parts of a successful strategy for overcoming the considerable barriers they faced. Other considerations also came into play, as this 1950s Pioneer reminds us:

> Women today forget that at one point, birth control was not a reliable option. You couldn't just choose the time you wanted to have children. Many of us saw family as a given, and a career as something to fit around a family. For us, choosing between career success and raising a family was not an issue—if you had a family, you just did what it took to make it work.

In fairness to today's professional women, it is important to remember that our Pioneers typically did not work at the same types of jobs that professional women hold today. Most Pioneers worked in female-dominated industries, often because such industries were the only ones open to them. Although their work was groundbreaking for its era, many of their jobs did not necessitate the kind of commitment currently expected of professionals today: commitments of round-the-clock hours, weekend work, and extensive overnight travel.

Although the Pioneers may have had a different experience in life than those working today, it would be clearly unwise to ignore the wisdom these seasoned veterans provide with respect to the options for successfully integrating career and family concerns.

Our Pioneers Suggest That Taking Time Out for Family or Downshifting Career Involvement Does Not End Careers

The finding that accommodating family needs does not have to derail one's career is perhaps the best news for the current generation of professional women. From their own experience in the workplace, the Pioneers in our survey suggest that it makes good sense for professional women to take a longer-term perspective in assessing the true costs of current career decisions. Their own experience suggests that there may be options that women do not consider when just looking at the immediate consequences of a particular career decision. In not taking a longer-term perspective, a woman may be considering her options too narrowly and thus limiting her choices. One 1970s Pioneer, a corporate president with two children, explained:

> If a woman is planning on having kids, she should do it whenever it is right for her. There is a small window for having a child, but you can work for at least 40 years. Careers evolve and develop in ways you can't begin to imagine. Life is full of choices. If you limit yourself to a particular career path, you may be giving up other more interesting possibilities, including the option of having children. Even the most rewarding career is just a job compared to the joys and challenges of kids.

The advice offered by the Pioneers about taking a longer-term career perspective is particularly important in light of the amount of anxiety this topic generated among the younger women in our survey. *Our most recent group of graduates, the Successors, were the ones least likely to believe that career success and family responsibilities were compatible.* The Successors, like the Settlers, are the women who are most likely to be either currently in the throes of raising children or to be seriously contemplating that prospect. Many of them report witnessing the struggles of the women ahead of them in attempting to integrate work and family concerns. As one 1990s Successor wrote:

> I don't have children yet, and I hope that I don't have to sacrifice my career in order to have a family, but the trials of my mentors suggest that things really look bad.

Observing the difficulties that many senior women had in trying to successfully integrate career demands and family life, many Successors expressed doubts about whether careers would have to be sacrificed once children entered the equation. As one 1990s Successor, a management consultant, observed:

> The senior women with kids who are left in my firm are all workaholics. I don't know how or when they spend time with their kids. They seem to be pretty good at managing and delegating their home responsibilities, but they don't ever seem to be at home to enjoy their families. It's not a model I want for my life.

As a group, the Successors questioned the wisdom of trying to integrate the demands of a career and family. *For them, trying to do both, particularly at the same time, was not viewed as an optimal strategy for achieving a balanced life.*

The experience of many of the most experienced women in our survey suggests that they may be right. Several women echoed the remarks of this 1960s Pioneer, who observed:

The career game is a long one. You have many years to succeed in your career. Being a mother and raising a family only is an option during certain times in your life. There is little reason to rule out the maternal option for a career. One can have a career before, during, or after having kids. Everything doesn't need to happen at once. Taking a longer-term perspective on things is important.

Looking at a career as an involvement that can be stepped up or down depending on what other issues are going on in one's life offers new options for women trying to decide on how best to balance their personal and professional lives. In Chapter 7, we will address the option of sequencing commitments as an important strategy for creating balance in our lives.

◆ ◆ ◆

ACTION PLAN: SEVEN-POINT STRATEGY FOR ENHANCING OPTIONS

Point 1: Negotiate Hard for What You Want: They Need Us Now

In working with women professionals in a variety of fields, I have been able to observe firsthand some very positive changes occurring regarding the question of whether a women has to choose between career success or family interests. For many professional women, not just MBAs, the opportunity to create work that blends more readily with the demands of parenting is increasingly available. Although the jury is still out on the long-term career effects of exercising these new options in the professional workplace (see Chapter 8), the fact that organizations are now more than ever willing to consider a variety of arrangements beyond the full-time at-your-desk work week is good news for any professional woman.

Because of the market demands for highly skilled professionals, professional women are in stronger negotiating positions than ever before. Recognizing this position of strength and using it to our advantage can be an important step in creating the balance we seek in our lives. As one of our 1980s Settlers suggested:

> It is in a woman's best interest to ask for what she wants in terms of schedule and work assignments, then negotiate hard to get it. There is no harm in asking for more than you actually expect. That way you can get at least something approaching what you want!

Point 2: Consider the Extraordinary: It Is Not Out of the Question

I am consistently surprised at the types of arrangements that woman are now able to negotiate for themselves in terms of flexible schedules and time-limited involvement in work organizations. Arrangements that just a few years ago were unheard of and, for much of working America, unthinkable, are now becoming quite commonplace.

I was recently amazed when an attorney in my practice reported that she had negotiated an arrangement with her firm that allowed her to work from home *five days* a week, going into the office only for client meetings. Clearly, she was a valued contributor to her firm, and her employer recognized that it was preferable to have her in some capacity than not to have her at all. This organizational response reflects a significant positive change in the options available to many of us.

Point 3: New Technology Is Changing the Game: Use It

Although the type of scheduling arrangement described in the example above is not typical for most professionals, many of the women we studied reported that telecommuting had become an increasingly accepted possibility for them, enabling them to work full time but to telecommute from home one or more days per week. Technological changes have irrevocably altered the workplace, and are making previously unthinkable arrangements both possible and palatable. Faced with strong demands for a professional workforce, organizations are increasingly willing to consider options such as home-based employment. Obviously, not every job affords such options, but recent technological changes contribute significantly to our ability to integrate our personal and professional agendas.

Point 4: Think Bold and Creative First

When my patients examine the choices they have to make to accommodate the demands of work and family, I encourage them to think broadly about their alternatives. Too often, we limit our options by not thinking creatively about the types of accommodation we need from our jobs. Whether it is because we tend to underestimate our own contributions at work or because we wish to avoid conflict in the workplace, we frequently do not ask for what we need. We assume that a work organization will not be responsive to or accommodating of our needs—particularly if it has never been so in the past—and we soldier on. This clearly works to our disadvantage.

It might be better to consider, as one 1990s Successor suggests, the following strategy:

> Everything is open for negotiation at work. Once you have established some credibility, it is surprising the things you can ask for and actually get. Today it's cheaper for them to give you what you want than to have to train a new person to take your place.

Point 5: Learn from Those with Experience

It is important to recall that the most experienced women in our sample, the Pioneers, were the ones who were most optimistic about the ability of professional women to successfully integrate career and family life. When asked about the effects of raising a family on one's career advancement, overwhelmingly the women responded: "Just do it! Everything else works out." As one 1970s Pioneer wrote:

> Having children is not something you can plan the way you'd like to think. There are too many unknowns and things often don't happen according to plan or schedule. If it feels right for you and your husband, then it is right. The other things sort themselves out. It's one of the few times in your life when you

are completely at the mercy of forces you can't really control. That's sort of liberating. You do whatever you have to do to make it work.

Point 6: Take the Lead from Fields That Are Changing

One of the best vantage points for observing the changing opportunities available to us as professional women is, oddly enough, the field of medicine. It was not so long ago that medical call schedules were created on timetables that were antithetical to the successful integration of work and family life. These call schedules clearly put professional women (and actively involved fathers) at a disadvantage. Surprisingly, this is no longer the case in many specialties of medicine. Even though it's not always easy to arrange, it's now possible for residents to complete their residency in some medical specialties on a part-time basis. Similarly, at some universities, the tenure clock for medical school faculties can be slowed to accommodate working mothers. If a woman chooses to work part time while raising her family, the time line for a tenure decision is proportionately delayed. Although not without some attendant downside, this type of accommodation was truly unheard of as recently as 1985.

Although few would identify academic medicine as a field that has been historically hospitable to women, but it is important to note that as more women have entered the field of medicine, healthier lifestyle accommodations are becoming increasingly commonplace. Recently, one of my psychiatry residents surprised me by describing medicine as:

> . . . a great career for women who want to raise families. With night floats and part-time residencies, medicine is far more accommodating than a lot of other professional fields.

This statement would *never* have been made earlier. Of all the dramatic changes occurring in medicine today, accommodating a healthier lifestyle for physicians is not one most of us would have predicted.

Point 7: If the Negotiation Fails, Keep the Pressure and Your Spirits Up

If a first-time negotiation with a work organization is unsuccessful, that is not atypical. For the most part, organizations are notoriously slow adapters—taking risks on novel approaches to workplace issues is not typical organizational behavior. When a request is made for a change in workplace involvement, the immediate response is almost invariably negative. If an organization is unresponsive to negotiations, however, there are other ways to deal with the situation. As an academic colleague of mine recently observed about her field:

> The way a person gets promoted here or gets any important concessions is by having other job offers, and then letting the university know about them. It's only once they realize that they run the risk of losing you [that] they get serious in their intent.

Not giving up at the first sign of unresponsiveness is an important part of an ultimately successful negotiation. You may have to make a request more than once, or with different terms or circumstances, to secure the desired positive response.

CHAPTER 6

Now, Later, or Never: Is There a Right Time in a Career to Have Children?

EXPERIENCE: WHAT PROFESSIONAL WOMEN SAY ABOUT TIMING

If you are trying to decide when to have a child, ask yourself, "Do I want to give this company or this boss the power to control my decision about having children?" When I asked myself that question, I stopped postponing the issue.

—1980s Settler, mother of a 9-year-old

"Exactly how late can a woman start having children and not risk conceiving a child with birth defects?"

That was the question that came from a member of the audience at a conference, "The Consequences of Delaying Childbirth," held at the Stanford Business School in the late 1980s.

The gynecologist on the panel began her response, "A woman could conceive a child with birth defects at any time, but the probability curve for genetic disorders associated with age—"

"Just give me a number!" said the student, cutting off the physician in midsentence. "I just want to know how long I can wait."

The other members of the audience shifted uneasily in their seats, as such acts of undisguised aggression were rare in the congenial setting of the Stanford Business School. Indeed, even the woman demanding an answer was herself taken aback by the urgency of her request. She sheepishly apologized for her outburst.

The physician lecturer handled the confrontation with grace, and the discussion proceeded in a more amiable vein. It was clear from what followed, however, that the distressed woman was not alone in her desperate search for the right answer. The questions that came from the audience, about equally from men and women, resonated with the theme of this woman's anxiety: how best to time the entry of children into their fully engaged lives.

The couples present were clearly struggling with the biological clock in the way that only professionals can do. They wanted to know exact answers, and they wanted them in terms and numbers that would tell the whole story. Probabilities were not exact enough— they wanted to be able to apply the same kind of spreadsheet analysis that worked so well in business to every facet of the decision-making process. Only then would they be able to find the right answer to the timing question that had so frustratingly eluded them.

That particular conference was memorable principally because of the palpable anxiety emanating from that audience. There was no doubt that the unfortunate convergence of career ascendancy and the biological clock was of tremendous concern to the hundred-plus couples that filled the auditorium to capacity.

As I thought about that conference recently, it occurred to me how much things had changed in the intervening years. It is not that the answers to questions of timing have gotten any clearer, nor is it the case that the issues have become less important. Rather, it seems that we as professional women have changed, and with that change have come new questions. Although we are clearly still concerned about the right timing of childbearing, it appears that the trend among professional women today is to not follow in the footsteps of the women who came before.

With respect to how and when to have children, today's professionals are profoundly aware of the problems confronting "the generation of women who forgot to have children," as a recent news show callously described them. Having witnessed the problems of a previous generation of women who put career priorities ahead of family, many of today's professionals are saying up front that having a family is a priority for them. Among the professional women in my practice, the question is no longer "How long can I safely postpone childbearing?" but rather "How can I best time having my children so it will have the minimum impact on my career?" An ancillary of this question is: "If I decide I want children now, how do I work out my career around that decision?"

As the respondents in our Stanford study span several generations of professional women, the answers they provided to the question of "Is there a right time in a career to have children?" are instructive.

◆　◆　◆

LESSONS LEARNED

There Is No Definitively Right Time in a Career to Have a Family

When we asked the women in our Stanford survey if they felt there was a "right" time for a woman to start a family, the answer we got most consistently was no. Take, for example, the response of this 1980s Settler and mother of three:

> I'm sure there is, but I had my kids late (age 37, 40, and 44) because I got married late (34), so I didn't have a lot of choice. I had a friend at another high-tech firm who had her children at age 20 and started a whole powerful career at age 40. So it works all different ways!

Another mother, a 1970s Pioneer who chose to work for several years before having her children, could also see advantages to doing things either way:

> I had a lot of business satisfaction before having my children at 36. But I can see the advantage to having children younger, then going to work when they are older. I feel concerned about my

possibilities after such a long time out of the career loop and turning 50 to boot! I think there is a lot of age discrimination, which complicates choices for women.

Certain Times Are Better Than Others to Start a Family

Nearly half the women in our study said that there might not be a right time to start a family but that there are probably some times that are better than others, as this 1980s Settler with two school-age children observed:

> There's never a right time, but the best time would be when you have a lot of independence with respect to time and maximum flexibility with respect to schedule.

Others, like this 1980s Settler and mother of two teenagers, believed that there are several right times to have children:

> There are probably several right times: when a woman is just starting out, when she's well established in her career, and when she's reached all her career goals.

Many women echoed the sentiments of this 1970s Pioneer with three children who advised that the best time to have children was once one had established one's credentials:

> I think a woman's best option is to complete her education and establish her credentials before having children. That way she has the choice of how she wants to manage her career.

Many women felt that the issue of when to have children was a decision that should be unrelated to career concerns. They felt, often quite strongly, that career considerations had no place in the decision process, like this woman, one of the oldest respondents and the mother of a 45-year-old daughter:

> When a couple is ready to make a lifelong commitment to children is the only right time to have children.

Another Pioneer, who herself had decided to forgo having children, counseled:

> [A woman should have children] when it's right for the child, and when a woman and her partner are ready to be good parents. The career is not the salient variable.

Similarly, said one 1980s Settler with two young children:

> Age, financial security, and health should drive the decision, not a career. A woman should have her children when she decides it is the right time.

And finally, as one successful corporate executive, whose two children are now teenagers, reminds us: "You don't always have a choice."

A few women, like one 1980s Settler, indicated that although there might not be a right time to start a family, there were definitely some wrong times:

> Don't think about starting a family if your relationship is rocky. Things only get worse after children arrive. My husband was gung-ho about having kids, but he basically is indifferent to the work they create. It's been a source of constant tension in our marriage.

Another woman, also a 1980s Settler, wrote:

> There may not be a right time to have children, but there definitely is a wrong time, and that's when you are trying to start a business.

The Successors, the Most Recent Graduates in Our Survey, Were Most Emphatic About Getting Established First

The group of women who felt most strongly about getting one's career on track were those who were, for the most part, the youngest women in our sample. Far more Successors than others believed that there is a right time to have children, and that is once a woman has gotten her career on track. This group recognized that there would be trade-offs to early or delayed childbearing, but they took highly pragmatic perspective. Advised one 1980s Successor, who, like so many others in her peer group, had not yet begun her family:

> Have your family after you're established and can put your career on cruise, but before you are too old, tired, or set in your comfy lifestyle to have kids.

Other Successors agreed, like this 1990s Successor, mother of two toddlers:

> As far as a career is concerned, it helps to get enough experience prior to having kids. That way, you can return to work at a respectable level.

And this 1980s Successor with two preteens:

> It's best to have your family when you have a degree of success and stability with a company. That way, they will be willing to provide some flexibility to keep you.

This 1990s Successor with three young children under the age of 5 chose a different path, which caused her some regrets:

> It's probably better to wait until you have made manager or partner so you can feel pretty satisfied with where you are and what you have already accomplished. I didn't wait, and there have been pros and cons to that. I am far more likely to be considered for staff rather than line positions because I'm only available 30 hours a week for work.

Finally, this 1990s Successor advised women to fulfill their career aspirations before starting a family because:

That way it's easier to say "been there, done that," and dedicate yourself more directly towards your family. A family is more rewarding than any job could ever be.

It is clear from the Successors in our survey that the current generation of professional women is adroitly poised between aiming to have children early enough to avoid fertility problems and being practical by seeking to be established in a career to alleviate some of the flexibility and autonomy concerns that are critical to achieving a balanced lifestyle as a professional and a mother.

Infertility Is a Significant Concern for Professional Women

I'm having to take shots every day, trying to get pregnant, and it's been a horrible experience. If you want to have children, make them the priority. Have them when you're ready—don't worry about what's best for your career. Sadly, I waited too long, and now I may never have them.

The experience of this 1980s Settler was among the cautionary tales told by the women in our study who had "waited too long." Not many women in our survey had direct experience with infertility, but we did have some who had, and their stories were uniformly similar. Like most professionals, these women had dedicated a significant portion of their twenties and thirties to their education and career development—often to the exclusion of other parts of their lives. Like many other professionals, this translated into either not meeting their partners until later in their lives or even if they met them earlier on, putting reproductive issues on hold until career issues were settled. Most had waited until their late thirties or early forties to begin families, banking on the assumption that a woman could have children until her mid- to late forties. Once they had begun trying to have children however, they discovered that their fertility was seriously impaired. Advises one of these women, a 1980s Successor in her early forties:

Young women would be wise to make having children a priority if that is what they want—do it while they can. I waited and now I cannot get pregnant.

Recently, a patient of mine, a 1980s law school graduate whom I will call Susan, shared the ordeal of her infertility. Because her experience is not uncommon but is so often absent from the literature on infertility, her story provides poignant testimony to the ordeal that many women professionals face.

SUSAN AND PETER'S STORY

I've never encountered anything like this. I'm having a hard time accepting that I can't have a child. It's really the first time in my life that I can't do something I want. I'm 40 and I feel like have nothing to show for it. Infertility is a loss like none other I've ever experienced.

Susan and her husband of a little less than two years, Peter, both in their early forties, are active, engaged professionals who had met late in life and had married after a short courtship.

Each had had some doubts about having children, particularly so soon after getting married, but they both felt that because of their age, they needed to try sooner rather than later. After nearly a year of trying to conceive without success, they decided to see a fertility specialist.

A series of tests and unsuccessful treatments with fertility drugs convinced their doctor that Susan and her husband were likely candidates for in vitro fertilization (IVF), a now relatively standard assisted reproductive therapy procedure. In that process, ripe eggs are removed from the ovaries and incubated with sperm, and the resulting embryo(s) is inserted into the mother's womb.

"I was worried that somehow our inability to conceive was divine intervention to keep us from producing biologically defective children," reported Susan, as she and Peter weighed the pros and cons of proceeding further.

Both of them shared a sense of shame about not being able to have children "naturally," and Susan felt additionally shamed by "my inadequacy as a woman." She questioned whether "my infertility, like my earlier ambivalence about having children, was indicative of the fact that I was not cut out to be a mother."

Entering into the IVF process, Susan was already somewhat depressed, and the series of regimented daily hormonal injections did little to alleviate that depression. In fact, the hormonal changes brought about by the medications significantly dampened Susan's already dejected spirits.

> I felt so helpless and overwhelmed by everything. There were decisions at every point—do we do one IVF or sign up for three at a reduced price? What was the most economical approach? It was like a sale at Safeway. And how many embryos should we implant, and what do we do with the leftovers? It was all too much. I really couldn't talk about it to anyone. Unless you've been there, you just can't know what it's like. Everybody just says it'll be all right, but obviously no one knows.

Despite her significant distress, Susan moved forward, overcoming her fears about self-administered injections and doing all that was necessary to proceed with the IVF treatment.

Peter was supportive throughout the process but clearly was more removed from the daily stresses inherent in the procedures. Susan reported that Peter also was having difficulty with the idea of infertility and became perceptibly more remote. He threw himself into his work even more than usual during this time. Peter particularly had difficulty dealing with the loss of control brought about by the infertility and coped by quietly withdrawing from the situation whenever he could reasonably do so.

Apart from the overall stress of the situation, the hardest time period for both of them, but particularly for Susan, was the two-week waiting period after the implantations. It was during this time that the success or failure of the entire process would be determined. Susan reported that the physical discomfort of the treatment was nothing in comparison to the emotional anxiety of this waiting period.

Almost two weeks to the day of implantation, Susan sadly began her period, signaling the failure of the fertility treatment. Both she and Peter entered a period of mourning.

> We could hardly believe it. After all we'd been through, to have it fail . . . the pain was indescribable—it was like a death. It was a death for us, especially when the doctors told us we could try again, but we had less than a 10 percent chance of success. We were so emotionally drained, there was no way we could go through it all again.

Deeply saddened and disappointed, Susan and Peter tried to move on, only to find themselves becoming increasingly irritated with each other and more disconnected. Susan was particularly hard hit by guilt.

> I felt like a complete failure. I couldn't see my friends who had kids; I couldn't stand to be around women with children. Everywhere I went, women with strollers showed up. It was really awful going to Peter's sister's wedding because everyone was asking us when we were going to try again.

Increasingly, Susan and Peter found themselves sniping at one another and frequently sought out opportunities to be disappointed in each other. At that point, they decided to seek couples counseling.

Nearly a year later, they are doing a lot better. As a result of the counseling, each has recognized the need to grieve the loss of their ability to have their own child. They have recently begun to consider adopting a baby, a profound stress in itself, but one that they are allowing themselves the necessary time to consider.

Susan and Peter's story is sadly reflective of the problems faced by other professional women and their partners when confronted with issues of infertility. Too often, the profound emotional toll taken by the inability to conceive children naturally gets lost in the dazzle of the reproductive technology currently available to infertile couples.

For professional women who are already concerned about how children will affect their lives, the issues involved in infertility are doubly stressful. If predictability and control are things that are important to us as professionals, then the problem of infertility strikes us where we are the most vulnerable.

> It's an invisible problem. It is not a sadness you share. Your friends with children feel badly for you and don't know how to respond, so often, it just doesn't get mentioned.

Only by recognizing the powerful effects infertility can have on our lives can we begin to assess the risks we are or are not willing to assume for the sake of our careers. Obviously, there are no guarantees of untroubled fertility, no matter how early we begin our reproductive process. As professionals, we have to or want to make a priority of our educational and career concerns, but inattention to what we want in other areas of our lives can result in unanticipated consequences. By assessing our priorities early and often, we can make choices that better reflect our own needs, and those of our partners. Recognizing that we are susceptible to fertility problems associated with age, and that our reproductive organs cannot be badgered into functioning on demand, will enable us to avoid making a decision by not making a decision.

More Advice from Our Stanford Women About the Timing of Children

The women in our study indicated that there is no definitively right time in a career to have children, with the prevailing wisdom apparently being that one should establish oneself professionally but not wait so long as to put one's fertility in jeopardy. Below is a sample of what the Stanford women had to say about the issue of timing:

> Don't overanalyze the situation. You may wait, thinking now is not the right time, and when you want to, it may not be so easy. Do it when you and your husband want children—the rest will work out.

> Get your career on track; get into a large corporation where you can get good job training. Leave when you have children,

then reactivate your career at 36 to 37 when the kids are in school.

If family is important to you, make that a high priority. Your family will always stay with you, but you can get laid off/fired from work. Also, I've known so many women who've worked to climb the corporate ladder only to find themselves hugely disappointed at their infertility later in life.

Definitely try to have [the first] child by [your] early thirties (before 35), to give you the opportunity to have two or more, and to give you options in case there is a fertility problem.

Your life and your career will be affected by kids. Make trade-offs and accept them early to avoid regrets later.

Listen to your heart and your husband's heart. That is the only thing that should play into this—your personal happiness is 100 percent your responsibility.

Don't make all your changes at once. Let things settle for two years or so after starting a job before deciding on children, so you know if you want another career change.

Do it at a time that you are satisfied with your mate and don't worry about your job. Three months go by so fast at work—they really won't notice you're gone!

Don't wait until your late thirties; you will be less physically fit for the rigors of caring for children and may have trouble conceiving.

Don't put it off too long—energy levels do go down as you get older!

Go for the family—it may take a while to get pregnant. Career women are already old biologically. Get your husband to help or hire lots of good help. It's worth the money for your sanity.

Make sure you and your spouse agree on time commitments and expectations with the family. If possible, choose a more flexible career path or enlightened organization.

Do it. I'm now having troubles—and it's partly age and partly letting work schedules, travel, and stress get in the way.

Be ready as an individual and as a couple. A sound/solid marriage and parental partnership is critical.

Wait a few years until you have established a track record of success.

There's no certainty anywhere anymore. Consider keeping skills current with consulting contracts; it's harder to get pregnant later, so go for it!

What does your husband do? Is he going to be an equal partner? If not, think twice about whether career or family is most important to you. If family is, go for it. If career is, then I'd suggest waiting.

Wait until you've worked awhile.

The sooner the better. It's physically exhausting work—very tough to do in late thirties, early forties. Plus, greater risks to you and the baby.

Better sooner than later. It's easier to have small kids when you are more junior. As you have more responsibilities, it gets harder. It's better if you have more flexibility.

There is never a convenient time. At the end of [their] life, many people (men, too) value their family more than their work.

◆　◆　◆

ACTION PLAN: DECIDING ON TIMING

The Right Time to Have Children Worksheet is a good starting point for a discussion of the issues involved in the timing of children. The worksheet helps to clarify priorities and concerns and provides an opportunity to discuss these issues in a focused way. As with several of the other worksheets, it is recommended that both partners complete the forms individually, each from his or her own perspective: What are the personal advantages to having children now for me? What are the career advantages to having children now for me? Once completed, the worksheets allow for a comparison of each partner's concerns.

THE RIGHT TIME TO HAVE CHILDREN WORKSHEET

Instructions: Make a copy of the Right Time to Have Children Worksheet *for each partner. After each partner completes an individual worksheet, discuss the findings.*

1.	ADVANTAGES TO NOW	DISADVANTAGES TO NOW
Personal	_____	_____
	_____	_____
	What could be done?	_____
		_____
Career	_____	_____
	_____	_____
	What could be done?	_____
		_____
Finances	_____	_____
	_____	_____
	What could be done?	_____
		_____
Housing	_____	_____
	_____	_____

What could be done? _____

_____

Help/support_____ _____

_____ _____

What could be done? _____

_____

Age/health _____ _____

_____ _____

What could be done? _____

_____

Other

children _____ _____

_____ _____

What could be done? _____

_____

Other _____ _____

_____ _____

What could be done? _____

_____

2. **ADVANTAGES TO WAITING** **DISADVANTAGES TO WAITING**

Personal _____ _____

_____ _____

What could be done? _____

_____

Career _____ _____

_____ _____

What could be done? _____

_____

Finances _____ _____

_____ _____

What could be done? _____

_____

Housing   _____   _____

_____   _____

What could be done? _____

_____

Help/support_____   _____

_____   _____

What could be done? _____

_____

Age/health   _____   _____

_____   _____

What could be done? _____

_____

Other
   children   _____   _____

_____   _____

What could be done? _____

_____

Other   _____   _____

_____   _____

What could be done? _____

_____

3.   **ADVANTAGES OF NEVER**   **DISADVANTAGES OF NEVER**
Personal   _____   _____

_____   _____

What could be done? _____

_____

Career   _____   _____

_____   _____

What could be done? _____

_____

Finances _____   _____

_____   _____

What could be done?   _____

_____

Housing _____   _____

_____   _____

What could be done?   _____

_____

Help/support_____   _____

_____   _____

What could be done?   _____

_____

Age/health _____   _____

_____   _____

What could be done?   _____

_____

**Other
children** _____   _____

_____   _____

What could be done?   _____

_____

Other _____   _____

_____   _____

What could be done?   _____

_____

CHAPTER 7

So Who's Doing It Right Anyway?
To Work or Not

EXPERIENCE: WHAT PROFESSIONAL WOMEN SAY ABOUT WORKING *AND* HAVING CHILDREN

"I don't see why we should schedule meetings in the evenings. Those parents never show up, so why should we be disadvantaged?" With that comment, the petite woman with tiny reading glasses perched on the tip of her nose had launched the opening salvo. . . .

"I resent that!" shouted another woman as she rose to speak. Her tailored suit stood out against the sea of sweats and khakis. Her voice resonated with barely contained outrage as she continued: "I am offended by what you just said! This school is supposed to stand for inclusion, not exclusion. I am here as often as most of you are, and I think it is important to include those [mothers] who can't make it during the day—and also the fathers. This is a parents' association, not a coffee klatch!"

The emotional tension in the room was palpable, and mothers assiduously avoided eye contact as the debate raged around them. Despite their best intentions to stay neutral, one after another was drawn inexorably into the eye of the controversy. They could not *not* join the fight. Every one of them had feelings about this issue. The stakes were too high and the outcome was too telling.

Here in the library of a suburban elementary school, the battle lines of an American cultural war were being drawn, between the mothers who worked and those who stayed at home. The emotional battleground on which these women clashed is rarely so littered with raw emotion. In most instances, the conflict simmers out of sight, just below a veneer of "good girl" civility. But this day, their discord was in plain view.

They were women, nearly all professionals, who had made a choice about how they wanted to live their lives once they had had children. Some, freely or by necessity, chose to remain at work and to balance the demands of a full-time career with those of their children and families. Others—many, in fact—chose to step off the career path for some period of time or to severely curtail their professional involvement to be at home with their children. Both faced difficult choices and consequences, and both wanted desperately to be right about their choice.

Why was it so important for them to have made the right choice? Why did they need to be sure that they were doing the right thing? The answers were pretty straightforward. It was important because they cared about the well-being of their children. They cared about the quality of their lives and they wanted to do whatever they could to ensure their children's happiness.

The issue of whether a woman should work after having children is of profound importance to all professional women. Everyone has an opinion, and the research to date has done little to resolve the controversy. To better understand the issues involved, we asked our Stanford sample to tell us how their decisions about working after motherhood were affecting their lives.

Here is the distribution of these mothers among the different employment statuses:

AT A GLANCE:
EMPLOYMENT PATTERNS FOR
STANFORD MBA MOTHERS

EMPLOYMENT STATUS	PERCENT
Full time	47
Part time	46
Stay at home	7

The information these women provide is useful in developing strategies for dealing with the hard choices about careers and children that every one of us confronts.

$$\bullet \quad \bullet \quad \bullet$$

LESSONS LEARNED

The Full-Court Press: Working Full Time with Young Children Is Not for the Fainthearted

Practically no one in our Stanford sample said, "It can't be done." Most of the women agreed that a woman can have a full-time career and successfully raise a family, but—and this is an important *but*— they said that doing it right takes an extraordinary commitment to both. It is clearly a tough choice to make, and not one without its physical and psychological costs. For those who had chosen to do both, however, it definitely had certain advantages.

By way of example, let's look at the experiences of three women employed full time who felt they had found a way to make it all work.

The first woman, whom I will call Ann, is a 1990s Successor with two toddlers and a new consulting business. She regularly works more than 40 hours a week to build her client base and to keep her business competitive. Couple that with rearing two children under age 4, and it is not at all surprising that Ann describes her life as "challenging to say the least." Many of the other working mothers in our sample agreed with Ann's observations that she doesn't believe that "you can be supermom and super businesswoman. However, I do think you can reach a compromise with yourself as far as being a success at both." Ann explained:

> I have my own business, so I have a lot of flexibility, and that is a tremendous plus. I know that working less hours (on average about 50 hours per week) and being less involved in all the details of my company has probably hurt its growth. But it's the choice I made. I keep business travel to a minimum, which definitely compromises my ability to network, and I don't work week-

ends, except for once in a while, and then my family always takes precedence. I have an office at home in case I can't get into work. My husband shares equally in child care when he gets home, although he's not usually home before 7:30 or later. But in general, it's really been pretty good.

Sarah, a 1980s Successor with elementary school–age children, wrote that she has "accomplished as satisfactory a balance as I believe is possible with two careers and a desire to be a good mom." She went on to describe her experience:

We live in a great house, have great kids, have good careers, and are happy and healthy. We own our home, have savings for college and for retirement. It seems greedy to want more! I think a woman can reach a balance or an optimal solution between work and family, but neither will be maximized. Men can maximize careers and still optimize family, but I don't think we can. I currently work about 45 hours a week. While I'm not terribly satisfied with my job (business development), I am not willing to make the time commitment required to do more exciting things while my kids are young.

For a third mother, Jill, a physician who currently directs a large medical facility, "the hardest thing . . . has been the lack of time to get all things done that I want to do. I regularly work 80 to 90 hours a week, and flexibility is not part of my work. I get around it by bringing my kids with me, as often as I can, to meetings and such." She wrote:

I think I have found ways to resolve career advancement yet allow time for my family. For me, there is nothing so wonderful as to have children. I don't think women have to choose between a successful career and a family. The stress of doing both well is definitely reduced by having great help—really good nannies and a housekeeper.

With these examples in mind, let's take a systematic look at what the women in our survey tell us about the pluses and minuses on combining a full-time career with raising a family.

AT A GLANCE:
THE PROS AND CONS OF FULL-TIME WORK

PROS	CONS
Contented with life	Time pressure
Career satisfaction	High role conflict
Career path	Advancement limits
Parity with partner	High child-care stress/costs
High efficiency/productivity	High services needs

As we saw in the previous examples, for many of the mothers who maintained a full-time career, there were distinct pros and cons to trying to manage both a family and a career. Although they were actively engaged in their careers, they were equally clear that when a conflict arose, their families took precedence over their careers in essentially every instance.

As to the upside of a full-time career, those mothers who were attempting to do both reported the most satisfaction with their careers. Of all the mothers in our study, the mothers working full time had the fewest concerns as to where their careers were headed.

Typical was one 1970s Settler who wrote:

I feel like I've managed to keep my career pretty much on track. [I enjoy serving as] a role model for the younger women in the firm.

A 1980s Settler, a mother of two school-age daughters, worked in high tech and saw her career commitment as important to her children's future:

I feel I have struck the right balance between a fulfilling career and raising my daughters. To me it's been an important legacy for my daughters—to see that my work matters to me and to know what I have been able to accomplish. It's not always easy, especially when [they were] younger, but I think it gives them a sense of their own efficacy that I never had.

Others felt that even if they were not advancing as rapidly as they would have had they not had children, they had learned to organize their time resources wisely and to be very efficient in their work. As one 1970s Pioneer wrote:

You learn to be very productive and efficient in how you use your time. It's not that the quality of your work suffers; it's just that you don't waste time on anything nonessential.

Several of these women commented on feeling parity with their partners, who were more likely to equally share in household and family responsibilities. Observed one 1980s Successor:

Because we both work full time, there is absolutely no question that he needs to pitch in. Of course, I still do more, but he really helps a lot, especially with the nonchild stuff—cooking, cleaning, etc.

Another mother, a 1980s Settler with two teenage children, wrote:

I think it is important to share equally in paying the bills as well as in raising the children. I wouldn't feel okay about not pulling my weight, and my husband would not have had the opportunity to be as close to our children if he had had to support our family alone. It's been hard at times, and both of us have had to compromise to do it, but I think it has worked out better for us this way.

And despite the fact these women were often exhausted from the sheer volume of the responsibilities they shouldered, as a group, the mothers who were employed full time were quite content with their lives.
Those who felt they might do things differently if they could do them again regretted not having or not being able to have more help

in the home with children or household chores. Generally, these mothers concurred with the 1970s Pioneer who wrote:

> There is nothing that I feel I've missed out on. I've done a career and I've had children, and now I get to reap the benefits of both. There's nothing I wish I would've done differently—except perhaps to have found a wife to make the whole thing a lot easier.

The principal disadvantages reported by mothers working full time focused on issues of role conflict. *Like others in the study, these mothers reported that they often found themselves concerned about work issues at home and family issues at work, and they reported significantly more role conflict than did any other group of mothers.*

In fact, the amount of role conflict that a mother experienced was directly affected by the number of hours she worked, as well as such variables as the age and number of her children and the amount of support the mother could count on from partners and others. In most instances, the role conflicts these women experienced arose as a result of their concerns about their family's well-being. "If child-care arrangements are not going well," wrote one mother, a physician with two young children, "I cannot concentrate at all. The reverse is not true."

In addition to juggling multiple roles, the mothers working full time reported that their careers were not unaffected by their choice to have children. *They reported having to tolerate slower career advancement because of an inability or unwillingness to put in the overtime and weekend hours that many professional jobs required.* Often this, translated into taking staff positions as opposed to direct line management, or, as one 1980s Settler wrote, "going from having 30 employees reporting to me to none" once she became a mother. For many women, managing the balancing act was just that—managing to make it look easier than it was, as this 1980s Settler described:

> Juggling a full-time career is difficult but not impossible. In order to make it work, you just can't look too committed to either. They must both appear to be equally important to you, regardless of how you really feel.

For most mothers, overnight travel was held to an absolute minimum, and, as we saw earlier, time to just hang out with colleagues was severely constrained when a child was waiting at the end of the day. For some women, "ambition and tolerance for workplace politics" were tempered by a focus on "what really matters."

Several women lamented that there was little or no time for themselves or their partners. Not atypical were comments like this from a mother of three children who works full time in biotech:

> It's keeping track of the details that kill you. You've got all these things to do at work, and the minute you walk in the door, you have a whole other set of responsibilities: who's done their homework, who has tests, which school form needs to be sent in, where are the clothes, who's doing what tomorrow. . . . Before a child gets to high school, the list is endless. It consumes every free minute. That's hard to accept sometimes.

Further, the cost of child care and other purchased services, like household help to make it all work, was not an insignificant consideration, and the presence or absence of a support system, not the least of which was a supportive partner, often determined the success or failure of the whole venture.

Clearly, there are distinct pluses and minuses to attempting a full-time career while successfully raising a family. However, the women in our sample who were doing both tended to agree with this mother, a 1990s Successor, who wrote:

> With a career and a family, balance is a constant challenge. They both want all your time. Superficial compromises will be necessary, but if you're flexible, you can find ways to make it work for you. It's hard, but it's definitely worth it!

Working Part Time Works Well, at Least Partially

If you asked most working mothers what their ideal job configuration would be, they would probably tell you it was some kind of part-time work. And for nearly half of the mothers in our study, working part time while raising their families was the alternative that they chose for themselves. When one considers that it would be hard to find a more career-oriented group of women than Stanford MBAs, this finding says a lot about the realities of balancing career and family interests.

To get some idea of how these women are faring, let's once again look at some typical respondents.

Amy, a 34-year-old senior business analyst at a large corporation, has two children under age 4. She cut back her work schedule to about 30 hours a week after the birth of her last child. She wrote:

> Not spending more time with my children never bothered me until I was home on maternity leave with my second child and my 3½-year-old and I had so much fun. I learned what I was missing! I don't really feel my career has suffered as a result of my having a family, but we'll see as time goes on and I continue to work part time. Because my husband travels a lot, I hold travel to an absolute minimum, and I say no to meetings if I've already got a fairly full week. Telecommuting has really helped my ability to truly work at home.

Laura is a 36-year-old 1980s Successor who had worked in management consulting before having children. Subsequent to the birth of her two children, the oldest of whom recently started grade school, she shifted career paths within her firm. Here is her report:

> My company has been incredibly supportive and accommodating of my work/family concerns. They've allowed me to go part time, change career paths from consulting to something more flexible. The downside is that the position I have will not lead to advancement. Having a family has either defined or clarified (I'm not sure which) my ambitions and my willingness to work hard towards them. The conflict I feel is created by the limits of the choice I have made. I want to be a success, but I honestly don't want to invest time or effort in doing it. I might have been more willing to stay on the consulting track had I had more confidence in my ability to manage it all—something that my firm did not instill.

Maria, a 32-year-old marketing manager, is a 1990s Successor. She is the mother of three school-age children and she currently works about 30 hours a week. She feels she has benefited greatly from the fact that the large corporation she works for has a clear commitment to retain women.

Managing a household full of children can bring its own stresses. That's why a balance of work and family is great. My company has policies that allow for part-time work. But even with that policy, I am precluded from certain jobs. It hasn't ended my career, but it certainly has caused it to move a whole lot slower. In order to succeed as a part-time employee, I have to be incredibly organized, have outstanding prioritization skills, and give the impression of always being available. You have to act like your job is your highest priority. I've chosen in some way to be less successful by prioritizing family over work.

AT A GLANCE:
THE PROS AND CONS OF PART-TIME WORK

PROS	CONS
Contented with life	Uncertain career path
Less child-care stress	Role conflict
Less time pressure	Financial concerns
Job satisfaction	Centrality concerns
Career maintenance	Dependence on partner

As a whole, the women who had elected to work part time while raising their families were very happy with their choices in several dimensions. They tended to like their jobs, and many echoed the words of one Settler who reported that she doubted if she would ever take a full-time job again:

At first I was pretty wary of what part-time work would mean for my career, but I discovered that it allowed me time not only for my children but also for me, and I really like that. I will never go back to work full time, unless I'm absolutely forced to do it.

Because these women tended to have less work demands on their time, they reported having more time to do the things that mattered to them in addition to work and family concerns. Many reported being able to reengage in exercise in ways their schedules previously had not permitted, and for many, the pleasures of volunteering, rediscovering hobbies, and often newfound domesticity were important parts of their lives.

In all fairness, it is important to note that several mothers reported that even working part time, they still could barely do all the things they wanted to do, as one 1980s Successor with two small children recounted:

> I can't believe I ever managed working full time. Now that I'm home 2½ days a week, I think I'm getting less done than before. I'm less organized and definitely less efficient. But it's really fun to be that way, and I really dread having to return to work full time.

For financial as well as practical reasons, mothers working part time often cut back on child care. Because they enjoyed being with their children, this was not typically viewed as a hardship. Rather, spending more time with their children was often the expressed purpose for their choosing to work part time in the first place. Of course, any mother who has ever ventured into a grocery store with a toddler in tow can identify with how energy intensive and "inefficient" that experience can be.

Like the other mothers in our survey, the women who chose to work part time were generally very contented with their lives and reported that they were in good spirits most of the time. Many of these mothers based their decision to work part time on their concern that "children are young for such a short time," as one 1980s Successor and mother of two children under age 3 explained. "It's important to make the most of it and to try not to get caught up in the rat race."

Several women expressed satisfaction at being able to keep a hand in their professions and not having to cede all the career territory they had previously acquired. The major drawbacks to working part time reported by these women centered on the continuity and content of their careers. Most of the mothers who had cut back their hours expressed some uncertainty about what the future held for them with respect to their work. Many were concerned about their lack of a viable career path, as this 1980s Settler, a self-employed consultant with two young children, explained:

> I've jumped off the traditional career track. When I first had children and was still in a corporate environment, I experienced a great deal of conflict. I left when my first son was 14 months old. If I could do it over, I would have left my corporate job sooner. I'm not sure where my career will lead, but I'm much happier not having to deal with the kind of discriminatory attitudes towards working mothers that I found in the corporate world.

Like this mother, many women working part time had real concerns about a lack of an obvious career path and an inability to be integrally involved in their work organization. Many questioned whether, in fact, part-time work could ever be truly meaningful.

Others expressed financial concerns once their salaries were no longer at their full-time level, and more than a few women echoed the concerns of one Settler who advised that "women need to be wary of taking a part-time salary and doing a full-time job."

Coincidental to these financial considerations was often some measure of concern about being dependent on the support of a partner to reduce one's time in the workplace. Although this did not appear to be an insurmountable anxiety for most women, it did occasionally surface as a negative consequence of working part time.

For these mothers, role conflict, when it occurred, most frequently arose in the context of trying to work from home. For many women, the lack of a clear definition of work time and workspace created significant role overlap. Wrote one 1980s Settler:

> It was hard when my children were younger to work at home, because they would always find me.

And another mother, a 1990s Successor with two young children, wrote:

It's great if you can work from home, but it's really hard to get any work done. You have to be very disciplined, and once your children turn two, forget it.

There clearly were career concerns identified by this group of mothers, but overall, *the women who worked part time felt that the choices that they had made were right for them, that the time and flexibility they gained more than compensated for any career or financial disadvantages they had incurred.* Given the opportunity to do things differently, they typically reported that they would make the same choice again.

The Stay-at-Home Option

Not surprisingly, some of the most detailed and reflective responses to our survey were those we received from mothers who had elected to leave the work force for some period of time to raise their children. These "stay-at-home mothers," as they often described themselves, had obviously thought long and hard about their choice. Many wrote at length about their decision process, and several wrote of their frustrations at often feeling compelled to justify their decision to leave the workplace and be at home with their children.

Let's take a look at some typical respondents.

Joann is a 36-year-old mother of two children under the age of 3. As a 1980s Settler, she regularly worked 50 hours a week before deciding to "retire" to raise her family. Here is how she describes her experience:

I made the decisions I did because I feel strongly that regardless of what anyone says, something will suffer, either your job or your family—because there are only 24 hours in a day. My children are my pride and joy, and for me it was definitely the right choice. I'm sure the time I have taken off now will come back to haunt me in terms of more limited opportunities or lower pay. I realize I am in a very small minority of women not working. For me, at first it was a difficult adjustment because I, like so many people, identified closely with my job. Not working does not mean loss of identity, but it does change your definition of a sense of self. I think one has to be ready to make many compromises regardless of whether or not you go back to work.

Julia is a 44-year-old 1970s Settler with two teenagers. She and her husband decided that it made more financial and practical sense for her to stop working when they had children rather than for both of them to attempt part-time careers. Here's how she described her decision process:

I stopped working (for pay) after the birth of my [first] child. My mother worked after I reached [fourth] grade—after that, I remember lots of talks with our housekeeper. I wanted my children to know their mother was always around, not the house-keeper/baby-sitter. I gave up my career temporarily (15 years!) so that I could be totally involved with my children and also have time for R and R. The long hours that companies expect from their motivated employees were lousy for our marriage even before we had children. My husband and I did not have time together, and I couldn't imagine trying to juggle two high-powered careers and children. Given my personality and drive—I give 100 percent to my endeavors—I knew that I'd be trying to be the supermom and the super career woman, and never satisfied with my performance in either.

When asked to describe the stress in her current "position," full-time mom Andrea, a 1980s Settler with two children ages 2 and 4, wrote: "No boss has ever made the unreasonable demands that a 2-year-old does, nor throw[n] complete tantrums when you can't deliver!" She went on to describe her experience:

Working during my [first] pregnancy practically killed me because of the late hours, travel, etc. I was put on bed rest during my last trimester. I think a woman would be smart to have her kids relatively early, like her late [twenties], because raising a family is physically exhausting work. I stepped out by choice because I don't believe in the phrase "It's quality time, not quantity of time." Having kids means being at home with them until they are school-age, which is the equivalent of an 8-year hiatus in my career. Right now, my career is at a standstill. It's my choice, but it does worry me.

AT A GLANCE:
THE PROS AND CONS OF STAYING AT HOME

PROS	CONS
Contented with life	Uncertain career path
Fewer time pressures	Career disruption
Less role conflict	Less career satisfaction
Least child-care stress	Financial pressures
More discretionary activities	Dependence on partner

Like the other women in our survey, the women who elected to remain at home once they had children reported that they were very content with their lives. They thoroughly enjoyed the opportunity to spend time with their families and luxuriated in the lack of time pressures in their lives.

Although not all felt they had unlimited expanses of time because they were actively engaged in raising a family, as a group, these women had more time to devote to activities that mattered to them. They could, if they chose to, do volunteer work on a regular basis, and had the time and energy to enjoy physical, domestic, and recreational activities.

They were obviously less concerned than the other women in our sample with child-care issues, principally because they were available, and for the most part, could afford child care as needed. For obvious reasons, they did not find themselves beset with worries about work issues at home and vice versa.

Sounds pretty good, and for the most part, it was.

As mentioned above, *the women who were not currently employed reported being quite happy with the way their lives were structured at the present time. The only rub came when they thought about the future.* Here, the concerns that did surface had to do with some guilt, but principally anxiety, about what would happen to their careers as a consequence of taking time out of the workplace. As Julia, the 1970s Settler with two teenagers, recounted:

> When I didn't return to work after three months' maternity leave, I felt *guilty* because I wasn't utilizing my degree! All my friends kept asking me when I was going back to work!

More than a few of the stay-at-home mothers echoed the concerns of this 1980s Successor with four children under age 8 who wrote:

> I didn't find an appropriate point of expertise before I stepped out of the workforce. I've done too many varied and unrelated things to leave me in a good position for reentry. While there was never a doubt in my mind that I wanted children, and I was blessed to be able to have them easily, the conflict I currently face is that I have some fears and insecurities about being out of the workforce. I don't know yet how this will all work out and I'm concerned.

Many of the women in this group indicated that even though they felt they had made the right decisions for themselves and their families, they might have opted for other career options if any existed that permitted the flexibility they currently enjoyed.

For most of the women in this group, however, time out of the workforce was by no means seen as permanent retirement. Nearly all indicated that once their children were grown, they fully intended to return to work. The question of what their decision would cost them in terms of career disruption and satisfaction, however, remained largely open.

More than a few of these women also acknowledged financial pressures attendant to no longer bringing in a professional-level salary. Here again, Julia's experience is informative:

> With only one breadwinner, and therefore only one income in our family, it was very stressful when my husband was laid off 10 years ago and only got two months' severance.

Despite these pressures, being able to stay at home while children are young was often described as "an incredible luxury afforded by the good fortune to have a husband whose income could support a family on a single paycheck."

The experience of the stay-at-home mothers was the envy of a lot of the mothers in our survey, but this option is not open to all working women. Certainly many women in our Stanford sample did not feel that they could financially afford to choose this option and at the same time provide the life experiences that they wanted for their families.

Summing It Up

From our research, it appears that *no one option has the lock on happiness for professional women with children.* As our survey respondents have demonstrated, trade-offs come with the territory no matter which option we select:

- *Working full time* means a full plate with little downtime for our selves or our partners, but it allows us to better keep our careers on track.
- *Working part time* allows us a lot more time with our families while letting us keep a hand in our work. The principal downside is the effect such part-time work has on career paths and advancement.
- *Staying at home,* although providing the gift of time to our families and ourselves, does create some anxiety about the future, particularly with respect to career directions.

AT A GLANCE:
COMPARING THE OPTIONS

	FULL TIME	PART TIME	STAY AT HOME
Pros:			
Contentment with life	+	+	+
Career satisfaction	+	~	−
Cons:			
Time pressures	+	−	−

	FULL TIME	PART TIME	STAY AT HOME
Role conflict	+	~	−
Child-care stress	+	~	−
Purchased service needs	+	~	−
Financial pressure	−	+	+
Dependence on partner	−	+	+
Career path uncertainty	−	+	+

+ = more; ~ = some; − = less.

From the data, three strategies emerge that suggest ways of optimizing our personal and professional goals:

- Sequencing
- Securing essential support
- Identifying needs and stresses

◆ ◆ ◆

ACTION PLAN: THREE STRATEGIES FOR "GETTING IT RIGHT"

Strategy 1: Consider Sequencing

For many of the women in our survey, the decision to gear down their career when they had small children was their preferred option. Even if their partners were willing to scale back their own career ambitions, these women felt strongly that they wanted to spend more time at home. For these women, our research suggests that sequencing one's career may be a strategy that incorporates some of the best of each of the options detailed above.

The idea of sequencing a career has been around for some time and was first described in 1986 by Arlene Rossen Cardozo. The idea behind sequencing is essentially tailoring career plans to a woman's life cycle: working full time and establishing yourself in the workplace before having a family—as recommended by many of our Stanford women—then either leaving (as Cardozo recommends) or gearing down (as our women suggest) once children come along, and finally reentering the workforce once the children are older. *Sequencing acknowledges that one's focus changes over time as family needs change, and that what was a central focus in one period of life may be less central in another. If our sample is any indication, this is an idea that is attracting a lot of proponents.*

Many of the Stanford mothers who work part time, as well as the stay-at-home mothers, espoused a sequencing strategy. They did not consider their current career choice to be a permanent arrangement, and many, if not most, of them, indicated that when their children were grown, they would return to the workplace in some capacity. Additionally, most felt that they could do so primarily because they already had the education and expertise required for such a transition.

Many of the Stanford mothers planned on sequencing their careers by working part time or not at all while their children were young; others adopted a different sequencing strategy. One of our respondents recounted how, in her case, it was fine for her to be working when her children were very young, "because they loved being with our nanny," but not when they became teenagers, because "they had sadly outgrown the nanny and needed more of a parental presence." Although she feared there would be a price to pay, she, like many of the other "sequencing" mothers, were clear that they would definitely reenter the workforce— "with a vengeance"—once their children were off to college.

Unfortunately, because very few women with grown children had themselves experimented with sequencing, we have little data on how well this plan actually works over time. This absence of data raises the question of why so few of our older professional mothers, especially the Pioneers, chose to adopt this strategy. On reflection, however, the answer is fairly apparent.

For most of us who started working as professionals in the 1970s, the option to stay home or work part time simply did not exist. You had to do everything you could to get your toe in the door. Once you gained that toehold, you could not afford to let go or the door would slam shut. There was no way you could opt for a part-time position and still be taken seriously. As so many of our Pioneers reported, you had to "do exactly as the men did, and then some."

The situation is thankfully different for today's generations of professional women. Although obviously there are still positions, and certainly advancement within corporate hierarchies, that require full-time—or rather, 150 percent—dedication, there are many more opportunities where less than a full-time commitment is considered a credible professional presence. The unparalleled rise of the internet economy and its e-business component has certainly created significant opportunities for home-based employment that never previously existed—opportunities that have significantly expanded the job horizons of many professional women. Similarly, the opportunity to telecommute is changing some of the professional landscape for women. Most importantly, perhaps, as more women enter the professional workplace, a critical mass of women is better able to demand accommodation, and we are now beginning to see the results of those demands.

Obviously, for some women sequencing might be too risky or simply might not work. For them, their careers are an investment that they can not afford to jeopardize. However, despite the fact that we have scant data on the efficacy of sequencing as a long-term career strategy, it is worth considering if one is unhappy with one's current career–family balance.

Being able to adopt a sequencing strategy, however, also assumes a certain financial solvency that not all professional women enjoy. If taking time out is not an option, then there is at least the possibility of recognizing that perhaps it is fine to find a "place to hang out" within a work organization, as one mother described her strategy. Finding a less demanding position while one is in the deepest throes of child rearing might not be a bad idea.

By adopting the broader perspective suggested by sequencing, we can feel less compelled to do everything at once and can feel more relaxed about setting our own priorities, not following someone else's game plan. In doing so, we can recognize that, as one early Pioneer put it, "there are different seasons in life. If you plant faithfully, you can harvest when you are ready."

Strategy 2: Secure Essential Support

As we have seen with other issues addressed in this book, each strategy has its advantages and disadvantages, and what works for one person may be completely wrong for another. There is, however, one thing that remains constant: Whatever choices a professional woman makes, certain essentials need to be in place to ensure the successful integration of a family and a professional life.

What is essential? Freud himself may have struggled with the question "What do women want?" but I'm sure his wife could have told him the answer in a heartbeat: We want help—help in the form of love and support, much like the love and support we offer to the other members of our families. Apparently Freud never asked, or perhaps Frau Freud was afraid to say. If the latter were the case, Frau Freud would not be unlike her contemporary counterparts. Few of us are very good at acknowledging that we need help. Even when circumstances reach absurd proportions, we are often reluctant to give voice to our needs. In fact, if there is one phrase that could be productively abolished from the lexicon of today's professional women, it is "I should be able to do this."

Hardly a day passes in my office that a working mother does not berate herself for being unable to deal with the stress of her complicated life: "Yes, I have a newborn and a toddler, and yes, I have no child care. And yes, we just moved into our new house last week, and okay, I am six thousand miles from any family other than my husband, but *I should be able to do it*—after all, I'm not working right now."

Then there is the young attorney, now four months pregnant with her second child, working full time at an exceedingly stressful public-interest job (not unlike her husband's) yet managing to superbly raise her 2-year-old daughter on a very tight budget. Her comment on the stress she was experiencing: "This shouldn't be so hard. I must be a wus."

Hardly. In fact, those early years of child rearing are among the most difficult and demanding for any woman. Chances are that at no other time in our lives will our emotional and financial resources be as sorely taxed as when our children are young and we (and/or our partners) are at the earliest stages of our careers. Yet I am consistently surprised at how hard it is for us to accept the challenging nature of the tasks that we have set out for ourselves.

"Today is the rainy day that we've all been saving for" is the best advice I can offer my patients who are caught up in the struggle of allocating resources and time to the competing demands of work and family. Now, when things are the most difficult, is the time to use the resources that we have been holding in reserve for a rainy day.

And in essence, that is exactly what our research has demonstrated. Whenever a woman becomes a mother, she needs help, and she needs lots of it.

In fact, there really is only one essential that mothers, working or not, require, and that is support—it just shows up in several iterations.

Childcare and Household Support

Our sample was replete with examples of how mothers, especially those working full time, required a whole host of support workers to successfully balance a professional career and a satisfying family life.

Susan, the physician who regularly worked 80 to 90 hours a week, advised maximizing support resources to ensure more time with family:

> Give up cooking and cleaning and grocery shopping [and have the baby-sitter do it]. Hire someone who drives and pay more to get better in-home child care. Be willing to take on debt to do it. I now have live-in and live-out help, because it's too much work for one person.

Another 1980s Settler, a mother with twin toddlers, recalled her initial reluctance to employ the help she desperately needed until her older sister offered her this advice:

> You can't buy time, but you can buy services. What you're doing is really shortsighted. You're wasting precious time doing things that you can have others do for you and you're not getting to enjoy your children. You wouldn't waste your time doing stuff like [photocopying] all day at work, so why do that at home?

Although obviously not every professional woman has the luxury of sufficient dispensable income to be able to purchase services at the level these women describe, doing whatever we have to do to provide the best quality and amount of child care and household help can be essential to our own well-being.

A colleague's research speaks directly to how indispensable support services are, especially when both partners are employed. A study on marital satisfaction done at the Stanford University School of Education found that the single most important predictor of marital well-being in dual-career couples was the amount of purchased services in their households. For *both* men and women, the proportion of available resources dedicated to purchasing services was directly related to the extent to which each partner claimed to be satisfied with his or her dual-career marriage.

If support is so critical to our well-being, then why is this concept so difficult for us as professional women to accept? Why do we consistently underestimate our needs? Perhaps it is something about our can-do spirit that does not allow us to accept the idea that we need more help. Or perhaps it has to do with not feeling alright about outsourcing activities that are traditionally "female." More charitably, perhaps we simply cannot afford the help we need, and even more likely, we are just too exhausted to figure out how to get the help we need and what it would take to organize that effort.

For whatever reason, clearly we often do not recognize or ask for the help we require. Similarly, for whatever reason, we routinely underestimate the physical and psychological importance of delegating nonessential activities to others. Delegation—that which we do well in our jobs—we often do less well in our homes. The question arises, of course, of just whom we delegate tasks to, which brings us to the next essential for professional women with children.

Support of Partner

Having a partner who "honestly buys into a dual-career family," as one Successor put it, is an invaluable asset to all professional women with children. This is true not only for mothers who are attempting to maintain a professional career while raising a family but also for mothers who elect to stay home with their children for some period of time.

Many of the mothers in our survey echoed the sentiments of one Pioneer who strongly advised women against ". . . attempting a full-time career and raising her family without the help of a supportive spouse. It's a prescription for unbelievable stress," she wrote. Sadly, her own experience spoke poignantly to the issue:

> . . . the strain of doing both resulted in my getting divorced, in large part because my husband refused to recognize and support my career. He paid lip service to the idea that I should have one, but when push came to shove, he never was really there to back me up.

To say that a supportive partner enhances the well-being of professional women with children is an understatement. The support or lack of support provided by the partner can, as one 1980s Settler observed, "make or break the success of the whole venture—and the more the mother works, the more essential that support becomes." And several mothers in our survey reported that their ability "to manage a full-time career was a direct consequence of a husband putting his career on hold."

So important is the support of a partner to any professional woman with children that Chapter 10 is devoted specifically to that topic. That chapter focuses on the types of support professional women need from their partners and discusses strategies for maximizing that support.

Before moving on to the other essentials for professional women with children, however, there is an ancillary point that merits some attention:

What if there isn't a partner, let alone a supportive one? Then what?

If a supportive partner is so critical to the well-being of a professional woman and her children, what if there isn't one? A recent study conducted at Cornell University answered that question by confirming that single professional parents can and do raise strong and healthy families. After a careful analysis of the children of single- and dual-parent families, the authors concluded the education level of the parent was far more influential in a child's development than was whether one or two parents lived at home. As professionals, we have the education piece in place, so obviously single parents can do a fine job of raising a family. It's just a lot tougher to do. There are few single parents who would argue that their lives would not be a lot easier with a supportive partner to shoulder some of the responsibility.

For a single parent to balance the stresses of a full-time career and children, other forms of familial and peer support become even more essential. A friend and colleague recounted recently that when she faced the prospect of single parenthood following her divorce, the image that came to mind was that of having to jump from the roof of a burning building and being concerned about who would be there to catch her. Only when she envisioned her friends and family, along with a cadre of professional helpers, holding the net could she conscience making the unavoidable leap.

Another colleague, a single mother of a college student, described her experience when her son was young:

> The only way I made it through law school with an infant was to send the baby to my parents during exams and when I was studying for the bar. I could not have done it any other way. It clearly gets easy as the child gets older, but when they're infants, it's so exhausting.

In either of these cases, there is no doubt that the stress these women experienced would have been lessened by the presence of a supportive partner, but nevertheless each woman found a way of obtaining the support they needed to create a successful life for themselves and their families.

Support of Family and Friends

As the above examples demonstrate, in the absence of a supportive partner, the support of friends and family becomes even more essential to professional women with children. Even when a supportive partner is part of the picture, friends and family who truly understand the choices a mother makes and who enthusiastically endorse our efforts are critically important to us.

There are clearly some services that one cannot buy, and there is no replacement for a friend or family member who is willing to pitch in when a mother is unable to attend to her children's needs. Assistance during times of family illness—help with shuttling children in an emergency or standing in for a parent who is unavoidably absent—are invaluable assets to working parents, and ones that are most often best addressed by those closest to them.

Without family members nearby or close friends, professional women are at the mercy of purchased service providers for family emergencies, if such providers even exist. The chronic lack of child care for sick children is an issue many women in our survey decried, and sadly, there are no indications that such service will be more forthcoming in the future. As one 1980s Settler, a stay-at-home mother of three young children, remarked:

> If I had to do it over again, I would have my mother-in-law come to live with us. As difficult as that would have been, it still would have made things a lot easier. I might have stayed at work had that option been a reality.

As the mobility of American families increases, however, the possibility of having family members nearby during child-rearing years is becoming increasingly unlikely, and for many of us, stable friendships are falling victim to similar demographic trends. For professional women with children, this often means less support that we can count on from family and friends at a time when we are most in need of such assistance.

Workplace Support

"When everyone around you either is not a parent or has a spouse at home, their expectations of you can be real obstacles to your success," wrote one 1980s Successor, a physician and mother of two elementary school children. She continued:

> Both my husband and I have experienced limitations because we are parents. The best way we've found to achieve a family–career balance is to have colleagues and superiors who are parents in

two-income households and who understand the constraints. Currently, my coworkers all have young children, so I feel very little pressure on work–family issues. It wasn't always that way. There was a time when I had to learn what not to talk about.

Several other working mothers described having coworkers or managers who had gone through the child-rearing experience themselves, an experience that sensitized them to the demands of trying to do it all. One 1970s Settler described sympathetic "bosses at the company I worked for when my son was a baby, who let me vary my hours according to my needs . . ." She recalled that such support, the exception at the time, was directly responsible for her being able to stay on her career path.

Interestingly, more than a few women commented on the fact that having a boss who herself was a mother did not necessarily guarantee support. One mother described a female boss who derided her reluctance to put her infant son in full-time day care. "It worked for me," was this woman's attitude, "so it should work for you." Needless to say, this mother quickly sought and found a far more empathetic work environment.

Financial Support

Despite professional-level earnings, many women in our survey complained about the high cost of securing the services needed to support their family and career efforts. Although most of the women we studied earned comparatively high wages, several reported that their earnings did little to offset their costs, once one took into consideration child-care costs, household help, clothing, food, taxes, and other expenses occasioned by a professional career.

One 1980s Settler with three children described her situation:

I sometimes wonder why I work. After taxes we really have very little to show for the money I make. We spend close to $30,000 a year in child care and schooling alone. But ultimately I think it's the right choice. It's an investment in maintaining my career, as well as my sanity.

For those mothers working part time or those staying at home, the financial pressures of living on a single income can be quite significant. Not having one's own income, particularly after years of pulling one's own weight financially, can create significant strain in a relationship. Issues of financial autonomy and decision making may require significant readjustment. It is not at all uncommon that the work one does as a mother gets inadequately calibrated in the fiscal (or power) equations of the family. This lack of financial equity can create serious problems within a family relationship if the appropriate financial and psychological support is absent.

Clinical experience suggests that for many professional women, issues of dependency, and particularly financial dependency, are difficult to handle. Further, for professional couples more arguments over financial matters erupt when there is an imbalance in financial resources (and subsequently power) within the couple than when those resources are restricted. As a result, having a truly supportive relationship that allows for financial parity regardless of who's bringing home the actual paycheck is a definite plus for any professional woman.

Societal Support

Support for working parents from the larger community or society is often absent from the daily experience of most professionals. For example, is it decreed somewhere that school *has* to begin exactly half an hour before most parents are expected to be at work, thus turning the morning drop-off into a speed derby? And is there an infantry commander who could best a professional woman when it comes to organizing the logistics of transporting several children to a variety of after-school activities?

Societal support that would truly address the concerns of working parents is by and large nonexistent or, at best, insufficiently present in American society today. This is particularly concerning for professional women because in many families the task of dealing with school schedules and delivering children to their appointed locales is primarily the responsibility of the mother. A recent study entitled "High-Mileage Moms," conducted by the Washington, D.C.–based Surface Transportation Policy Project, documented that the average married woman with children spends 66 minutes a day behind the wheel of her car, and the average single mother spends 75 minutes a day driving around. Even mothers who do not work full time are spending an increasing percent of their time behind the wheel, reported the study's authors, as fewer children are allowed to walk to school or neighborhood activities unaccompanied.

Interestingly, 61 percent of the women studied made at least one stop on the way home from work, and 30 percent made two or more stops. In comparison, only 46 percent of men surveyed made a stop on the way home. Aptly dubbing us "chauffeur moms," the study's authors wrote:

> It speaks to the additional demands (on women): that this is "your job" and that you are driving all over the place to satisfy the increased complex demands of "your clients."

Even though chauffeuring duties can certainly be stressful, many mothers considered the time spent shuttling children around as a rather valuable and unparalleled opportunity to spend time alone with their children. What is problematic is that no viable societal alternatives exist for those times when the need to attend to one's work conflicts with the needs of one's family.

Despite the fact that in 1999 nearly 80 percent of mothers with children between the ages of 6 and 17 are working outside the home, we still do not have institutional supports in place that reflect that reality. Child care remains largely an issue that each working parent must essentially address on her or his own. Corporations have tended to shy away from on-site day care, and child care for sick children is woefully absent in most areas of the country.

That our society consistently fails to recognize, let alone accommodate, the needs of working parents speaks to the ambivalence that we as a society feel toward mothers in the workplace. Although the recent economic boom has certainly begun to cause institutions to rethink their policies for retaining their professional workforce (see Chapter 9), any changes in this arena have been, at best, glacial. From our study it is clear that selecting a company that provides institutional support for balancing the demands of one's career and one's family is obviously an excellent strategy for professional women with children. As one 1990s Successor, a consultant with three young children, suggests:

> Working mothers might consider choosing the company [they] work for with an eye on their attitude towards family concerns. I thought long and hard before I chose a place of work, and I decided not to work for a company that required frequent relocations or a lot of travel. As a consequence, I haven't found any particular limits to my career since becoming a mother.

Several women cautioned working mothers to carefully examine the reality of "family-friendly" corporate policies and noted that *"what a company says may differ from what the corporate culture actually supports."* They suggested that a prospective employee talk with other working mothers at the firm to determine the reality of the situation.

Strategy 3: Identifying Needs—the Getting It Right Worksheet

Our research suggests that any of the three options available to professional women—that is, working full time, part time, or not at all—can be successfully integrated with raising a family. Rather than there being a single inherently right or wrong choice for professional women, any of the choices *can* work. How well they work depends on a range of variables, not the least of which are individual preference and needs and the existence of critical support systems, to enhance their success.

If that is true, then the question that emerges is not really "Should I work or not?" but rather "Do I want to (or have to) work?" And if so, "How best can I do this?" And, most importantly, "How can I get the support I need to successfully accomplish my goals, regardless of the option I choose?" To that end, the following exercises are designed to answer some of the questions posed above. The Getting It Right Worksheet will help identify the stresses associated with each work option. The second section of the worksheet allows you to assess the support systems you have in place to act on your decision.

GETTING IT RIGHT WORKSHEET

1. Stress checklist

Below you will find a list of the stresses associated with each work situation and a column for your use in planning how you can best offset these stresses.

If I am going to work full time while raising a family, I can expect:

What I can do to offset this:

High time pressure   _____

_____

High role conflict   _____

_____

High child-care stress   _____

_____

High need for purchased
services   _____

_____

If I am going to work part time while raising a family, I can expect:

What I can do to offset this:

High partner dependency   _____

_____

Some career concerns   _____

_____

Some financial pressures   _____

_____

Some role conflict   _____

_____

If I am going to stay at home while raising a family, I can expect:

What I can do to offset this:

High partner dependency   _____

_____

High career concerns   _____

_____

Some financial pressures   _____

_____

2. Essential support checklist

This part of the worksheet was designed to help you assess the support resources you have in place to ensure a positive outcome regardless of the work option you choose. Obviously, how much you actually need each support resource will depend on a range of variables, including the age and number of your children and the nature of your work. This exercise will help you identify those areas that may be inadequately addressed by your current arrangements.

Do I have good and sufficient:

1. Child care?

	Yes	Somewhat	No
	3	2	1

If not, why not? _____

_____

What needs to change? _____

_____

2. Household help?

	Yes	Somewhat	No
	3	2	1

If not, why not? _____

_____

What needs to change? _____

_____

3. Partner support?

	Yes	Somewhat	No
	3	2	1

If not, why not? _____

_____

What needs to change? _____

_____

4. Financial support?

	Yes	Somewhat	No
	3	2	1

If not, why not? _____

_____

What needs to change? _____

_____

5. Institutional support?	Yes	Somewhat	No
	3	2	1

If not, why not? _____

_____

What needs to change? _____

_____

6. Workplace support?	Yes	Somewhat	No
	3	2	1

If not, why not? _____

_____

What needs to change? _____

_____

7. Support from friends/family?	Yes	Somewhat	No
	3	2	1

If not, why not? _____

_____

What needs to change? _____

_____

17–21: good to excellent support resources
13–16: moderate support resources
7–12: inadequate support resources

When you have completed your Getting It Right Worksheet, you should have a better idea of the kinds of stresses you can anticipate in a particular work situation, as well as a better idea of how you can begin to address those stresses. Additionally, you will be aware of the support resources you have in place (or need to put in place) to enhance your ability to get it right.

Whatever you decide is right for you and your family at the present time, however, may change as your children grow older. As different needs emerge during the course of the family life cycle, revisiting this worksheet can help you address these changing needs.

CHAPTER 8

If I Work, What's the Best Way to Do It?

EXPERIENCE: EVALUATING WORK OPTIONS

What professional woman with children has not fantasized about living out some variant of Diane Keaton's role in *Baby Boom*? What a terrific idea—running off to Vermont to start one's own baby-food business as a way of resolving the competing demands of corporate life and motherhood. Start your own company and throw off the bonds of workplace oppression. Sounds pretty good, but one patient's brush with "mamapreneurship" tells a somewhat different story:

> I actually thought that starting a business when I had my first child made a lot of sense. I could be at home with my baby and still earn a real living. And I could choose the kinds of projects I took on. It seemed ideal. What a joke! My first child didn't sleep for four months, and I was working day and night to deliver on my projects. I didn't have enough child care and I knew nothing about kids—their needs are higher in the first few years than at any other time. I was exhausted all the time. It was just about impossible to try to build a new business and nurse a baby at the same time. There's a lot of legwork and marketing that goes into that first year of business. I felt pulled in all directions, and the business limped along for several years. I definitely would not recommend it. It would have been better to have started the business before the kids showed up.

Although my patient's description of her experience is probably closer to the reality of what it is like to be a new mother and an entrepreneur, the temptation to escape the pressures of corporate America provides a strong incentive for many professional women.

Many of us see independent employment as a strategy for coping with the relentless and often inflexible demands of corporate life. For some, such employment has worked very well, as in the case of this new mother, a former editor who recently took a contract position as a technical writer in Silicon Valley:

> In order to be on a fast track, most corporations demand a level of commitment that I was not willing to make. Right now what's important to me is being in control of my time. While I miss being at the center of things, I enjoy the flexibility and a schedule that allows for a family life and for other activities that are important to me.

To get a sense of how corporate versus independent employment compares for professional women, we asked the women in our Stanford survey about their experiences in the workplace and about how they saw the advantages and disadvantages of corporate life versus independent employment.

◆ ◆ ◆

LESSONS LEARNED

AT A GLANCE:
PROS AND CONS OF CORPORATE
LIFE FOR WOMEN

TOP 5 ADVANTAGES	TOP 5 DISADVANTAGES
1. Visibility	1. Male corporate culture
2. Benefits	2. Lack of flexibility
3. Security	3. Discrimination/sexism
4. Training	4. Glass ceiling/politics
5. Hours	5. Prejudice against mothers

The Top Five Advantages of Corporate Life for Professional Women

We asked the women in our Stanford survey to tell us what they saw as the major advantages of corporate life for professional women. Here's how they saw them.

Visibility

Being visible by virtue of gender topped the list as the most frequently cited advantage of corporate life for professional women. Several women wrote about the advantages of being a woman in the corporate workplace, particularly if the organization valued a diversity. One 1980s Settler, a mother of three, described her corporate experience:

> As a woman you're noticed more, and if you're good, it's easier to stand out in the crowd. I was noticed, and in a large corporate setting, that's a great advantage. The lack of flexibility for family concerns was a distinct disadvantage, though.

Several other women, like this 1990s Successor, a product manager, cited increased opportunities for women, at least at the less senior levels in work organizations:

> Some companies have a commitment to women, at least on paper, and I have found that my advancement, particularly at this stage of my career, has benefited from my company's desire to promote women.

Along similar lines, the opportunity to be around other professional women was seen as a distinct advantage of a corporate setting, often because such women could serve as role models for newer and less-experienced professionals.

Benefits

Access to employment benefits like health insurance, paid vacation, maternity benefits, and sick leave was also rated as a highly attractive feature of corporate life, particularly for working mothers. Several women echoed the feelings of this 1980s Successor who discovered:

> I've had my own business—no question, corporate life is easier. You have vacations, a steady paycheck, and you can limit your hours to 8:30 to 5:30. You can't do that in your own business.

Security

The financial stability of a corporate organization, as well as legal protections against discrimination in hiring, promotions, and terminations, were also attributes of corporate life that professional women identified as important. Wrote one 1980s Successor with two children:

> I have certainly thought about leaving my company, but I can't really do it financially without considerable sacrifice. At 39 years old, I'm less willing to take the financial risk.

Similarly, in terms of other protections for women, some women felt that large corporations are more overtly conscious of, and responsive to, issues of sexual discrimination and harassment. Noted one 1980s Settler who works in consulting:

> Larger, better managed firms have more programs in place to deal with gender discrimination and harassment. They attract better people and are also more willing to promote women.

Training

Training and other corporate opportunities that provide professional women with the opportunity to learn new skill sets "on the job" are options that many of the women in our Stanford study identified as being of significant professional benefit. One 1990s Successor wrote:

Good companies have training programs where women can learn skills, particularly management skills, that they might not have been exposed to otherwise. There are also others who have paved the path ahead of them. It's easier to chat people up and get them to tell you things you need to know.

Working Hours

Also among the big pluses of corporate life, particularly for mothers with young children, were working hours that were more limited, with less need to work on weekends and holidays.

The issue of corporate hours, however, cut both ways for the women in our sample. Although many women, as we shall see below, cited inflexible and long work hours as a distinct downside of corporate life, others felt that the corporate setting offered some distinct benefits on this score, as this 1990s Successor observed:

> Contrary to expectations, I have found that in corporate life, the bar for success is lower. They expect less and you can succeed more easily.

Even women working in corporate America in the 1950s, like this 1950s Pioneer, observed similar advantages to the corporate setting:

> The hours tend to be pretty set, but you can get lost in the crowd. And that's the point—you can get lost in a crowd—which can be an advantage at times.

Interestingly, for many of the Pioneers in our study, the most frequently cited advantage of corporate life was "none." From their experience, it appeared that whatever advantages may accrue to women working in corporate settings, the disadvantages they experienced far outweighed the advantages. Several of them echoed the comments of this 1970s Pioneer, a business manager:

> I have found no particular advantage to working in a large corporation. Even financial security is no longer a reality.

The Top Five Disadvantages of Corporate Life for Professional Women

Male Corporate Culture

Male corporate culture topped the list of disadvantages that women saw to corporate life. Many women described the "pervasive, overwhelmingly male atmosphere in the executive suites and boardrooms" as the norm in corporate life, as this 1990s Successor in consulting observed:

> It's still a good ol' boy network in corporate America. Women still have to work twice as hard to be considered for promotions or to have their opinions considered seriously.

Many women observed that despite gains made by professional women, the top levels of most major corporate hierarchies were still the sole purview of men. Often, these male executives were seen as "operating under their own rules" and establishing a corporate culture that "is often very strong and hard to adapt to"—a culture that "can be oppressive to a women's natural style or inclination." Exclusion from male-bonding events and locales, and having to deal with the biases of older or more conservative men in the corporate workplace were included in the negative assessments of male corporate culture. The experience of one former consultant, a 1980s Settler, at a men-only event was far from unique:

> In my previous job, part of what was expected of us involved going to strip clubs on sales trips. While I found them distasteful, they were only annoying, not prohibiting. I certainly could have done without them.

In general, the women we surveyed tended to agree that corporate America was very much a man's world and that "men still feel a lot more comfortable with other men." As one 1990s Successor summed it up:

Institutions may have a certain image of the type of people who will one day run the company, and that person may not wear a skirt.

Inflexibility

The lack of flexibility evinced by many corporate bureaucracies made it into the Top Five Disadvantages category by virtue of the frequency with which the women we studied felt that corporate life did not allow for the autonomy and flexible work schedules that so many of them desired.

A mother of a 1-year-old, a 1990s Successor currently employed as a corporate vice president, observed:

> On the one hand, large corporations tend to be meritocracies, which is a real advantage, but on the other hand, it's very hard to have the lifestyle choices and flexibility that I need.

Rigid corporate policies and tightly regulated or client-driven work and travel schedules were frequently cited as distinct disadvantages of corporate life, as this 1980s Successor recounted:

> My job required 50 percent travel. My manager was distressed about my pregnancy and the required maternity leave, and vocalized his concerns constantly. No matter how flexible [bosses are], they want you when they want you, no matter who is sick at home.

Interestingly, the gender of one's boss did not necessarily make a difference in terms of work expectations. Several women pointed out that their experience with female bosses was no better on the issue of flexibility than their experience with male bosses.

Discrimination and Sexism

Discrimination and sexism also appears to be alive and well in corporate America, judging from what our respondents wrote, like one 1990s Successor, an entrepreneur:

I found that, in general, corporate life has a way of stifling sensitivity and creativity. Being a corporate team player often calls for compromises and turning the other cheek in certain situations of sexism, racism, and other ignorant behavior.

In terms of discrimination, several women shared experiences similar to that of one 1980s Successor, now self-employed, who described sexual harassment from bosses and vice presidents in the early days of her career, as well as limits to career advancement because of being a woman:

> I had to toe the line on bureaucratic silliness that women had to follow but men didn't—things like unspoken dress codes, flex-time for men but not for women, and hostile secretaries.

In general, the climate in some corporate environments, particularly for the women in our survey employed the longest, was pretty chilly. Interestingly, the percent of women reporting sexual harassment in our survey decreased from 38 percent for the Pioneers to 27 percent for the Successors, which suggests some improvement in workplace cultures. On the downside, however, overall the percent of women reporting some negative effect of gender remained about the same for each of our three groups.

AT A GLANCE:
WORK CLIMATE ISSUES

	PIONEERS	SETTLERS	SUCCESSORS
Have you ever experienced:	Yes	Yes	Yes
Sexual harassment	38%	30%	27%
Negative effects of gender on career	33%	39%	29%

While many women cited examples of corporate policies as potentially protective, others decried the extent to which such policies were observed "on paper only." One woman looked at the bright side of this issue, by observing that women could "sue for greater amounts" in the corporate setting.

Glass Ceilings

Glass ceilings, or in some cases, *lead* ceilings, as our several respondents reported, were evidenced by the fact that there are "few women in senior management." As one 1980s Settler, a product director, said:

> The picture of success is still a man. Women don't fit the prevailing corporate culture at the highest levels in terms of management style.

Many of our respondents advised professional women to sharpen their political skills and to take lessons from their male peers to make it through what they perceived were the cracks in the glass ceiling that were starting to appear in certain industries. That can be a painful experience, as one of my patients, an executive in high tech, recently recounted:

> I broke through the glass ceiling to the senior VP level, but it may take me the next several years to pull all the shards out of my back.

Prejudice Against Mothers

Prejudice against mothers rounded out the top five corporate disadvantages cited by the women we studied. As one director of a telecommunications company, a 1980s Successor, described it:

> Typically, males in their [fifties] and [sixties] are in senior management, and although their hearts may be in the right place, there can be misperceptions about women in the workplace. I've seen women who desire children or a home life taken less seriously, or given less substantive roles.

Often seen as most debilitating was the mind-set of senior management that they had had to sacrifice personal life to make it, so you should, too.

Several women reported biases from other women against mothers in the workplace, as this 1980s Settler, currently working as a financial director, explained:

> I was booted from my last position by a woman manager who told me I should be more realistic about my options, since I had had two pregnancies in two years. I was replaced by a woman without children. Now I work at a somewhat liberal company, but even here, other working mothers discriminate against pregnancy and motherhood. It is sad.

Other issues identified as distinct disadvantages of the corporate environment included extended travel, long and client-centered hours, and the fact that, as one Settler remarked:

> Most of the successful men in my company have stay-at-home wives—what an asset. I want one, too!

The Pros and Cons of Independent Employment

Although we did not specifically ask the women in our survey to assess the positives and negatives of independent employment, we did hear from many women, particularly those with young children, who chose that type of work. The responses they provided offered considerable information on their experiences with independent work.

AT A GLANCE:
WORKING FOR YOURSELF

PROS	CONS
Flexibility	High work commitment
Autonomy	Low security
Financial upside	Low stability
Validation/recognition	No benefits
Work content	Isolation
	Low centrality
	No career ladder

The Upsides of Independent Work

For professional women with children, working for oneself has many clear advantages. Perhaps the most important one was the amount of flexibility offered by such work. *According to the respondents of our survey, flexibility outweighed all other advantages for working women, particularly those with children.* For many of the women, like this 1980s Settler, the ability to exercise control on one's schedule while still engaging in meaningful work was an important consideration in deciding to step off the corporate track:

> I've chosen to be the primary caregiver of our three kids, so my flexibility issues have limited my upside. But that's been rewarding in itself because I love my job in a women-owned business of which I am a 25 percent owner. I sell our products and consultants, in a defined geographical area on my own terms, and I make good money. An added plus is that I'm surrounded by great, successful women. The downside is that even though I get to choose my hours (24/week), I am in a service/client-driven environment. Even though I'm home a lot, I often feel I shortchange the kids. I'm very lucky to have a successful career and a successful family, but even with my job, I often feel that both sides suffer a bit.

The ability to control one's work hours, to avoid unnecessary travel, to schedule vacations that coincided with family events, and to take time off when desired were all among the flexibility issues that mattered to the professional women we studied. Wrote one mother of six:

> I made the decision to work for myself "for the kids' sake." Eventually I said, "Who am I kidding? You'd never choose it any other way." For me, there was a time to be a mom and a time to have a career. I can't imagine being anywhere near as good at my work as I am if I hadn't raised [six] kids!

Autonomy, or the freedom to exercise control over one's work product and work flow with no reporting obligation, was another frequently cited plus of self-employment. The freedom to choose what projects one works on and the ability to control one's involvement in those projects were also touted as positive features of independent employment.

So were the financial upsides of independent employment. Although most of the women we studied did not list financial rewards as significantly contributing to job satisfaction, the opportunity to fiscally benefit directly, and perhaps significantly, from one's work was an important consideration, particularly for working mothers. Additional financial upsides included decreased spending on child care, clothing, dry cleaning, and so on.

Additionally, having one's initiative, ideas, and innovations validated and recognized mattered to the women we studied. As a group, these women valued the ability to choose interesting work and to define the scope of the work they did. In short, they wanted to be in control of their work lives, as this 1990s Successor, a business consultant, described:

> I have been doing independent consulting for a while and fear reentering the "real world." I left there because I wanted more control—I really hated face time. I wanted to take vacations when I needed to, and I wanted better pay and more control of the work I chose to do. If I had my druthers, I would only work 20 hours a week. To me, success is defined by having a balanced life.

The Downsides of Working for Yourself

The work commitment needed to start and keep an independent enterprise afloat was one of the principal disadvantages of stepping off the corporate track. The sheer amount of work and the number of hours required to get any business off the ground and to keep it running were noted as being among the most significant negative aspects of independent work. Often, working for oneself meant having no support staff and few opportunities to delegate responsibilities. There is no time to slack off, and as one business owner described it, "In my own business I have to ask myself for permission to take time off—and I don't grant that permission very often."

The lack of financial security and of work stability, along with nonexistent benefits, also presented some formidable challenges for professional women who worked independently. As one self-employed mother of two wrote:

> I'm the main breadwinner for our family, so I'm really on the line much of the time. If I don't work, we don't eat—it's as simple as that. I never feel like I can turn work away. It's how men feel when they are under this kind of pressure. It's incredibly stressful.

More than a few women spoke of the isolation that often comes with being self-employed, particularly in independent consulting, and several decided that the lack of a structured career ladder made it hard to determine where they would wind up if they ever decided to rejoin corporate America.

Some self-employed women, particularly those in consulting roles, found their work lacking in centrality. For the women who enjoyed executing plans and strategies, the lack of centrality inherent in a consulting role played poorly to their talents. They did not enjoy being less integral to their work organizations, and they often missed the power and authority they previously wielded in corporate life. Said one self-employed 1980s Settler:

> I could not play the "boys" game very well [because of] my own personality, so I chose to "drop out" and give my time to my kids. I have interesting work, but I miss the challenge and continuity of full-time work. I revisit the pros and cons of my decision all the time. I love what I do, but I make very little money. Fortunately I have a husband who earns enough money to underwrite our expenses and to let us live well on essentially one income.

Summing It Up

For working mothers, *staying in a corporate environment can provide some important backstops:*

- Job security
- Health and vacation benefits

- A regular paycheck
- The opportunity to "just hang out"
- Not having to always monitor the bottom line

But often *the benefits of the corporate environment are offset* by:

- Inflexible work demands
- Inflexible schedules
- Inhospitable corporate environments

Working for oneself has distinct advantages:

- The freedom to choose what to do
- The autonomy to decide where and when to do it
- The opportunity to be recognized for one's efforts
- The opportunity to financially benefit from one's efforts

The disadvantages of working for oneself include:

- The high level of work commitment needed
- Variable job security and stability
- The absence of employment benefits
- Interpersonal isolation
- The less central work
- The lack of obvious career ladder

Because for most working mothers, flexibility is *the* primary consideration in achieving work–life balance, it is not surprising that independent employment was a popular choice for the professional women with young children in our study. As we saw in the survey, these women often reported being willing to endure work instability and financial uncertainty to have more control over their work life. For them, having a partner who was able to provide financial and emotional support was particularly important, as was their ability to tolerate the isolation, effort, and uncertainty that often goes along with being one's own boss.

◆ ◆ ◆

ACTION PLAN: FINDING WHAT WORKS

Figuring out what works for you both personally and professionally involves understanding what matters to you about your work and why. The following exercises were designed to help clarify those issues.

Discovering What Matters About Work

The What Matters About Work Worksheet is designed to help you identify the values and attributes of your work that are the most important to you.

WHAT MATTERS ABOUT WORK WORKSHEET

Step 1. Rate how important each of the following is to you. (Definitions of each factor are provided below.)

	Importance		
	Low		High
	0	5	10
Recognition			
Interaction with coworkers			
Financial upside			
Power			
Authority			
Respect			
Flexibility			
Autonomy			
	Low		High
	0	5	10
Stability			
Security			
Benefits			
Training			
Work-time commitment			
Centrality			
Work content			
Career focus			

Step 2. Once you have rated each of the above issues, circle the top five. These represent your most *central concerns.*

Step 3. Underline the next five responses to clarify your *secondary concerns.*

Step 4. The rest of the responses are of significantly lower interest for you and can be your *trade-off concerns.*

Step 5. Apply the findings. The *central concerns* are obviously the ones you want to focus on in your decision process. Even though you may not find a perfect fit for all five central concerns, you can easily eliminate certain work situations as being clearly incompatible with the issues of greatest importance to you. The *secondary concerns* are just that—important, but by no means deal breakers in and of themselves. The *trade-off concerns* are those issues that are really not that important to you personally—for example, health insurance may not have any particular value to you because you and your family can be covered under your partner's policy. These trade-off concerns, then, are things that you are willing to give up if other needs are met.

This list of concerns can be particularly useful in designing a job search and/or to determine which of several work options might best meet your needs. Finding what's right for you is a matter of comparing the various work options in light of what you have identified as the most important aspects of your work.

Definitions:

Recognition: being visible and recognized for accomplishments at work

Interaction with coworkers: ability to interact with coworkers

Financial upside: opportunity to make money

Power: ability to get people to do what you need

Authority: institutional recognition of your ability to exert power

Respect: gender-neutral environment

Flexibility: ability to control work schedule, vacations, leaves, etc.

Autonomy: freedom to control work flow and content

Stability: consistent opportunity to work

Security: financial protection to cover expenses

Benefits: health care, maternity leaves, vacations, etc.

Training: opportunity to learn new work skills

Work-time commitment: willingness to invest long hours and weekends in work/travel

Centrality: being integral to the function of an organization

Work content: having interesting work

Career focus: existence of a clear career path and continuity

Optimizing Time

As we have seen, the primary reason professional women take time out of the workplace or work part time is to have more time for their families. Clearly, cutting back on work and not working at all are options that will increase the amount of time available for family life. In reality, however, these may not be the most desirable, or even available, strategy for every working mother. As we have seen, even mothers who cut back on their work complain of never having enough time to accomplish all they set out for themselves. Because time is such a critical issue for all mothers, the following exercise is designed to help identify ways of optimizing the time that is available.

In doing this exercise, it is important not to shortchange the exploration process about this issue. Too often, our thinking can be short-circuited by fear, misinformation, or limited reality testing of possible options. Ideas get raised and dismissed as untenable without being given truly careful consideration. As is very common when one is anxious or uncertain, tunnel vision sets in, and the horizon of available options is severely constricted.

In answering the question of how to find more time for yourself and your family, consider the following steps:

- Work through the Optimizing Time Worksheet with as broad a perspective as possible.
- Oblige yourself to think expansively, creatively, and imaginatively when answering the questions.
- When answering the question "What can I do about that?" allow yourself to brainstorm.
- Remember, you're just thinking about the issue, not committing to act on it immediately. This kind of thinking, even if it brings up some pretty far-out possibilities, results in many more creative solutions than does a narrowly focused search for answers.
- Talk with others who share this concern: Talk with your partner, and most importantly, talk with your kids (if they are old enough to understand!).

OPTIMIZING TIME WORKSHEET

1. **On a scale of 1 to 10, how important to me is finding *more* time for my family or myself?** _____ (1 = not important; 10 = very important)
   (If your answer is less than 6, you're doing pretty well already and probably do not need to continue with this exercise.)

2. **Does finding more time for my family/self mean I have to cut back on work hours?**

   _____ Yes _____ No _____ Perhaps

   Are there other options?

   _____ Yes _____ No _____ Perhaps

   List other options (e.g., outsourcing nonessential activities, hiring a cook, getting partner to contribute more time, getting more cleaning help, simplifying lifestyle)

   _____

   _____

   _____

   _____

3. **Is my partner supportive of my desire to cut back on work or change my work situation?**

   _____ Yes _____ No _____ Perhaps

   If not, why not?

   _____

   _____

   _____

   _____

   What can I do about that? (e.g., do I know what my partner's concerns are? Are there ways of addressing them?)

   _____

   _____

   _____

   _____

4. **Would changing my child-care situation help?**

_____ Yes _____ No _____ Perhaps

If yes, how?

_____

_____

_____

_____

What can I do about this? (i.e., having a caregiver do errands could reduce stress and increase time spent with children)

_____

_____

_____

_____

_____

5. **Can I financially afford a change in my work situation?**

_____ Yes _____ No _____ Perhaps

If not, why not?

_____

_____

_____

_____

_____

What can I do about this? (e.g., could spending cuts offset lost income?)

_____

_____

_____

_____

_____

6. Could I still afford child care?

_____ Yes _____ No _____ Perhaps

If not, why not?

_____

_____

_____

_____

_____

What can we do about this? (i.e., for sanity's sake, some child care would still be necessary; how can we handle this?)

_____

_____

_____

_____

_____

7. Do I _want_ more time to spend with my family members, or do I feel I _should_ be spending more time with them?

If it's the latter, what is the _should_ about? (If the _should_ is about guilt, check out Chapter 3.)

_____

_____

_____

_____

_____

What can I do about the _should_? (i.e., is it really a matter of my spending more time with the family?)

_____

_____

_____

_____

_____

8. Am I willing to risk some career detours?

_____ Yes _____ No _____ Perhaps

If not, why not?

_____

_____

_____

_____

_____

What can I do about this? (i.e., even under the best of circumstances, trade-offs need to be made; what am I willing to trade off?)

_____

_____

_____

_____

_____

9. Am I willing to tolerate less important or no work for a time?

_____ Yes _____ No _____ Perhaps

If not, why not?

_____

_____

_____

_____

_____

What can I do about this? (i.e., if need be, would I be willing to "stay afloat" in my profession for a period of time?)

_____

_____

_____

_____

_____

10. Am I willing to pay reentry costs, if necessary?

_____ Yes _____ No _____ Perhaps

If not, why not?

_____

_____

_____

_____

_____

What can I do about this? (i.e., given the uncertainty, am I willing to be a trailblazer in terms of the unknown costs of reentering the workforce?)

_____

_____

_____

_____

_____

11. Am I willing to tolerate some isolation?

_____ Yes _____ No _____ Perhaps

If not, why not?

_____

_____

_____

_____

_____

What can I do about this? (i.e., am I willing to create my own sources of support for myself, and if so, how?)

_____

_____

_____

_____

_____

12. **If I were to change my work situation, could I protect the time available to be with my family?**

_____ Yes _____ No _____ Perhaps

If not, why not?

_____
_____
_____
_____

What could I do about this? (e.g., I could arrange my schedule to do the after-school pickup, to guarantee that I left the office on time)

_____
_____
_____
_____

13. **Summarize "To Do" lists to arrive at my optimal time strategy** _(What are the things you can do now to optimize your time?)_

_____
_____
_____
_____
_____
_____
_____
_____
_____
_____
_____
_____
_____
_____
_____
_____
_____
_____

Applying What You've Learned

The best way to apply the information gathered from the above exercises is the following:

- *Focus on your central concerns* when making a work or career decision.
- Begin to *implement the things you can do immediately* to optimize your time.
- *Create a "perfect" job description* that takes into consideration your central concerns and optimal time strategy.
- *Negotiate hard for what you want,* either in your current situation or in any other that you might be considering. Included in this is a thorough discussion and negotiation of options and alternatives with partners.

We have seen that there is no one perfect way for a professional woman to integrate a successful career and a successful life. *The most important points in creating a work–life balance are (1) to strive to find the options that work best for us and (2) to not shy away from making hard choices on the issues that matter.*

CHAPTER 9

Once I Have Children, What Do I Do with Them? The Best Child-Care for Professional Women

EXPERIENCE: HOW PROFESSIONAL WOMEN RATE CHILD-CARE OPTIONS

By 5:00 in the evening, the rustle of papers as faculty members prepare for their escape exceeds the enthusiasm for the debate at hand. It is no secret that being the last agenda item of the day is not an enviable slot. The issue slated for that position at the April 1999 meeting of the Stanford University Faculty Senate, however, held the audience transfixed. Hardly a soul exited when the discussion began, and most of those present were acutely aware that the issue under consideration could, as one faculty member explained, ". . . provoke a serious decline in the quality of the scholarship and the educational offerings of this university . . ." It was an issue that could cause ". . . the erosion of our ability to appoint and retain excellent faculty . . . now, today. Not soon, but now."

And what issue could hold such an august body so transfixed?

Child care! Hard to believe, but true. Child care—the bane of every working mother's existence—had finally become an issue of serious debate and consequence for the university, as it has for many industries. Child care, a problem that has far too long been considered a "woman's issue," has finally made it into the mainstream of acceptable workplace dialogue, at least in certain settings. As one male Stanford faculty member described it, and as most professional women with children can appreciate, "the situation is such that it is common for faculty to register their fetuses and even pay for day care before their baby is born in order to secure a spot. As someone who had to register not only one but two fetuses to gain access to the Arboretum [the campus child-care center] . . . I have gone on the record in the past expressing my concerns about . . . child-care issues—not the least of which were fee increases that average 5 percent to 10 percent a year while salaries did little to keep pace."

As a working professional who has spent the better part of two decades dealing with the problems involved in finding the right child care for my own children, I can only applaud the fact that this issue has moved out of the closet and into the realm of serious debate and attention. I regret that it took so long for it to rise to its present level of concern and legitimacy and decry the psychological toll it has taken on all of us, as well as on our families, in the interim. Finally, we are beginning to see some movement away from the philosophy of "you decided to have kids, so you figure it out" to "well, we need to hire and retain talented professionals, so we have to figure out how to accommodate their needs."

Although industry is only marginally motivated by concerns for the welfare of working parents and their children, the issue of child care is finally getting the attention it deserves. Clearly, the economics of employing and retaining a skilled professional workforce are fueling the child-care debate, as is the increased presence of committed parents, both male and female, who are making their families a priority in their lives—and not insignificantly—in boardrooms and executive suites. Even at Stanford, were it not for the fact that a critical mass of senior faculty and administrators, again both men and women, had confronted serious child-care issues—particularly for sick children—in their own life, I doubt the debate would ever have moved forward to its current state of prominence.

Obviously, we have a long way to go, but the psychological warning bell has tolled. And, as Stanford's first female provost, Condoleezza Rice, proclaimed, "we've got to attack the problem, which is a substantial one." The notion of giving child-care issues serious consideration is the philosophy that most forward-thinking institutions are now adopting.

That this national dialogue about child care has commenced is indeed good news. Barring major economic reverses, attention to the issue of child care portends well for working parents, but what about right now? Turning corporate talk into action will take quite some time. How do we, as parents, deal now with the issue of securing the kind of child care that is right for our family's needs?

For most working professionals, the lockstep of our lives is thrown into chaos when the carefully articulated relationship between our children and their caregivers is disrupted. Because the care of our children is our primary concern, every working parent can identify with the sentiments of this 1970s Settler when she wrote: "The most depressing news I ever got was when my child-care person said she was quitting." Finding a new person to assume this vital role, finding someone who can adjust to and fit in with the family's needs and schedules, and, most important, finding someone we trust to care for the "most important people in our lives" can be an exceedingly daunting task.

And the cost is not insignificant. Even among professional women who are fortunate to be able to afford good child care, the going rate for top-quality care often taxes the resources of any but the most financially successful. It is not uncommon for women to spend a significant portion of their after-tax dollars on child care. The premiums offered to find and retain an excellent child-care provider are often more beneficent than any of the workplace perks that most professional women themselves enjoy. It is not unheard of for families to provide cars, bonuses, paid vacation travel, school tuition, health-care, unemployment insurance, and a range of other benefits, in addition to room, board, and a healthy salary, to attract a quality nanny. "It's the cost of doing business," acknowledged one woman resignedly.

If my practice is any indication, more arguments have erupted among professional women and their friends over shared caregivers or the hiring away of a capable nanny than most other issues combined. When a quality nanny is "in play," the maneuvering involved in hostile corporate takeovers pales in comparison with the tactics used to hire that nanny. By and large, the angst and responsibility for screening, securing, and retaining caregivers lies principally with the busy professional woman. In this, as in other family arenas, women generally assume the major portion of psychological as well as actual responsibility for ensuring a quality outcome.

To understand some of the issues involved in the child-care needs of professional women, we asked the women in our Stanford survey to tell us about their experiences with child care:

- What kinds of child care worked best for them?
- What advice they had on this subject.

• • •

LESSONS LEARNED

Finding the Right Child Care Is, Unsurprisingly, a Major Stress for Professional Women

It comes as no surprise to any working mothers that finding quality child care was a major stress for the professional women we studied. Over half of all respondents reported a great deal of stress associated with finding the right child-care arrangements, and for many, the stress associated with child-care issues was *the* most significant stressor in their lives at present. They, like other working mothers, reported that the sheer amount of physical and emotional energy consumed by this issue was significant, and a lot of sleepless nights were dedicated to working out appropriate arrangements.

Perhaps the most depressing news coming out of our survey was the fact that child care represented a major stress in the lives of all three groups of women we studied. Regardless of whether a woman had her children in the 1940s or the 1990s, finding quality child care appears to be every bit as difficult now as it was then. This 1970s Pioneer recalled the situation that existed when her now-grown children were younger:

The biggest obstacle to my career was not being a woman, it was the lack of child care. There is no adequate professional child care in this country, and my job involved long work hours and overnight travel. Hiring nannies is haphazard at best. They stay for [one] or [two] years, and then you have to start all over again. It's way too much turnover! If I could do it over, I would screen for someone who wanted lifetime work with a family, and I would pay more to get her. In fact, I would advise women to demand as much and pay as much for good child care as for a good secretary/administrative assistant. It's worth it.

The Best Options for Working Professional Mothers Are Either Live-In Caregivers or In-Home Child Care

Any professional who has ever engaged in the morning marathon of bringing children to day care or a sitter before work can identify with "feeling like I've put in a full day's work even before I've left my house," as one patient, a mother of three children under 9, recently described her morning routine:

> Not only do I have to deal with my two-year-old who screams every time I try to get him to put on shoes, but there's making sure the lunches are made, the homework is packed, and that my husband knows where the soccer practice is for the afternoon pickup. It's thoroughly exhausting, and it's every day. Sometimes I fantasize about getting ill, nothing really serious, just enough so that I would have to take to my bed. It's a sick thought, but I feel that desperate at times.

For the women in our Stanford study, the difficulties this mother confronted were a familiar scenario, and from their own experience, they suggested that the best type of child care for professional women were live-in nannies and in-home child care.

All three groups agreed that having someone come into the home to provide care was a real benefit for working mothers. Not only did such an arrangement obviate the need for time-consuming pickups and deliveries, but often such caregivers were able to be more flexible and able to adjust to the unanticipated demands of a busy professional schedule.

This 1980s Settler, a mother of four children under 6 years of age who is currently employed half-time as the managing director of a money management firm, advised:

> Good help and lots of it is key to making the whole thing possible. In order to work in a professional capacity, you have to be able to separate your home life from that at work. For me, it's clear that when I'm with the kids, I'm with them. When I'm at work, I know the kids are well cared for. It's hard to get men to understand that part-time work is OK and that I really am working when I am at work. I have a lot of help on the home front, a housekeeper and a nanny. I don't cook, clean, or do laundry. (Men haven't done them forever!) It's still a tough balancing act, but it can be done. You probably can't have it all, but you can get pretty darn close.

Although obviously not everyone can afford to have in-home child care, and such arrangements can have a downside for the care provider, it is also true, as Princeton sociologist Marta Tienda points out that "because we rely on other women to take care of our children, two women can enter the labor force for every one that takes on a new job . . . all of [whom] are driving economic growth in a profound way."

Political economics aside, it is clear from our survey that if you can do it, and particularly if you are working full time and/or have more than one child, having in-home child care can greatly decrease the stress of balancing work and life priorities. For some lucky mothers, their child-care providers not only help reduce the sheer volume of work associated with having a family but also play a nurturing role in the lives of the professional women themselves. One of my patients recently described her son's nanny as one of her best friends:

> Julia is a lifesaver. I enjoy talking to her about Matthew because she knows him almost as well as I do. And with no grandparents

around, I can brag about him [only] with her. She loves him, and it's really fun to have someone to share that with. She takes care of me practically as well as she does him. She's my friend and confidante.

Not every mother in our study was as fortunate with her child care. Several mothers wrote about a lack of family privacy that existed with live-in child care, and others described their delight when they were finally free of an "extra person living in their house." Having to deal with chronic turnover, or having to tolerate "an extra child," as one woman described her "au pairs who were either too immature or too entitled to stick around," also created significant stress for the employed professionals we studied.

In all, however, none of the women who had live-in help felt that given the available alternatives, they would prefer to do without it. Most women, although not necessarily thrilled with these arrangements, recognized them as an essential support to their careers. As one woman described it, for her family the important issue was "how well our nanny deals with our children's needs. The rest of us kind of fall into line around that."

Lack of Seamless Child-Care Options Are a Major Issue for Professional Women

Not only was the lack of quality child care a serious problem for most of the working mothers we studied, but the lack of what one woman described as "seamless options" for children as they progressed from infancy to toddlerhood to school age and beyond was also of significant concern for working professionals. One Settler described these changes:

What worked right for us when our son was an infant (an in-home nanny) worked less well when he turned 2 and started to need more social interaction. Whereas early on it was fine for him to be at home all day or at the park down the street, once he got older he needed more interaction with other children, and our nanny didn't drive. She was a wonderful woman, but his needs changed, and he needed someone who could interact with him on a different level. I dreaded it, but I had to find someone else, and that was a tremendous stress.

Unless there is in-home child care or a healthy supply of willing friends and relatives nearby, most working parents lack a truly reliable and trustworthy conveyance for their children during the workday, let alone someone available to care for children who are ill or out on school holiday. These are significant concerns even before one begins to consider the cost of the entire venture. With child-care costs running on average $1,300-plus per month for American parents in 1999, not to mention the high end of the live-in spectrum where even $3,400 a month is not unheard of, the stress and cost of keeping the whole enterprise on track are clearly not insignificant.

Because as professionals we are acutely aware of the developmental needs of our children, finding the right child care is of significant concern to us. Yet no one option appears to be best for all ages of children, and the chronic need to reevaluate child-care situations, especially as children grow older and/or when family size increases, is an additional burden to working parents. In reality, however, no matter how burdensome it is, we do whatever it takes to ensure the best care for our children. More than one mother in our survey echoed the feelings of this Successor when she wrote:

> My husband and I are willing to do whatever it takes to secure the right child-care situation for our children, up to and including leaving our jobs for a period of time if we feel that our children's needs are not being met. It is one issue on which neither one of us is willing to compromise.

Top Five Things Working Mothers Say They Would Do Differently If They Could

We asked the mothers in our survey what, if they had to do it again, they would do differently with respect to their work–life balance. Not surprisingly, the issues of child care and household help topped the list.

AT A GLANCE:
TOP FIVE THINGS TO DO DIFFERENTLY

1. Spend the money and get the help needed

2. Get more help with the nonchild things

3. Start having a family sooner

4. Quit work earlier and take more time off with each child

5. Have more work experience under the belt before starting a family

Spend Money for Good Help

Among the women we surveyed, the most frequently offered advice to professional women contemplating children was essentially to "spend the money—take on debt if necessary—but get the best child care and household help you can possibly afford."

Get More Help with the Nonchild Things

Ancillary to the idea of getting good help was the notion that a working mother should secure as much household help as possible to free up her limited time so that "you can be the nanny," as one Settler wrote:

> If spending time with your family is a priority, then set in place the needed support staff to make that a reality. Get rid of any nonessential, nonkid tasks, and delegate those that don't interest you. It's the only way to ensure that you enjoy the time you have with your family.

Taking a child's nanny along on family trips, atypical for most professional women, was seen as a plus by some of the mothers we studied, particularly as it allowed parents to have some vacation time together. By having child care available during the vacation, working parents were able to spend time together, apart from the children, but not entirely without them.

Another mother suggested that "things like family vacations should be just that, vacations." She recommended:

Take a cruise or go to Club Med where everything is arranged and you don't have to make any decisions or plans. You do enough of that in your regular life; you need a real vacation and so does your family. If you can afford it, do it.

Throwing money at the problem does not solve all things, but it can make a difference, and the prevailing advice was essentially that if you have the resources, spend them on the things that are going to make your life easier.

Start Having a Family Sooner

Among the other significant pieces of advice reported by the mothers in our study was a wish that they had started to have their families earlier. The topic of the timing of children is the subject of Chapter 6, but it is important to recognize how often the professional women we studied felt that, as one mother described it, "If I had known how I was going to feel about having kids, I would have started sooner and had a whole bunch!" Difficulties with delayed pregnancies and a lack of energy for the rigors of child rearing were also among the concerns expressed by this group.

Quit Work Earlier and Take More Time Off with Each Child

An ancillary issue to starting families sooner was that of leaving work sooner, particularly for those mothers who decided to quit their jobs entirely or to cut back their work commitments. Many of the women we studied expressed utter surprise at how much they enjoyed staying at home with their children. As one mother wrote, the "sheer joy of spending time with my little ones was such an astonishing surprise" that she wished she had bucked the tide earlier and left the workplace sooner. These women suggested that *if you're thinking about leaving work, "definitely quit sooner rather than later, and take more time off with each child, regardless of what others think of you."*

Not extending their maternity leave as long as possible was something that many mothers regretted. Again, as we saw earlier, being unable to predict how one was going to feel as a new mother too often resulted in not negotiating adequate maternity leave, where such negotiations were possible. Although clearly there is no right length of time for a maternity leave, for most professional women, "the longer, the better" appeared to be the prevailing wisdom. Obviously, if one were bored, one could always return to work earlier than expected; however, the opposite was not always true.

Have More Work Experience Under the Belt

Finally, the issue of gaining the necessary experience prior to taking a maternity leave so that, as one mother put it, "you can say you've been there, done that" was also an important insight offered by our mothers. As we saw in Chapter 6, many mothers suggested that having gotten appropriate work experience prior to starting a family enabled them to negotiate a better deal for themselves. Wrote one mother:

> Once you become invaluable in the workplace, it's easier to get what you want in terms of maternity leave, flexible hours, etc. You need to build your personal capital before you go into that negotiation.

Summing It Up

What we have learned from our research underscores how critical finding the right child care is to the well-being of working mothers. For mothers who could afford it, in-home child care appears to best meet their needs, particularly when their children were infants and toddlers.

As children grow and develop, however, such in-home child care needs to be augmented by other activities—play groups, preschool, and so on. This often signals the need for a different kind of child-care arrangement. As with many of the other parenting challenges we confront, transitions in child-care arrangements often spell more work for us.

Finding the right person or situation is a task that if poorly conceived or executed will result in infinite grief and unnecessary emotional and financial aggravation. Yet how we go about selecting that person often is far less systematic than the way that we might interview candidates for positions in our workplaces.

◆　◆　◆

ACTION PLAN: SECURING THE RIGHT CHILD CARE

Asking the Right Questions

Detailed below are the major issues of concern for parents in securing child-care providers. When you are working through the list, remember that not every item is going to be answered during an initial interview, and obviously not every question needs a full assessment to allow you to make a good choice. The issues addressed, however, are ones that should be at least considered in the decision-making process.

First Impressions

One of the things that you learn as a clinician is the importance of first impressions. What was the first thing that came to mind when you met the patient in the waiting room? What was her handshake like? Did he smile? How about her appearance? What did he look like? How was she groomed? What was your experience once you sat down with him in the office? Was he perched at the end of his seat or did he sit back in the chair? Each bit of information provides more information about the person you are about to interview.

So, too, when we met a prospective employee, particularly one to whom we entrust so much, our instincts and observations can help us in taking the person's measure. If your first impression is not very favorable, knowing why is important. Consider the following information:

- **Appearance:** If a person shows up for a job interview looking unkempt, what will that person be like once he or she is no longer trying to make a good impression? If concerns about cleanliness or hygiene arise this early in the game, it usually does not portend well for the future. A caregiver who does not take care of his or her own appearance and grooming will most likely not make a priority of your child's appearance or hygiene.

- **Affability:** Pleasantness, courtesy, and kindness all are part of the definition of affability. The last thing an already stressed professional woman, let alone her children, needs is a sullen or unhappy caregiver. Obviously, anyone can have a bad day, but a lack of affability could signal real problems.
- **Attitude:** Attitude problems don't usually show up at the initial interview but generally tend to surface over time, often in subtle, somewhat imperceptible, ways. "I feel like I always have to be careful not to ask too much of her," one of my patients said of her caregiver. "Even when she sees that I'm struggling with one of the children, she never jumps in and helps out. I have to ask her to do everything. And she generally does it, but in a somewhat begrudging manner."

  Such concerns as offending the caregiver by asking him or her to do things the way the parent prefers and sensing an unwillingness to pitch in can lead to resentment and frustration, not to mention additional work, for an already stressed parent. As one patient who struggled for months trying to work things out with a difficult sitter recently concluded:

  > If the fit is wrong, the fit is wrong. I've found that it's almost impossible to work through major issues with a caregiver because I'm not there all day to provide the necessary coaching. Once I've lost my trust in the person's ability to do the job, it's over. From my experience, I would advise that if a person is not working out, cut your losses early. There is often little to be gained by trying and retrying to make the situation work. It almost never does.

  Certainly not all mothers would feel this resolute in their decision to fire a caregiver; however, it is important to recognize that open, honest two-way communication is critical to the success of the child-care experience.

Personality
- **What is this person like and would I want to spend time with her or him?** If you would not enjoy spending time with this per-

son, you would not expect that your children would, either. For example:

- Is the person warm and loving?
- Does the person seem to love children, and is he or she good with them?
- Does he or she project empathy and concern?
- Is he or she fun to be around?

A person who is "just flat—not really bad—just not a lot of personality," as one of my patients described a prospective baby-sitter, is not going to miraculously transform into the kind of person your child will enjoy. Clearly, trade-offs are necessary, but chances are that the younger your child, the more time she or he will be spending with this person. Finding someone who your child will enjoy is an important consideration.

- **Does the person appear to be energetic, healthy, and generally in good spirits?** A child-care job requires enormous resources of energy, patience, and good health and spirits. A lack of any of these resources is inevitably problematic.

Experience
Checking out the experience of the person you are considering for a caregiver position should involve the basics of investigative inquiry: who, what, when, where, why.

- Whom did the person work for?
- What did he or she do?
- When [how long] did he or she do it?
- Where did he or she work?
- Why did he or she leave?

Talking to References
If there is a step of the child-care screening process not to ignore, it would definitely be talking to references. This process can reveal a lot about the person under consideration. Even in today's litigous environment, the tone of voice used in discussing the caregiver often gives more important information than what is actually said. Is the

reference enthusiastic or are damning with faint praise? Does he or she seem hesitant in providing answers to your questions? If you detect this type of hesitancy, a very direct approach may be effective: "You seem somewhat reticent to talk about X. Can you give me some idea about why that might be?"

Having a list of questions (see the Child-Care Checklist at the end of this chapter) can make it easier to approach the task of talking with references. There are other questions you might want to add or substitute, but the basics can tell you a great deal.

Background Check

- **Given the nature of the job under consideration, a background check is an important step in the hiring process.** Knowing what others—for example, an employment agency—have done with respect to background checking is a critical part of the decision process. One patient of mine recently recounted her surprise at an agency practice of including in the contractual statement about background checks something to the effect of "we do not guarantee the accuracy of any of the information" obtained. This may get them off the hook legally, but it certainly puts the responsibility for doing a thorough reference check on the individual employer.
- **What do you need to do to feel comfortable?** This question is subjective, and you really have to decide what you are comfortable with doing or not doing, as the case may be. For some, a reference check is an acceptable way of securing information on a person's background; for others, more extensive background checks are the only way to feel comfortable.
- **If a background check is desired, there are agencies that conduct such checks on license-exempt child-care providers.** Some agencies will check for criminal convictions and substantiated child abuse reports. Local child-care coordinating councils or law enforcement agencies can be a good place to start.

Basic Job Skills

- **Do you feel comfortable with the person's ability to think and reason** through the types of situations that might arise in the course of caring for your child?

- Would the person respond appropriately to questions your child might ask? Can they answer questions appropriately and are they cognizant of the level of response needed by your child?
- Would your child listen to and respect this person's ideas and directions?
- Does the person understand and communicate effectively? This is particularly important from the health perspective, and in terms of modeling language skills for the child.
- Could he or she be stimulating to your child? No one wants to spend time with someone who is boring or unable to engage them, and certainly this is not what you want for your children.
- Does he or she share your child-rearing philosophy? Consistency in child rearing is important, and the security of knowing that your child-care provider shares your basic philosophy is critical to feeling comfortable with your choice.
- What does he or she know about child development? Has he or she taken any courses? Encouraging a caregiver to attend child-rearing classes at a local college or health center is helpful to both your family and the caregiver.
- Does he or she understand and respond to the needs of your child? The ability to know your child's needs is an important part of proper care. An inattentive or unresponsive person is not an adequate caregiver.
- Will he or she follow through with your wishes/instructions? Can you trust that the person will do as you ask and follow through on the things that you feel are important for your child's well-being?

Trust/Judgment
- Would you trust this person with your life? That's essentially what you are doing. This is the hardest issue for most parents. Obviously, you can never be absolutely certain, but there are some things that you can do to help you assess the situation correctly.
- Look for red flags—disconcerting comments from previous employers, direct observation of concerning behaviors, suspi-

cious information on background checks, etc. Perhaps the best red flag is our own reactions. If you get the "raised hair on the back of the neck" feeling, as one patient described a recent interaction with a nanny applicant, take a pass.

- Evaluate the person's judgment—discuss possible scenarios with potential caregivers, much as you might in other employment situations. Having a few "what ifs" on hand to review with the potential caregiver would provide you with some idea of the type of judgment the person would use in real-life situations. (See the Child-Care Checklist at the end of this chapter for some examples.)
- Once you employ a caregiver, assess his or her trust worthiness and judgment. Use direct observation; ask your child directly for feedback, if this is age appropriate; use unanticipated monitoring—anything from returning unannounced to video monitoring.

Safety Issues

- Does this person share your levels of concern about safety? Is there anything in the interview that would make you question the person's attitude toward safety? Is he or she knowledgeable and respectful of basic child-safety issues—car seats, seat belts, safety locks on cabinets, poison control, and so on?
- How is the person's driving record? How much driving experience does he or she have? Has he or she ever had accidents, tickets, or DUI (driving under the influence) or DWI (driving while intoxicated) convictions? Some of this may be included in the findings of background checks.
- Does the person have specialty safety training? Infant and child cardiopulmonary resuscitation (CPR) is important for any caregiver. Swimming ability and lifesaving skills are critical if pools or water sports are a part of your child's life.

Responsibility

- Is the person responsible? Does he or she show up on time and in the right place? Can you rely on him or her to fulfill commitments? What do previous employers say about that?

- **Is the person honest?** This is difficult to assess before the fact, but if the person seems too good to be true, he or she probably is. A trial run of unobtrusive on-the-job observation can be helpful in assessing honesty and responsibility.

Flexibility

- **Is the person willing to accommodate a professional woman's schedule?** Many working mothers complain about the "out-the-door syndrome," characterized by a caregiver's racing past them the minute they step in the door. Obviously, respecting the caregiver's time commitments is essential to a good working relationship, but having someone who can be somewhat flexible and willing to pitch in as needed is extremely helpful—if not essential—for working professionals. Someone who has the "it's not my job" attitude can be more of a hindrance than a help.
- **Is the person available for the extras you might need?** Professional schedules may require weekend or evening work and travel. Can your caregiver be there when you need him or her? Would the person be willing to travel with you, if you should want that? What about caring for sick children—is the person available? Working out expectations and compensation issues early on can prevent a good deal of stress later.
- **Is the person interested in longer-term employment?** This averts frequent, costly, and emotionally draining transitions. The mothers in our survey saw longer-term employment as a distinct advantage.

Relationship Quality

- **What do you know about her/his friends and family?** This issue can be complicated, but the recent experiences of several of my patients demonstrated the wisdom of getting to know a caregiver's background and family. One woman recently described her child-care person, whom she adored, coming to work with obvious bruises inflicted by an on-again, off-again boyfriend. With great effort, my patient asked the woman about the marks and discovered in the course of the conversation that the boyfriend had been coming to the patient's house during the day. In addition to talking with the woman about her personal safety options, she had a clear discussion prohibiting the boyfriend's visits to the family home. Clearly, good people sometimes get involved in difficult circumstances, but it is essential to be aware of who is spending time at your home.

- **Is the person mature enough to handle the job?** This issue is one raised by several women in our study who indicated that having a nanny or caregiver who did not have some measure of maturity often resulted in difficulties for the family. For some caregivers, not taking care of themselves—not getting enough sleep to do their job properly, working other jobs, interacting with questionable people, and so on—meant poor, and sometime dangerous, work performance.

Using the Child-Care Checklist

The Child-Care Checklist is a shorthand version of the questions considered under Asking the Right Questions. The checklist is designed specifically for inhome care providers but can easily be adapted to caregivers in any child-care setting. Once you have made a decision on a caregiver, the checklist can be helpful over the course of time in reassuring yourself that you made an appropriate choice.

CHILD-CARE CHECKLIST

1. First impressions	+	−	Comments
What are my first impressions of this person?	_____	_____	_____
How was her/his appearance?	_____	_____	_____
Did he/she seem affable and friendly?	_____	_____	_____
How was his/her attitude about the job?	_____	_____	_____
2. Personality			
Did the person seem warm and loving?	_____	_____	_____

	+	−	Comments
Does the person seem to like children, and is he/she good with them?	_____	_____	_____
Does he/she project a quality of empathy and concern?	_____	_____	_____
Is he/she fun to be around?	_____	_____	_____
Does he/she appear to be energetic, healthy, and generally in good spirits?	_____	_____	_____

3. Experience

For whom did the person work?	_____
What did the person do?	_____
How long did he/she do it?	_____
Where did he/she work?	_____
Why did he/she leave?	_____

4. Talking to references—questions to ask

How long had X worked for you?	_____
What were X's responsibilities?	_____
What do you particularly like about X?	_____
What are some of the things that you do not particularly like about X?	_____
Have you had any particular problems with X?	_____
If so, what were they?	_____
How does your child feel about X?	_____
How do you feel about X?	_____

Do you find X to be:	+	−	Comments
Easy to get along with?	_____	_____	_____
Trustworthy?	_____	_____	_____
Able to exercise good judgment?	_____	_____	_____
Safety conscious?	_____	_____	_____
Reliable?	_____	_____	_____
Flexible?	_____	_____	_____
Why did X leave your employ?	_____		

	+	−	Comments
Is there anything else you think that I should know about X?			_____
Would you recommend him/her to our family?	_____	_____	_____

5. Background check

| Have I done what I need to do to feel comfortable? | _____ | _____ | _____ |

6. Basic skills

Do I feel comfortable with his/her ability to think and reason?	_____	_____	_____
Would the person respond appropriately to questions my child might ask?	_____	_____	_____
Would my child listen to and respect this person?	_____	_____	_____
Does the person understand and communicate effectively?	_____	_____	_____
Could he/she be stimulating to my child?	_____	_____	_____
Does he/she share my child-rearing philosophy?	_____	_____	_____
Does he/she know about child development?	_____	_____	_____
Has he/she taken any courses in child development?	_____	_____	_____
Can he/she understand and respond to the needs of my child?	_____	_____	_____
Will he/she follow through with my wishes/instructions?	_____	_____	_____

7. Trust/judgment (See sample scenarios below.)

| Would I trust this person with my life? | _____ | _____ | _____ |
| Are there any red flags? | _____ | _____ | _____ |

	+	−	Comments

8. Safety issues
Does this person share my
levels of concern about
safety?

Does he/she have a
clean driving record?

Does he/she have training in:
CPR?
Lifesaving?
Swimming?

9. Responsibility
Does the person appear
to be responsible?

Is he/she on time?

Did he/she bring
necessary forms,
information, etc.?

What do his/her
references say?

Does the person do what
he/she says he/she will?

10. Flexibility
Is the person willing to
accommodate a
professional woman's
schedule?

Is he/she available for the
extras I might need?

Is he/she interested in
longer-term employment?

11. Relationship quality
How are his/her relations
with friends and family?

Is he/she mature enough
to handle the job?

Sample scenarios:

- What would the person do if my child were asleep in the car and he/she needed to run in and pick up the dry cleaning?

  _____

  _____

  _____

- What if another nanny invited my child and the nanny to her family's home for a visit that afternoon? _____

  _____

  _____

PART III

Children, Careers, Relationships, and You

CHAPTER 10

The Right Partner

EXPERIENCE: ATTRIBUTES OF THE RIGHT PARTNER FOR A PROFESSIONAL WOMAN

Ever noticed how so many of us have become the husbands we always wanted to marry?

—Gloria Steinem

"I spent so much time trying to find a good guy," complained one colleague, a newly wed physician. "Now you're going to tell me I have to toss him out?" Obviously, the idea of a "right" partner for a professional woman raises some justifiable concerns, not to mention more than a little anxiety. The notion of a one-size-fits-all perfect partner is, of course, absurd, but there are certain traits and personality characteristics that lend themselves better to the life choices of professional couples, particularly when children enter the picture. For such couples, professional life can often be the source of significant stress, and the last thing they need is a stressful relationship. Days that are chaotic and demanding of their own accord do not warrant the additional burden of dealing with relationship difficulties. In fact, *among the professional women in my practice, the principle cause of profound personal unhappiness is often a relationship that is not working.*

Our research supports this observation. When we asked the professional women in our study for advice on how best to successfully integrate a career and family, a committed partner topped the list of assets. Many of the women cited their relationships as being integral to their ability to "have it all." Advised one 1990s Successor:

> You need a great relationship to make it work. My husband and I are able to talk about things, argue and work them out. That's absolutely essential.

Another Successor, a physician with three children, advised that for a dual-career family to work, the stresses inherent in that arrangement needed to be understood and borne equally by both members of the couple:

> Find a spouse who is dedicated to making it work. My husband and I have both experienced limitations on our careers because we both are parents. You both have to be willing to deal with that.

A spouse who has not fully "bought in" can be a real limitation for professional women. Not only does one not get the needed emotional support but one also has to contend with an unhappy partner. One of our Stanford women who found herself in this situation wrote:

> Be very picky about selecting a mate. Make sure he's willing to really be a partner. My husband has been pretty baby-phobic, but now that the children are older, he's more involved. I still feel he would prefer to do less, and that is *very* stressful.

For professional women, having a partner who is either uncaring or just "doesn't get it" sets the stage for chronic unhappiness. Reserves on both sides of the relationship equation are seriously depleted by the demands of professional involvement and an active family life. Emotional energy, a commodity already in dangerously short supply for most professionals, can be absorbed by endless, repetitive, go-nowhere arguments. Some measure of conflict is inevitable in any relationship, but certain personal characteristics can enhance or diminish the prospect of making it all work.

◆ ◆ ◆

LESSONS LEARNED

The Right Partner Is a Two-Way Street

The characteristics described below are personal attributes that ideally belong to both partners in a couple. The best relationships result when each person is cognizant of the qualities that go into creating a good relationship and works hard at maintaining that alliance. *Most of the characteristics listed below are qualities that can be learned or enhanced if they are not naturally part of a couple's skill set.* Some of these qualities, like stable moods, may be part of a natural disposition that can be enhanced through awareness, cognitive change, and/or professional help. Some, again using the example of mood stability, may change because of untoward circumstances. The important point is that the presence of the attributes cited can enhance the relationship of a professional couple, and their absence over a period of time can be a source of significant stress and disharmony.

12 Personality Positives

AT A GLANCE:
12 PERSONALITY POSITIVES

1. Positive emotional attachment

2. Empathy

3. Trustworthiness

4. Generosity

5. Emotional stability

6. Differentiated self

7. Reasonable limits

8. Healthy sexual interest

9. Good communication skills

10. Basic compatibility

11. Healthy work ethic

12. Commitment

Positive Emotional Attachment

Human affect ranges from warm to rejecting. At the positive end of the emotional spectrum is what psychologists call positive emotional attachment. Essentially what that means is that a person has the capacity to be affectively available: to feel things in real time and to project a sense of warmth and caring. A positive ability to form attachments is critical to the survival of any relationship.

A case in distinct counterpoint is that of the couple below.

LYNN AND STAN'S STORY

Lynn, a successful writer, complained bitterly that Stan, her husband of eleven years, was truly unavailable to her and her children. Not only did he not seem to enjoy spending time with her, but he also expressed no interest in her life, in her work, or for that matter, even in their children's lives. He was, and always had been throughout the course of their marriage, preoccupied with his work, the stock market, his exercise, and little else. He wasn't overtly hostile or even depressed—just indifferent. In my office, he dismissively declared that he loved his wife, and he couldn't understand why she would have thought otherwise.

A telling moment in their relationship had occurred just a week prior to their coming to see me. Lynn described driving herself to the hospital for an elective, but not insignificant, surgical procedure, only to have Stan call and inquire when he could expect her back. "He needed to know, so that he could plan his day," Lynn explained.

Her husband's glacial response to her medical needs was overlooked by Lynn, ostensibly because "he's not bad to me, he doesn't beat me or anything, and he is a good father—he's just quiet."

Lynn's own work suffered from her one-sided efforts to keep her marriage and family afloat. Her mood was often severely compromised by her husband's lack of affection and support. She felt that she was the problem; she had been in therapy for six months, and she presented as the "identified patient" in the couple. Lynn felt alone and miserable in her marriage, but she was truly conflicted about leaving the father of her two sons.

Could Stan change? Perhaps somewhat, but in this case, there was little evidence of a willingness to do so. He refused to engage in therapy in any meaningful way, and he frequently missed their joint appointments. As such, it was impossible to learn what lay at the root of his disengagement. From what I could tell, however, I seriously doubted whether someone as temperamentally cold, self-focused, and rejecting would be able to muster the necessary positive emotional attachment to save this relationship.

Within seven months of starting couples counseling, Lynn asked her husband for a divorce. At present, she and her children live a less affluent life but are doing fine. Rather than engage in a protracted legal battle with her husband, Lynn accepted less financial support in exchange for more favorable custody arrangements. As a result, she has had to support herself and her children by returning to full-time work. But despite these difficulties, she reports being far happier with her current life, and her children seem to have made the adjustment well.

Even though the husband in this couple fell on the extreme end of the emotional attachment–detachment continuum, this couple's situation illustrates well the absolute necessity of positive emotional attachments in any relationship. Issues of emotional rigidity and the withholding of affection have profound negative effects on any relationship, let alone one challenged by the unique stresses of a professional couple. When one considers the special needs of such relationships for qualities like patience, consideration, and cooperation, the essential importance of an ability to form warm, loving, and emotionally generous attachments is all the more obvious.

Empathy

Empathy is the ability to put yourself in the place of another. It allows you to emotionally identify with another person and to consider things from that person's perspective. It requires a certain measure of insight and compassion that enables you to step out of yourself and your own experience and adopt that of the other person.

Not surprisingly, empathy is often confused with pity, an emotion that conjures up images of shame and disappointment. On the contrary, empathy, or even sympathy for that matter, has little to do with pity. Rather, the ability to be empathetic is the ultimate compassionate and unselfish act.

Women, in general, tend to be high in empathy, perhaps as a consequence of our hardwiring for biological motherhood, or perhaps because of our sociological role as relationship sustainers. Which-ever it is, when one looks at empathy from the perspective of a professional woman, especially one with children, it is easy to see how having a partner who is truly able to be empathetic is a distinct advantage.

For professionals, empathy in a partner translates into essentially two things:

- *Active support*—the willingness to do what it takes to make things work: Active support means not reading the newspaper when there are children to be put to bed, and not being helpless and inept at doing things to keep the family personally and professionally on track. Active support is being willing to go the extra mile.

    One patient of mine described the active support she received from her husband as "his willingness to trade off being the baby entertainment committee for the first half hour or so when we walk in the door." This allowed her to catch her breath before launching into the demands of home life.

    This type of active support can extend to recognizing the need to take the family out to dinner after an exhausting day, to involving oneself in the hiring of child care and/or household help, coordinating activities, and so on. Basically, active support means *doing whatever it takes*—being attentive to a partner's needs and being thoughtful and responsible in turn.

- *Proactive support*—seeing what there is to do and doing it without having to be asked: One of my patients, a mother of two children under age 5, described how it was not that her husband was unwilling to help—he would do whatever she asked—but he rarely took the initiative:

He's more than happy to help out if I ask him to, but he never sees what needs to be done, particularly with the children. I always have to tell him. But then we both wind up getting resentful—I because I have to remind him, and he because he hates the reminder.

This type of partner has sometimes been referred to as the *salad maker*—a person who is quite willing to make a salad, but only if told that a salad needs to be made in the first place and given explicit instructions on how to do so. Absent a direct request, the main course never materializes because salad makers generally do not take the responsibility or initiative for anticipating and executing what needs to be done.

Proactive support means anticipating needs and figuring out how to go about accomplishing them. Given all the stresses that professional couples confront, such proactive support is a significant contributor to relational harmony.

Trustworthiness

"There is so much duplicity in my line of work, that the last thing I need is to be worried about whether I can trust my husband or not." This patient, a defense attorney and mother of two young children, worked with clients and fellow attorneys who played hard and fast. For her, having a partner whom she could trust—a partner who would not deceive her, who was loyal, dependable, and honest—who "would be there for me no matter what, just as I am for him" was an absolutely essential part of her well-being.

The element of trust in a relationship is a given—no one would deny its necessity. Yet *trust is something that many professionals have difficulty with, often because it brings up other emotions, not the least of which is dependence.* If autonomy is at the emotional core of all high achievers, then dependence as its antithesis is something to be avoided at all costs. Yet *no relationship can survive, or even have reason to exist, without some measure of interdependency.* It is this interdependency that professional couples often have difficulty modulating. *Leaning how to trust one another—learning how to be dependent on each other without compromising personal au-*

tonomy—*is a delicate relational balance that confounds many professional couples.* The subtleties of interdependence are not readily apparent, but a little professional intervention can often go a long way toward reequilibrating relationships when problems arise in this area.

Trust is a complicated issue that touches on all aspects of a relationship. Take, for example, how issues of trust are expressed financially. Is each partner willing to trust and be trustworthy around issues of money? Are other issues being expressed in the complicated financial calculus of professional couples? And what about sex? Would any discussion of trust be complete without an acknowledgement of the role of sexual trust and fidelity in the well-being of a relationship? As important as it is, such trust takes some measure of work for most couples. Once established, however, trust forms the foundation on which other uncertainties in life can be tolerated. As the attorney from earlier in this section explained: "My work life is one big, uncertain nightmare. I couldn't deal with having to live with that insecurity at home, too."

Generosity

Ancillary to the issue of trust is that of generosity. In busy professional couples, reserves of goodwill are often so severely depleted by the frenetic pace of life that neither partner can demonstrate anything even remotely approaching a generosity of spirit. "There just simply isn't the bandwidth" is the way it is usually described. If ever a relationship demanded a generosity of spirit, it is that of a couple (or family) whose life is going at full tilt. Yet such generosity is often what is least available for many couples, and a chronic inability to deal with the small stuff makes for unhappiness on the day-to-day level. Explained one of my patients, a mother of infant twins:

> It's the constant assaults of little things, like the thousand pounds of feathers analogy, that smothers the good feelings I have for my husband. I have lost the ability to forgive and overlook the small mistakes and petty errors. I just don't have the patience anymore.

This tolerance for life's imperfection is critical to promoting relational harmony, yet it is often the first thing to go when the situation gets stressful. One patient described constantly feeling barraged by the demands of her life with her husband:

> We barely find the time to eat when we come home from work— cereal is as gourmet as we get. We're too tired to even go out. I don't know how we'll cope when we have kids—we're so exhausted now. We get into stupid fights because we each think the other one isn't doing enough. It's dumb and it wastes so much energy, but we do it anyway.

For many couples, generosity, like trust, can also be expressed financially. As we saw earlier, for professional couples, financial inequities can give rise to countless variations on the themes of power and the withholding of it. "He treats me like a child," complained one stay-at-home mother of two school-age children:

> He expects me to be on a budget, and to ask him when I need more money. It's completely insulting. I'm used to having my own income and not having to ask for what I want. Does he think I'm going to be irresponsible just because I'm not working?

The issue for this particular couple was the husband's anxiety at becoming the only breadwinner in the family, coupled with the wife's discomfort at becoming financially dependent on her husband. Helping the husband to be more generous in his assessment of his wife's contributions and helping each become more comfortable with their new financial arrangement was critical to resolving their problems.

Emotional Stability

The professional women I see in my practice who are most satisfied with their relationships describe their partner as "a good person" or "a good guy"—someone who is substantial and predictable and who is, by their definition, "solid and steady." Take, for example, this entertainment executive's description of her significant other:

I couldn't do what I do without Jon. He's my bedrock. When all hell is breaking loose, he's very steady. He's honest and encouraging, and he'll tell me when I'm going overboard. He's on my side—he's really there for me, and he makes me feel more complete. I love that about him.

Not surprisingly, having a "solid" partner—one who is mature in outlook, who is in pretty good spirits most of the time, and who manages to keep a sense of humor about the difficult, and occasionally irrational, adventure that both partners have embarked on—can be the defining characteristic of a successful relationship for professional couples. There are distinct advantages to having a partner who is generally well-balanced, relatively easygoing, not plagued by labile moods, and possessed of a "twisted appreciation of the absurd," as one professional woman described her mate. As mentioned earlier, these characteristics play equally well on both sides of the relational aisle.

A Differentiated Self

When psychologists speak of a "differentiated self," essentially what we mean is someone who is able to accurately perceive where "I" ends and "you" begins. Such a person can tolerate and appreciate the differences that necessarily exist between one's self and another person. The situation of Deborah and Jeff provides a useful illustration.

DEBORAH AND JEFF'S STORY

Both Deborah and Jeff work in high tech, but contrary to the usual pattern of gender roles in that industry, Deborah works as a software engineer, whereas Jeff works in marketing. Both are fairly driven in their work habits, but Jeff's tendency to spend "every hour" at work was a constant source of frustration throughout their six-year marriage. Here's how Deborah described her husband:

He's very critical of me. He comments on everything I do—if I've put on weight, if my clothes aren't right, if I'm not animated enough when we meet his business friends. He gets on my case about not being organized and keeping my office a mess. He never asks me how I feel about things. He treats me like a child, and I resent it.

In addition to being very focused on externals, Jeff seemed to have very little insight into the person he had married:

We each have to take care of our end of the bargain. If she wants to live a good life, to have nice things, she has to be willing to help me accomplish that. I can't be expected to worry about taking care of things around the house and still support this family.

In this case, Deborah earned significantly more than Jeff as a software engineer and was, as both confirmed, raising their two children without much assistance from Jeff. As for the "nice things," Deborah's relaxed manner and casual style of dress suggested that she was less motivated by "nice things" than was Jeff.

As in this case, a person like Jeff is often blinded by self-focus and disguised insecurities. Such people have absolutely no idea who their partner really is. They see others, and particularly those closest to them, as extensions or reflections of themselves, or agents for their own self-fulfillment. They have little incentive to learn, or to care about, anything or anyone who does not fulfill their own needs. Lacking the capacity to tolerate and appreciate differences in priorities and ways of accomplishing those priorities, such people tend to take the world on either narcissistically or competitively. You're either with them or against them, and good luck if you fall into the latter group. Empathy is in short supply, and often such people are mystified by their partner's unhappiness in their relationship, as Jeff complained in an early session:

I don't understand why she's unhappy. We have a very good life. She has a husband who loves her, who provides well for her, who doesn't run around. We're healthy, we have two wonderful children, and a great house. I don't get it. Everything would be fine if only she felt better.

Despite his protestations to the contrary, Jeff had barely heard his wife's expressed concerns about his workaholic tendencies and his lack of meaningful interaction with the family. Deborah felt quite alone in her marriage and strenuously resisted what she saw as her husband's attempts to control her.

For this couple, the resolution was actually positive, in large part because Jeff was genuinely committed to his wife and their marriage. Although not without some difficulty, he made serious efforts to learn strategies for improving his emotional availability and learned how to be more aware and attentive to his wife's feelings and needs. In the year since I saw them last, a recent holiday note from Deborah indicated that things were working better in their marriage.

Reasonable Limits

All high achievers tend to have problems in the area of limit setting. In part this is because there are so many things of interest to us, and in part because our capabilities create innumerable opportunities for engagement. *As professional women, we tend to also be highly conscientious as well as unwilling to disappoint others' expectations. Combining these positive qualities with a somewhat less benign penchant for self-criticism creates the consummate prescription for the overcommitted professional woman.*

If one suffers from the malady of the overcommitted self, it can only be made worse by a partner who is unwilling to set and/or support realistic expectations. Take, for example, a patient of mine, a married woman who had worked in retail for years and who desperately wanted to leave work to be at home with her school-age daughter. She described recently finding herself "weeping uncontrollably the whole way back to the West Coast" after an extended business stay in the Far East:

> It wasn't just the exhaustion that bothered me, it was more the sense that no matter what I said, Alan wouldn't support me. He just doesn't see why I would want to stay home. He's really worried about the money and points out all the other working mothers we know. But they don't have the hours I do, and they don't travel like I do. Their jobs seem to demand a lot less of them. He just doesn't get it. I have trouble justifying not working. It does

seem unfair. After all, he says he'd like to stop working, too, and that's not an option for him. But I'm desperate. I get physically ill on Sunday nights just thinking about the next day.

It is apparent from her description that this woman's own difficulties setting boundaries on her desired work involvement were exacerbated by her partner's inability to appreciate her concerns and to support her desire to establish reasonable limits for herself. *It is not at all uncommon for high-achieving couples to place inordinate expectations on themselves, expectations that are synergistically amplified by those of their partners. If no one in the couple is capable of setting realistic limits, expectations on either side can easily spiral out of control.*

Healthy Sexual Interest

To me, sex is just one more thing I have to do. I'm so exhausted, I'm never in the mood. Frankly, right now I wouldn't care if we never had sex again. But I know it makes my husband unhappy. He hasn't given up, but he's angry. We can't even talk about it. I feel so guilty and so resentful. It's ruining our marriage.

Unfortunately, this woman's concerns about a lack of sexual intimacy in her relationship are far from unique. In recent years, I have heard a similar tale from surprising numbers of young professional couples. In fact, I find it rather remarkable how many healthy and relatively happily married couples report that sexual intimacy has been distinctly absent from their relationships for months, and even years. The toll this lack of intimacy takes on their relationships is often despairingly, but silently, endured. It becomes the great unspoken issue in the relationship, and one that often precipitates significant misidentified fallout.

That a lack of sexual interest should be such a pronounced part of so many professional couples' experience is cause for concern. How do we explain it?

One could hypothesize that changing gender roles have contributed to changes in the sexual politics of the bedroom—that is, as more women have begun to excel in the workplace, they no longer have to accede to the sexual needs of their partners. In this hypothesis, economic ascendancy in the workplace would translate into sexual power at home. This would suggest, however, that professional women would be less inclined to robust sexual needs to begin with, a proposition not borne out by clinical experience.

An ancillary hypothesis posited by one of my residents, who observed this phenomenon among her friends, was that perhaps because women have to act like men, using so much of our limited testosterone to succeed in the workplace, we have nothing hormonally left for sex. A hormonal hypothesis definitely holds some appeal, but this particular one does not explain why this phenomenon appears to be equally present in couples in which the woman is not in the workplace.

So what has happened to the sexual needs of professional women? Not every professional woman claims a decreased interest in sex and sexuality. But of those that do, there seems to be a combination of factors at work.

First, biology and the delicate hormonal balance attendant to childbearing and nursing infants play a distinct and often underappreciated role in our sexual desires. It is not uncommon for new mothers to be repelled by the notion of sexual activity, perhaps as the result of an evolutionary protective mechanism. As one young mother described it recently:

> All my kisses and hugs go to the baby. I'm totally focused on her. The thought of sharing my body with my husband—I shudder just thinking about it. I feel awful about that, but it's so intense. I just can't imagine how I'm ever going to be with him again. It scares me because I love him and don't want this to interfere with our marriage.

For many new mothers, issues of body image and the role changes arising out of pregnancy and childbirth contribute to confusion about their sexual attractiveness—the classic post–baby belly blues. Such concerns can lead to tense, infrequent, or nonexistent sexual encounters. Even where biology is not contributing to the problem, exhaustion from juggling the obligations of family and/or a career can conspire to sap the sexual interest of any professional woman. As one colleague recently described the phenomenon: "We tend to pencil in sex at the bottom of our to-do list, so we can erase it if we run out of time." Male patients often describe sexual activity as a desired tension release after an action-filled day, but many women experience things differently. For busy mothers, sex can often feel like a chore rather than a pleasure, and finding time to "get in the mood" becomes increasingly rare as other demands on one's energies take precedence. Rather than an opportunity to relieve the pressures of a busy life, sex can become an additional to-do.

For professional couples, problems most often arise when a desire gap between partners emerges, in which one person's desire for sexual intimacy is out of step with his or her partner's. Most often, neither person understands what is going on, and each assumes some measure of responsibility, sadness, or guilt for the sorry state of affairs.

What is the recommended recourse if a partner is uninterested in sex, is too busy and stressed out to enjoy it, and generally not into it? Four factors appear to be of significant help in getting a sexual relationship back on track—provided, of course, that it was on track at some earlier point in time.

- **Understanding:** The first step to reestablishing a healthy sex life is understanding what is going on. Appreciating that sometime biology can play an important role in determining sexual interest and understanding that men and women frequently differ in the way they approach sex are important parts of reestablishing intimacy. *Knowing how stress and biology can affect sexual interest and knowing that something can be done about this issue can be beneficial in eliminating guilt and psychological blame.*
- **Reassurance:** Encouraging a partner to explore the underlying causes of any decline in sexual interest is also a critical step in readdressing the sexual balance in a relationship. One patient, a new mother with two other small children, recalled how her husband's reassurance that "we had always had a great sex life before the babies, and his willingness to help me figure out what I needed to feel more comfortable sexually, was a lifesaver." *Know-*

ing and acknowledging that sexual interest can wax and wane, that there are ways of reviving that interest, and that over time you can return to an earlier level of robust sexuality can all be important parts of reviving intimacy in a relationship.

- **Addressing the issue:** Although there are lots of ways in which a sexual relationship can get out of kilter beyond biology and work-related stress, whatever is causing the sexual problems for a couple can best be addressed by acknowledging that a problem exists and talking about it. Often, we refrain from saying anything about a problem, particularly a sexual problem, for fear of making it worse, but the "let's not talk about it, and maybe everything will be fine" approach inevitably results in failure. Not overanalyzing problems is one thing, but not dealing with them at all is quite another. With sexual problems, most often both persons are acutely aware that a problem exists, but the conspiracy of silence short-circuits any efforts to ameliorate it. The longer the issues go unaddressed, the more opportunity exists for negative feelings to develop and proliferate. Eventually these feelings get expressed, often in confusing and indirect ways that further complicate an already difficult situation. An open, frank discussion of the situation almost always results in a better outcome than does the silent endurance by both partners of the psychological pain and isolation attendant to sexual discontent. Again, professional help can be very beneficial in sorting through these issues, and arriving at a more satisfying resolution.

- **Persistence:** Optimism and persistence can do wonders for a couple trying to get through a rough period, sexually or otherwise. In fact, most of the other personality positives listed in this section come in to play in the sexual arena as well. Having a positive attitude, being warm and empathetic, communicating well, and so on, can be important in working through any difficult situation. For an issue as emotionally charged as sex, such personality positives are even more essential. A partner who is willing to do the hard work—to persist in attempting to resolve sexual difficulties, who chooses not to use such problems as an excuse for infidelity, and who remains optimistic about the probability of success—

can be an extraordinary asset in redressing sexual problems. Because professional couples are often unaware of the extent to which such problems exist for others like them, they are more likely to engage in a destructive cycle of silence, guilt, and resentment in their intimate relationship.

Good Communication Skills

Almost inevitably when a professional couple seek psychological counseling, they describe their problem as "difficulty communicating." In fact, communication difficulties have spawned a whole new genre of popular relational insights that focus on male–female differences in communication styles. Appreciating how sex differences can affect and distort communications within a couple is an important first step in reducing the number of repetitive arguments that spring up in any relationship. For professional couples, it is especially important because the extraordinary demands of highly leveraged lives leave little time to waste on endless arguments that result in little or no change.

When professional couples seek counseling for communication difficulties, most often what they describe is a situation in which the "talk" and "listen" functions in the relationship are defective. In many cases, it is the woman who complains that her partner does not hear or listen to what she says, whereas the man complains about not understanding what the woman wants, often accusing his partner of "expecting him to read her mind." Take, for example, this couple who came to see me after several years of recurrent and escalating arguments:

JUDY AND MIKE'S STORY

Judy and Mike had been married 12 years and had three school-age daughters. Both worked full time in highly demanding positions, and each had a fair share of business travel to contend with. Both loved their work and relied on part-time baby-sitters to care for the girls while they were working.

They were a family with multiple time demands that left little downtime. What communication took place was often on the run. The way Judy described their problem was that Mike consistently ignored her requests to focus his attention on family matters. She cited as an example what happened while she was at a business conference on the East Coast.

Prior to leaving on her trip, Judy left a voice-mail message for Mike about how he could properly prepare the girls for their school play in her absence—which costumes to put on, how to arrange their hair, and so on. When pictures from the play arrived several weeks later, Judy was dismayed to see her daughters' smiling faces peering out from disheveled hair and the wrong clothing. Needless to say, Judy was sorely disappointed in Mike's efforts, and an all-too-familiar argument ensued.

Mike claimed that he understood his wife's desire to have their daughters look presentable in the play, but he thought they looked fine. He did not understand or recognize how important it was to his wife that they be "all decked out" for the occasion. Additionally, he reported that he often felt like he "was dealing with a moving target" in terms of the issues that mattered to his wife—he could not tell what was really important to her.

Although clearly there were many issues other than just faulty communication at play in this scenario, both Judy and Mike felt disappointed, misunderstood, and frustrated by their interaction.

From the communications perspective, Judy needed to learn how to better identify and articulate what was important to her and why. Mike needed to hear his wife's priorities, to learn to be up front with his own needs and feelings, and to negotiate their differences better.

Like so many other professional couples, Judy and Mike had to do a fair amount of work to get to the point where Mike was able to ask more questions and listen more attentively and where Judy learned to appreciate their differences in perspective and style. All of this took time—time to discuss issues, time to disagree and negotiate, time to resolve—time, the one thing that was in short supply in the life of this busy professional family.

Only when the couple saw the wisdom of working on their communication issues rather than wasting time in endless rounds of unproductive arguments did real change begin to take place. Once they learned to communicate more effectively, other issues in their marriage slowly began to resolve, and at their last visit, the couple reported a renewed appreciation for the need to spend more time with each other.

Having a partner who is willing to do the work—who is willing to learn how to communicate needs, feelings, and thoughts—is an asset to any relationship. In professional couples, the ability to communicate effectively under time constraints is even more critical. In the absence of this skill, the tensions that develop in the relationship are likely to overwhelm even the most dedicated relationship.

Basic Compatibility

If a professional couple do not share a certain measure of basic compatibility, the chances of their making it through the long haul are exceedingly low. Any two people need to have some interests in common, shared passions that sustain them over the years, be they intellectual, physical/athletic, or avocational. For the professional couple, this is particularly true, as the competing demands for time make nonwork hours scarce. If there are interests and activities that both members of the couple enjoy doing, and doing together, the opportunity for them to share pleasurable time together is maximized. The pull of such a shared enthusiasm can be a potent antidote to the prototypical workaholism of most professionals.

Unsurprisingly, many of the couples in my California-based practice enjoy outdoor activities together. One couple, who prior to starting a family spent a good deal of time backpacking and trekking throughout the world, currently limit their adventures to local day hikes, often with small children in tow. Both partners acknowledge that their mutual love of the outdoors is a bond that has sustained them through otherwise difficult times. Similarly, another couple consistently employ a weekend baby-sitter so that they can go for long bike rides together on Saturday mornings, during which they can catch each other up on their busy weeks.

Other couples share an intellectual interest or a love of theater, art, or music, which they indulge with varying degrees of passion. Some just enjoy going to Home Depot together and checking out the latest plumbing fixtures. *Whatever the interest is, the most satisfied couples tend to enjoy spending time together, find things to talk about, and generally get along well.* This doesn't mean that they don't disagree, bicker, or even fight, but by and large, they genuinely enjoy each other's company.

Healthy Work Ethic

What exactly do psychologists mean when we talk about a healthy work ethic? Basically, what we are attempting to describe is the ability to balance an active investment in one's career with a perspective on the importance of other aspects of life. In the case of working professionals with families, this translates into keeping one's work life in its proper perspective. Although it is easy to endorse, such a balance is far from easy to attain. From the perspective of a professional woman, having a partner who can "walk the walk and live the talk," as one working mother described it, is a distinct asset. "Having a partner who could and would be there" was identified by the women in our Stanford study as significantly instrumental in their ability to successfully cope with the demands of work and family. To truly "be there," a person has to actually be present, and that usually translates into wanting to be there in the first place, and, second, into working in an environment that supports this balance.

Among the women in our Stanford study, the ones who expressed the greatest amount of stress in integrating full-time careers and families were those women whose partners were never around to pick up the slack or who were unwilling to fully participate in family life. One mother of two children described a husband (now an ex-husband) who was unwilling to be there when she needed him:

> He'd never come home when he said he would, and if he was home, he'd put his own needs ahead of everyone else's. He'd hole up in his office and work. If he heard the kids needing help, he'd ignore them, or call for me to help out. He buried himself in his work to avoid having to do anything. He wanted the benefits of a family without having to do the work!

Even if a partner desires participation in family life, work commitments can get in the way. One mother, a 1960s Pioneer with two older children, explained her experience with her husband's demanding travel schedule:

> The most stressful thing for me was not being able to share the household work—child care, laundry, bill paying, etc.—because I have a husband who travels more than 30 percent of the time. If your partner is not around much, it's very difficult, if not impossible, to really share responsibilities.

Several other women concurred with the advice of this 1980s Settler who felt that something has to give in a relationship where both partners have demanding work schedules. She suggested that professional women have a choice:

> Either marry a man who is less driven than you are and who is willing to be flexible or accept the fact that you will have to be the flexible one. Two high-powered, big-ego people just cannot do it. Something has to suffer, and from my perspective, that would usually be the kids.

Trying to make it work with a workaholic spouse was another nonstarter for professional women, as one working mother, an attorney married to an investment banker, recently described to me:

> Not only is David never around because of his work schedule, but even when he's not traveling he's always working—24/7. He goes from one project to the next—no time out, no time for anything but work. I think he likes things that way—no responsibility for us—because he's too busy working. I'm basically a single parent and I resent it.

Shortly after the meeting in which this woman described her dissatisfaction at home, she decided to actually become a single parent:

> I almost think he was relieved when I told him I was leaving. He's so obsessed with his work, he can't even stop to recognize it has cost him his family.

While many professionals suffer from some measure of workaholism, or at least excessive dedication to their careers, a partner who is unwilling or unable to keep career interests in proper perspective is highly detrimental to the well-being of a family. Even in those instances where the partner wishes to invest more time in family life, certain career tracks are clearly incompatible with that desire. One mother from our Stanford sample wrote:

> If my husband could acceptably go to work late, after taking the children to school, then things would be a lot easier for us. But it's not acceptable in his field to do so on a regular basis, especially not as a man. If he wants to stay on the fast track to partnership, he has to be there when they want him, just like everyone else.

Another woman, a stay-at-home mother with three young children, wrote:

> Until it is really okay for both men and women to downshift for a period of time, to have flexibility in their schedules and not suffer any adverse career consequences, we can't really expect that both partners will be able to put their families first. My husband would love to take time out like I'm doing and be home with the kids, but it would be professional suicide for him to do that. The business day goes on no matter what is happening in your family, and companies expect you to be there. Sadly, this is even more true for men.

Just as the professional woman in our survey overwhelmingly endorse the notion that family comes first for them, many men describe family is *the* most meaningful part of their lives—with the proviso that it is often a lot harder for them to act on that priority and still feel successful in their lives. Unlike most women who derive a sense of self-worth from a variety of roles—as professionals, wives, mothers, friends, and so forth—most men still derive the principle share of their identity from their work. If they do not feel good about their work, they tend to not feel good about much else.

Even when men wish to keep their work life in its proper perspective, sex-role conventions—such as "men don't do children"—not to mention the new nonstop global economy, can conspire to limit their success at establishing a healthy work ethic. Having a partner whose chosen line of work constantly infringes on active participation in family life creates a tremendous burden on professional women. As we have seen, many mothers in our survey report that they felt they had little choice but to downshift their own career aspirations for some period of time rather than attempt to have both parents working at breakneck speeds while raising young children.

For some families, a two-career marriage simply does not work. Not because the parents are not committed to making it happen but rather because of a simple demonstrable fact: The less available both partners are—the higher their work and travel expectations and the less flexibility they have in their respective schedules—the less likely it is that two professional careers can happily survive under one roof, particularly when there are young children in the picture.

This does *not* mean that two active, successful, working professionals cannot raise a family and do it very well. On the contrary, our sample includes scores of working parents who have successfully managed to integrate careers and healthy family lives. What it does mean is that *for maximum success, one or both partners need work situations that are high in flexibility and autonomy and/or low in time and travel commitments. Barring this, very significant external supports are needed to keep the enterprise afloat.* The various resources that need to be in place are more fully explored in Chapter 12.

The scenario of the unavailable partner spells serious trouble for professional couples already feeling the strain of family and career responsibilities. Having to interject boundaries on a partner's work life and compete for airtime with a partner's career is something that no sane person would desire to do. Having, as well as being, a partner who is able to maintain a healthy work ethic, despite compelling pressures to the contrary, is clearly a distinct asset for any professional couple.

Commitment

It is obvious from all of the above that it takes a strong sense of dedication and optimism to make a relationship work for professional couples, particularly those with children. Each partner must be fully committed to attempting not just the possible but often the improbable in dealing with the planned and unplanned challenges that life tosses in our paths.

When we asked the women in our Stanford survey to identify the characteristics that were most instrumental in successfully accomplishing their life goals, the women frequently cited a commitment and belief that it could be done. Having a partner who shared that commitment was equally important to achieving their goals. In fact, many women echoed the feelings of this 1980s Settler, a mother of four children who works full time:

> My husband and I both really want to make this work and we are both committed to doing whatever it takes. We have each paid a price for being committed parents, but neither of us wanted to give up our careers. You have to be willing to put in the extra effort, to make the time for family no matter how tired you are. It's hard, but it definitely can be done. If you are determined to make it work, it can and does happen.

Another woman, a 1980s Settler and executive officer of a large corporation wrote:

> I never doubted for a minute that I could have a career and a family, until I tried to do it. It was much harder than I expected. Having a husband who supported my efforts, who was as committed as I was, has helped me through some difficult transitions. I think the important thing was that he never pressured me into working, he left the decision completely up to me, and then he helped out a lot. He really believed in what I wanted to accomplish by working, and didn't just pay lip service to my career. His own career has taken something of a backseat to mine, but we're both okay with that.

In many ways, a commitment to a relationship entails all the other personality positives we have already outlined. For a professional couple, commitment calls for being emotionally attached and empathetic, in addition to being relatively stable, generous, and trustworthy. A commitment involves setting reasonable expectations for yourself and your partner, as well as the ability to communicate past the hard issues. Some measure of healthy sexual interest and loyalty is also a necessary part of any couple relationship, as is a basic compatibility on the things that matter: life, work, and family.

When children enter the equation, all of the above must be coupled with a sense of dedication and optimism that ensures that the nearly impossible can occur on a fairly regular basis. Is it any wonder why so many people have trouble with commitment?

Summing It Up

Obviously, no one is a perfect 10 on all 12 personality positives; in fact, most of us manage to limp along hoping for a middling score on most items. The traits listed above are those which enhance the overall quality and viability of any relationship. Taken together, the 12 personality positives are neither necessary nor sufficient to ensure a trouble-free union. The more of these qualities that each partner brings to a relationship, however, the more likely it is that the couple will survive the tough times that they will inevitably face. Perhaps the best way to think about these positive personality traits is as a place to start when attempting to assess why things are or are not working in a relationship.

From all of this, one question that might arise, of course, is what to do if only 2 of the 12 personality positives are present in one's chosen partner. Obviously, one could chuck out the partner and start all over again. That might work for some, but for most of us, a more considered approach might be to bear in mind that very few people who have managed to be in long-term relationships are truly lacking in all, or most, of the characteristics described. More than likely, a person who scores poorly on say, the emotional empathy trait, will have some other compensating features to offset a deficiency in the empathy realm. Although learning to be more empathetic is not easy, it can be done if one has the dedication and desire to do so. Outlined below is a worksheet for assessing what each partner brings to the relationship in terms of the 12 personality positives.

• • •

ACTION PLAN: RELATIONSHIP ℞

RELATIONSHIP ℞ WORKSHEET

Instructions: Assign a value from 1 to 10 to each personality positive, with 1 being the lowest and 10 being the highest, for you and your partner. Duplicate the worksheet and have each partner rate separately, then compare.

	Partner	Self	What can we do differently?
	1...5...10	1...5...10	
1. Positive emotional attachment	——	——	—————— —————— —————— ——————
2. Empathy	——	——	—————— —————— —————— ——————
3. Trustworthiness	——	——	—————— —————— —————— ——————
4. Generosity	——	——	—————— —————— —————— ——————

	Partner	Self	What can we do differently?
	1...5...10	1...5...10	
5. Emotional stability	____	____	_____ _____ _____
6. Differentiated self	____	____	_____ _____ _____ _____
7. Reasonable limits	____	____	_____ _____ _____ _____
8. Healthy sexual interest	____	____	_____ _____ _____ _____
9. Good communi- cation skills	____	____	_____ _____ _____
10. Basic compatibility	____	____	_____ _____ _____ _____
11. Healthy work ethic	____	____	_____ _____ _____ _____
12. Commitment	____	____	_____ _____ _____ _____

CHAPTER 11

Okay, So What Are the Essentials of a Successful Life?

EXPERIENCE: WHAT MATTERS TO PROFESSIONAL WOMEN AND WHY

Success is getting what you want. Happiness is wanting what you get.

—Anonymous

After all this research and all this discussion, what is the bottom line? Is it possible for us as professional women to do it all and do it all well? And if so, how do we do that?

Obviously, the answers to those questions are neither simple nor straightforward (or this book could have been a lot shorter), but there are some key elements that we have identified that are critical to successfully integrating personal and professional goals. *Given that time is our most scarce commodity, let's "cut to the chase," as my children so often implore me to do, and examine the most important essentials for professional women in creating a work–life balance.* The essentials detailed below are those which both clinical and research experience have shown to be the most important assets for women professionals in accomplishing the difficult, and often exhausting, tasks that we set out for ourselves.

◆ ◆ ◆

LESSONS LEARNED

To better understand the concept of personal/professional balance, we asked the women in our Stanford study to tell us about what mattered in their lives and why. Specifically we asked them to tell us what they felt were the essentials for creating a personal sense of balance in their lives. Here's what they said, in order of frequency:

AT A GLANCE:
THE 10 ESSENTIALS FOR
CREATING PERSONAL/PROFESSIONAL BALANCE

1. Love and support

2. Drive and determination

3. Spirituality

4. Open perspective

5. Good genes/good sense

6. The right preparation

7. The right work situation

8. Financial resources

9. Courage

10. Luck

The 10 Essentials for Creating Personal/Professional Balance

Love and Support
Just like the Beatles said, "All you need is love"—or perhaps love and support—but even those musical geniuses would have had trouble crafting a lyric out of that mouthful. From our research, it does appear that love and support definitively top the list of essentials that professional women need to make it all happen.

When we asked the women in our Stanford study to identify what it was that sustained them and gave them a sense of well-being and balance in their lives, their overwhelming response was "the love and support of people who care about me." Not surprisingly, a principal player in this blueprint for balance was a willing and supportive partner.

As one 1980s Successor said of her partner, "he taught me that there was much more out there beyond work." Having a partner who can help you keep things in their proper perspective can be an extraordinary asset in the 24-hour, 7-day-a-week nonstop world of many business professionals.

A 1980s Settler, a management consultant who regularly worked 60-hour work weeks, described how her husband got "mad" if she worked weekends or too late in the evening. "This forced me to make trade-offs during the week and be more productive with my time." Having a partner who is not a workaholic and who enjoys spending time with you (and vice versa) can be a potent enticement to disengage from a workcentric mind-set that is inconsistent with a balanced lifestyle.

Not only are supportive partners beneficial in helping us set boundaries on unwieldy career demands, but, as detailed in Chapter 10, a partner who is willing to actually assist in accomplishing the tasks of life is mission critical. Proactive support, availability, trust, communication skills, and all the other positive characteristics that we reviewed in that earlier chapter go into creating the kind of supportive environment that professional women need for optimizing success.

Having a family—having children who need and love you—is an important complement to a supportive spouse, as they, too, significantly affect the sense of balance we have in our lives. Many professional women spoke of the "clarifying effect" the arrival of children had on their sense of priorities. Like this 1980s Successor, most mothers acknowledged that without children, their lives would be considerably less meaningful:

> I love my children and learn from them every day, even though they sure can be difficult! I can't imagine a life without them. I would probably be a miserable workaholic!

Another Successor, a working mother of two young children, wrote:

Nothing is so wonderful as to having children. They bring new life and perspective (and stress). But they remind you of why you are on earth and they help you get your priorities straight.

Even though children often place significant demands on our time and energy, not surprisingly, very few of us see our children as the reason our lives feel out of balance. We don't blame them for taking up our time and depleting our energies. Rather, we view our children as the reason we seek balance in our lives, not the reason we don't have any. It is the desire to spend more time with family that has motivated many of us to seek alternative employment or to create new work options for ourselves. It is the compelling nature of a 3-year-old's insistence that you watch *Toy Story* for the four hundredth time that elicits near-universal compliance from working mothers. We love having children and we love spending time with them, and that simple truth makes us quite determined to find the balance that might otherwise elude us.

Rounding out the picture for professional women is the love and support one receives from one's family beyond partner and children—the extended family, the family we grew up in—as well as the affection and nurturance one receives from good friends and loyal supporters. Many of the women we studied spoke of how important early encouragement from family, friends, and teachers had been in helping them set their course in life. "I trace back much of my dedication and self-confidence to my upbringing," wrote one 1990s Successor who recently became a parent herself:

> My parents and my sisters provided a strong, loving foundation which has kept me focused on what is important in life. My dad died a few years ago, and it made me realize that family will always be more important to me than any career can ever be. Family is what it's all about.

From our research, it is clear that much like the progeny of the terry cloth monkeys that many of us learned about in Psych 101, we all need the love and the ministrations of others to ensure our safe passage on life's journey. Such nurturance and support is not a need that we ever outgrow, no matter how old we are or how accomplished we become. As women and as professionals, we have a track record for achieving remarkable successes, but we can accomplish our goals a whole lot more easily and considerably better, in an environment that nurtures and supports our efforts.

Determination and Drive

The second most frequently cited essential for achieving a balanced life was the determination and drive to make it all work. The subject of a following *Wall Street Journal* article provides an interesting take on these two traits. The headline read MBA, EYE SURGEON AND TWINS AT 53. It went on to report: "When MK gave birth to twins 14 months ago at the age of 53—after working at her venture-capital firm until her delivery date—some acquaintances couldn't believe it. 'Others thought I was crazy,' she says. And some, aware that she always has been a pioneer, weren't surprised at all."

Two distinguished professional careers begun at a time when "women didn't do that," and three children to boot, with the last two—the twins—born when their mother was 53! Just when you think you've heard the ultimate "impossible" story about a professional woman, you come across an article like that one. Amazing, but it's all true—I went to college with this woman. I recall her regaling an audience of undergraduate women with her life story at a mentorship luncheon a few years back. Against a backdrop of rapt awe and amazement, one could hear barely audible sighs of despair emanating from the audience. The younger women left the talk energized and scared. Those of us who were older left just plain exhausted.

Although not everyone has such a superstar résumé, what makes it possible for all of us to succeed as professional women is our determination and a remarkable dedication to getting the job—or the jobs, as is usually the case—done. The positive side of our tendency to be hard on ourselves and to demand excellence in all areas of our lives is our ability to produce truly excellent work. As Margaret Thatcher once aptly observed: "In politics, if you want anything said, ask a man. If you want anything done, ask a woman." When we put our minds and our determination into a project, we get it done and we do it well.

In terms of drive and dedication, the women from our Stanford study were clearly no exception. Many of them spoke eloquently of their determination to accomplish the goals that they had set for their lives. When asked to identify the factors that have been most instrumental in her success, one mother of two preteen children, a principal in her own consulting firm, attributed her accomplishments to "my driving ambition, focused goal setting, high energy, low blood pressure, indifference to other's opinions, and a supportive (second!) husband." She described herself this way:

> I work hard to minimize the stress in my life. For me, this has meant that I work part time out of my home to have the flexibility to be with my children, to do volunteer work, etc. As I have achieved all my career goals and I'm financially secure, I am very grateful. I have always proactively addressed the fact that I have children, what my child-care arrangements are, etc. I don't care what other people think, so I speak out for what's important to me, even if there are negative consequences for me personally. I saw having to fit into corporate culture as real disadvantage of being in a large company; while one can be financially very successful, one can be pretty unhappy with the work situation. Right now, having a family has dampened my enthusiasm to keep running flat out, but I'm staying connected in industry without working full time. I still have a conscious desire to have it all and a willingness to compromise to get it.

Dedication to accomplishment often entails coming to terms with less-than-perfect solutions. One mother of two school-age children, the managing director of a consulting firm, described the obstacles she had to overcome to achieve a successful, if "imperfect," lifestyle:

> To make it in my field, you have to be tough and competent. In my case, I have gone from being a "bitch" to being someone who is respected and successful. It's painful to have to be perceived as being so tough, but it's essential for survival. I have been lucky, but there have been many bumps along the road. To succeed at my work, I've needed energy, drive, a thick skin, and a good sense

of humor. It's not easy to balance work and family; in fact, it's pretty stressful at times. I chose a part of the business where my 80 percent travel days are over. Still, it's hard to do it all. I never let my office know about competing demands, never talk about family issues or stress. Companies tend not to be sympathetic. There's still a lot of conflict in my life because I often want to be in two places at once—I don't think I've really achieved balance yet. But having children is the best decision I ever made. They are truly life's greatest gifts, and I want to be the primary care-giver for my children. Some things can't be delegated.

Not surprisingly, responses to our questionnaires included plenty of examples of ambition, drive, discipline, and hard work—the basic building blocks of success. Also not surprisingly, these characteristics were among those most highly valued by the professional women we studied. These women are no strangers to hard work and dedication. As developmental psychologists have frequently reminded us, as women, we tend to be very disciplined—as young girls, we live by rules, and we even make them up where they don't exist, for our own psychological comfort. Even though in some instances this may have unintended negative consequences in the form of less risk-taking behavior, the upside is that we live up to expectations, our own and those of others. We do not like to let people down, and we work really hard to accomplish what we expect of ourselves. This tendency can spell trouble in the form of professional overcommitment, but generally it results in extraordinary accomplishments. Our success is the direct consequence of our efforts, and our efforts in most instances are really rather good.

How all this relates to creating a successful life is actually rather simple. The same drive and determination that are integral parts of professional experience can be directed at creating balance in other areas of our lives. If we believe we can manage a career and a family—if that is what we really want to do—then we will figure out how to do it best. We may not all configure our solutions the same way, but we will figure out what works best for our families and ourselves.

A can-do spirit is an integral part of our professional success. It is this spirit that impels us to seek out work opportunities that previous generations of women might never have considered (or have been able to consider). We have found or created opportunities for ourselves that are unique and that require a commitment and dedication that is equally unusual. On the whole, we tend to be reasonably optimistic and self-reliant, and if we are not particularly self-confident, at least we know how to put on our game face and go to work.

This spirit of determination and accomplishment is equally present in our desire to integrate our personal and professional lives. The keys to success appear to be in knowing what we wish to accomplish and in believing in our ability to resolve the challenges we face.

Spirituality

Given that our Stanford survey did not include a question on the topic of spirituality, the fact that so many women volunteered this issue as essential to creating balance in their lives was significant. *For these women, a guiding faith or some measure of spirituality was the third most important essential for achieving balance in their life.*

"It's almost uncivilized to talk of spiritual practices in a university community," explained Stanford's Associate Dean of the Chapel, Kelly Denton-Borhaug, when I met with her to try to better understand what the women in our study were saying about the importance of faith and spirituality in their lives. "So it takes some courage to speak about one's spiritual beliefs in a questionnaire.

"But I'm not surprised," she continued, "that so many of the women you studied indicated that [a] foundation of beliefs and prayer [was an] important [part] of their lives. Americans in general are really searching for ways to experience spirituality. For many of us now, it's different from the ways our parents experienced it, through an affiliation with organized religion. Today there is a deep and evolving longing for spirituality in our lives. As women in a changing society, we have even more of a need to claim our spiritual balance."

And indeed many women in our survey reflected beliefs and values that spoke to the importance of the spiritual side in their lives. Some addressed their spirituality through religious practices and wrote of the meaning of prayer in their lives. One 1980s Settler with three young children wrote about the importance of her faith in God:

God has been there to guide me through the difficult times in our lives. My husband lost his job shortly after our second child was born, and I had to return to work and support the family on my part-time job. Prayer helped me to find the courage to get through it all.

A 1990s Successor who was about to begin a family of her own wrote of the comfort she found in a personal connection to a higher power:

I feel less alone when I know that God is there to guide me. I trust in his divine wisdom to help me chart the right course in my life.

For some, like this 1990s Successor, "finding balance has meant constantly seeking opportunities to better myself, to solve problems and be humble before God." For others, spirituality took the form of deeply held beliefs and values that served as moral compasses enabling them to maintain or reclaim a sense of balance in their lives.

"For me," wrote one 1980s Successor, a single mother with one school-age child, "balance means thinking about what is going to be important to me in 20 years when I look back—that, and believing in God."

"Being true to myself, and staying on my own path—not doing it for the résumé," wrote a 1990s Successor who took some time off to think through what's important to her, "that's what has made a difference for me. Getting in touch with my needs and making them a priority has been the mainstay of my life."

A fundamental belief in and respect for people, coupled with a willingness to look beyond one's immediate concerns, was a guiding principle for many of the women we surveyed.

As one 1990s Successor, who recently left her corporate post to be at home with her infant daughter, wrote:

For me, the things I learned growing up have been the most important in finding balance in my life: to respect others and to keep things in perspective; to be thankful for my good fortune in life. And to know that work alone does not mean success, and that you have to look within yourself to know what you want. It's hard not to be swayed by what others are doing. Listening to my own heart and that of my husband has enabled me to put our family first and come to terms with not having it all.

Because of the demands of our professional lives, we often find ourselves bereft of the opportunity to reflect on what is truly important to us. From our research, it is clear that having some connection to our fundamental beliefs and the values that sustain us is of critical importance in finding balance in our lives. For some, this may come from the meaning of prayer and other religious practices in our lives. For others, it may come from the introspective journey of the psychotherapeutic process. And for still others, it may simply be a mindfulness of what matters to us and why, and the commitment to make those things the center of our lives.

This need to focus our already overtaxed energies on the spiritual side of life may strike some as yet another demand. The time spent in mediation, reflection, or spiritual pursuits, however, is an emotionally rich investment, returning far more in terms of well-being than the effort we invest. "Attending a religious service," as Chaplain Denton-Borhaug said, "is one of the few times that we as professionals don't have to produce anything. We are not being judged on our performance. It's a great relief and a wonderful opportunity to relax and reflect."

Open Perspective
"If possible, enjoy as you go along—see the other side of the picture—don't get set in your thinking or ways." That's the advice offered to professional women by a woman who had "been there and done that." She had worked in retail for 12 years prior to starting her family of four children, the first of whom she "adopted at 6 weeks of age after 9 years of marriage. She then had another child, and finally twins all within 3½ years." She continued to work as a CPA while raising her young family, and being additionally available for "assisting her husband and parents, and taking care of everything on the home front."

The quintessential superwoman of the new millennium! Except for one thing—this superwoman graduated from the Stanford Business School during the 1930s. Now "79+" by her own description, this dedicated woman not only took the time to fill out the relevant parts of our questionnaire but even enclosed a letter written in her beautiful prewar script. It read:

> Being a woman in business—MBA, 193_—till flood of children in 1950—very different than picture today.
>
> Had worked in merchandising during vacations from 193_ to 193_. Was paid $114 a month. Went to Bis School so I could get a job other than merchandising. After graduating with my MBA, school didn't come up with anything except as an assistant copy editor at $60 month. Couldn't live on that, and I was on my own. Went back into retail. The company I worked for developed no loyalty—everyone had to be replaceable within 24 hours.
>
> After 2½ years I married a classmate. During the war years I worked for a company dispatching troops, securing businesses, scheduling, etc. Realized as a woman I had great advantage. Military people could always find me and they liked the wit and energy I employed in that industry.
>
> Since 1946, served on non-profit boards. Often a battle to get good business practices instilled. Difficult to observe untruths and social games played.
>
> I admire the Public Management classes at the Bis School. Sorely needed and timely with private funding coming into the void of available funds for community projects.
>
> Sorry I couldn't fill in more of the blanks. We've always saved 10 percent—so, the accounts have forged ahead. We are a good team on fiscal policy, so our retirement has been with travel and pleasure.
>
> Sincerely,
>
> ———

How's that for a postmodern heroine? The point of including this letter is to underscore the fact that there is a wealth of information, expertise, and just plain inspiration out there for those of us striving to make things happen for ourselves and our families. In fact, a principle motivation for undertaking the research in this book was the sense that considerable wisdom was going untapped by each of us as we went about our demanding lives in relative isolation.

Because work and family leave little time for contemplation or for the sharing of experiences, even those experiences that could save us a fair amount of time and trouble, we see life filtered through our own set of lenses. Too often, we are unaware of the distortion that that creates. We rely heavily on our own limited experience and have limited insight into how others are dealing with many of the same issues.

Our research suggests that to achieve a healthy balance in life, we must adopt an open perspective. Most simply this means recognizing that life does not begin and end with the present, that taking a look at the larger picture is essential to accomplishing our goals. We must learn from those who have gone before us, regardless of how different lives or times may have been, and we must add to the collective wisdom with that of our own. As one of our 1970s Pioneers advised:

> Most women who have worked for 20 years have learned that careers are not enough to get them personal satisfaction. Be prepared for several chapters in life . . . only one of which is total dedication to career.

Another woman, this time one of our 1990s Successors, offered a similar perspective:

> Choosing between career success and having a family is a balance issue that takes planning and some luck. The career game is a long one. The average woman professional has about 13 years to start a family and 38 years to have a career. For me, being a mom is the most important thing I'll ever do. A job or company would never love me back.

Finally, one 1980s Settler put her decision process in very clear perspective:

> I went for family with no regrets. If you want a family, have it. Your boss won't be there for you in old age (he'll be dead). For

me, it's been a much more rewarding way to make an impact on the world.

Whatever choice we make regarding career and family, we can anticipate that we may feel differently about our priorities at different points in our lives. For some of us, sequencing family and career priorities is a way of acknowledging and responding to the changing priorities at different points in our lives. Although the ability to sequence priorities may not be the available or optimal strategy for all working mothers, knowing that we do not have to do everything at once and that we can and do shift priorities during the course of a lifetime is an important part of maintaining an open perspective.

Whatever route we chose, it is clear that adopting a philosophy that allows one to fully invest in the present while appreciating the larger context of our lives is important to finding the balance we seek. Worrying (as opposed to doing something) about the future does precious little to change its course, and it robs us of the opportunity to revel in what we currently have. Keeping an open perspective allows us to capitalize on the changes that will occur during the course of our lifetime and, as one Pioneer wrote, "lets us live our life as a play with many acts."

Good Genes—and the Sense to Take Care of Them

Fifth on our list of essentials is the issue of our health and well-being. WORK THOSE GENES exhorts the logo emblazoned on the back of a jacket belonging to employees of one biotech firm. And indeed, working those genes is just what we as women and professionals are all about.

As a whole, we have been blessed with good genes that have enabled us to accomplish all the things that we have. This blessing is not to be ignored. Good health, energy, intelligence, and even an optimistic frame of mind are, to a large extent, a by-product of our genetic makeup. We got lucky in the Darwin pool—and if we made it this far, we did indeed get lucky—we got a pretty good set of genes. So recognizing our good fortune and doing whatever we can to ensure its continuation is an important piece of finding balance in our lives.

We all know what that means. In fact, is there a professional woman alive who doesn't know that exercise and healthy eating is good for us? And judging by the responses of the women in our sample, it is clear that many of us make a priority of exercise as a major stress reducer in our lives. But, just like so many other things that we have on our long list of priorities, exercise, healthy eating, and lots of rest can get lost in the morass of the "woulda, coulda, shouldas" that litter the landscape of our good intentions.

In fact, several of our Stanford women indicated that the ability to "get by on little (occasionally no) sleep" was a critical element in their being able to balance the competing demands of their very full lives. And not surprisingly, more than a few new mothers indicated that their greatest joy in life was getting a full night's sleep.

Even in California, the state where exercise mania was invented, not everyone finds the time and energy in what's "good for you." I recall a group I ran for faculty with children several years ago where the most consistent form of exercise among the female members was determined to be "just breathing"—and not in some exotic yoga way.

Making the time to take care of ourselves is something we too often put at the bottom of our proverbial lists, only to have it carried over to another day. We all know that in ignoring our own health and exercise needs, we are working against our good genes, but the hectic pace of our lives makes it difficult to make ourselves a priority. The question for us is not *whether* we should eat right and exercise—that's a no-brainer; the question for hardworking professionals is *how* to make those things happen in our lives. And for that there is no simple answer.

With respect to exercise, the best strategy seems to be to find something you like doing and if possible, find someone to do it with—a trainer, a friend, a family member. As one of my patients remarked, "It's a lot easier for me to live up to my commitments to others than it is to keep a promise to myself when other needs get in the way."

With respect to food, in addition to all the complicated psychological and physiological variables at play, for professional women the sheer demands on our time often result in abysmal eating practices. Too many of us spend our lunch hours chained to our desks, eating whatever is at hand. And I trust there is no one among us who has not been too exhausted to cook, has not eaten one too many take-out meals, or has not spent a disproportionate amount of time doing dashboard dining. Time is our enemy when it comes to food, and whatever we can do to improve the quality of our eating is obviously time well spent.

Taking care of the self, however, encompasses lots of things beyond exercise and eating alone. *Doing things that are good for us psychologically can include a whole range of other activities—art, music, hobbies, volunteering, spiritual activities, and so on.*

One interesting, but not unexpected, finding from our Stanford study is the fact that as women, our commitment to volunteer work appears to have diminished over time, with fewer younger professionals finding time for that kind of involvement. Although this is not at all surprising, it does speak to the loss of an opportunity that can be both rewarding and regenerative in our lives. Several of my patients have reported that volunteer day projects are one way of being involved without overcommitting one's limited time.

Any working mother with young children would be, of course, clearly justified in her outrage at the thought of adding yet another commitment to her life. Cognizant of that fact, I do recommend, however, that we give ourselves what I call "spa days" every once in a while. Of course, going to a real spa is not in any way an essential part of spa days, unless that is what you happen to like to do.

Rather, what I am suggesting is taking a day, an afternoon, even a lunch hour on a *consistent* basis to do whatever we love to do. Go to a concert, take a walk, shop, volunteer, have a nice meal—do whatever it is that is good for our hearts and souls.

For example, on a recent business trip to the East Coast, I made a point of avoiding unnecessary interactions with anyone—no phone calls, no faxes, no pager, nothing—just quiet. (I spend a lot of my life talking to people, so for me a "spa day" is not having to talk.) On that trip, I took care of my business in the mornings and visited art museums in the afternoons, reveling in silent bliss. Being able to order dinner in and watch a movie with no intrusions was an added perk. Pretty pathetic, but for me, it was heaven. Needless to say, I could settle into my indulgent bliss only after checking in with my family and finding out that they were enjoying their own version of a spa day without Mom's incessant vigilance.

If we are to sustain the high level of energy and discipline that our professional and personal commitments demand, then we must make it a priority to do things that make us healthy *and* happy, and to do them on a regular basis. No matter how small and insignificant the things that sustain us may be, we owe it to ourselves, and to those who love us, to "make time for the occasional guilty pleasure" as one of our septuagenarian Pioneers advised.

The Right Preparation: Credentials and Capabilities

By virtue of being professionals, we have the right preparation, but what happens to our confidence about our credentials and capabilities is subject to internal and occasionally external fluctuation. Take, for example, the following:

"My brain has turned to Play-Doh. I can't imagine going to trial like this. How will I ever do a closing argument?" lamented one trial attorney who was anticipating her return to work after a three-month maternity leave. "I've got a really bad case of mommy mush brain."

Although mommy mush brain is not a clinically documented syndrome, it certainly does exist—just ask any nursing mother who tries going back to work soon after giving birth. The convergence of the recent hormonal changes and prolonged sleep deprivation can produce a wide variety of symptoms, mommy mush brain being only one of several.

For the most part, the current generation of professional women is unique in attempting all manner of work that requires extended periods of concentration and focus. While there have always been women who worked at difficult jobs, more women today engage in professional work that demands that they be on their game at all times. Although our male colleagues clearly have their off days, they do not have the potent combination of maternal hormones and sleep deprivation to deal with on the workfront.

Does this mean that we don't perform well in our jobs? No. Clinically, what I have observed is that although we may lack energy, we generally power through the most difficult tasks regardless of how we feel. But the combined stresses of sleep deprivation and hormonal change does put a strain on us—a strain that we would do well to recognize for what it is: tough and temporary. Tough, we can handle—no problem. Temporary, we sometimes forget. We need to remember that we do start to feel better once our bodies return to their earlier state (not nursing every two hours or so), and that we feel even better after a few consecutive full nights of sleep. The good news is that child rearing has no known long-term, negative effects on our IQs. Raising children may drive us crazy, but it is completely benign from the intellectual functioning perspective.

So if our intellects will survive the onslaught of parenthood, do we really need to worry about the survival of our credentials and capabilities? Not surprisingly, many of us do, especially if we seriously contemplate leaving the workforce, even for brief periods of time. This concern is very real because in certain work environments, playing catch-up can be costly, if not impossible. And there definitely are some work situations in which once you take a step off the path, you're out of the game. However, I think in our anxiety about remaining competitive in the workplace, we often neglect some important facts.

First of all, many of the women we surveyed indicated that they felt they had to give up certain options to combine their careers and home lives successfully. But most indicated that they were happy with the trade-off they had made, and many felt that having to give up certain options motivated them to find other opportunities that turned out to be actually more attractive.

Second, does anyone (male or female) really like 80 percent travel, even in business class? It gets old really fast. Cutting back on overtime and extended travel is something that most people would prefer to do, so as professional women, we may be ahead of the curve on that one.

Third, as we discussed in Chapter 6, although there may be no perfect time in one's career for having kids, most of the women we studied felt that it was important to establish credentials and skill sets early on, to be in a better bargaining position when it comes time to have children. Obviously, with respect to credentials, it is a matter of simple supply and demand—the more we have of what is needed, the better our negotiating position.

It is important to also remember that once we have a certain credential and skill set, no one can take it away from us. Even after a serious case of mommy mush brain, we still recover all our previous faculties, and as we saw from our research, we even manage to gain some wisdom and insight in the process. Of course, we may be out of touch with technology that changes in a heartbeat if we step out of the workforce, but at the pace of change today, we stand a pretty good chance of being technologically obsolete no matter what we do. The two things that don't change are our ability to learn and our determination to succeed. From the clinical perspective, past performance is the most powerful predictor of future attainment, so if we did it once, we can do it again. "A good mind, a great education, and the determination to get the job done [are] the most powerful allies in creating a successful life," as one of our Settlers reminded us.

The Right Work Situation

Find out what you like doing best and get someone to pay you for it.

—Katherine Whitehorn

By and large, this was the philosophy of the women in our Stanford survey. To them, finding or creating the right situation for oneself is an essential part of attaining a more balanced lifestyle. How did they propose we do this? Our Stanford women offered three points of very direct advice:

- **Don't outstay your welcome:** "Keep your options open—if they don't appreciate you, move on," advised one woman, an executive who had successfully practiced what she preached over the course of her career. "Pursue something you like," advised another Successor. "They can't pay you enough to be miserable."

  Obviously one can afford to be a bit more sanguine when one has a graduate degree from a place like Stanford, but regardless of how well credentialed and established we are, we often underestimate our ability to find or create the type of work situation that is right for us.

- **Negotiate hard:** One of our 1970s Pioneers recommended the following negotiating strategy:

  Learn to play hardball [italics mine]. Negotiate adamantly for whatever you want. Don't settle too easily. Even if you think it's impossible to get, ask for what you want, and you'll be pleasantly surprised at the outcome.

A 1980s Settler who took the corporate route to the executive suite described her own job history as one in which she was down-sized twice. She offered the following insight:

Each time I had to face looking for a job, I was pretty scared, but I forced myself to hold out for what I wanted, and I got more than I expected each time. If I hadn't hung tough in my demands, I would have been starting from a much lower point each time I had to look for work.

- **Network ruthlessly:** Although the whole idea of networking has acquired an unfortunate association with work-obsessed cell phone addicts, networking is a concept of significant merit, particularly for women. As one Settler discovered:

  You can learn an extraordinary amount just by knowing the right people—and you never know where you're going to meet them. People love to share war stories, and *once you have a network in place, it's amazing what you can turn up* [italics mine].

Primate research has shown that the female of the species tends to be quite adept at maintaining kinship networks. If we can loosely extrapolate from that research and add our own findings—that as professional women we like to talk—then we can loosely derive that networking is something that should and often does come quite naturally to us.

It is important to remember how vital a good network is to all of us. Information is power in any work setting, and among other things, a good network at the very least can help us identify desirable work or business opportunities.

Perhaps more important, a good network can also provide the inside scoop on any situation we may be considering. "Is the environment as supportive as the headhunter would like us to believe?" "What's X really like to work for?" And so on. Given all the other considerations that go into our decisions about work, such information can be invaluable in helping us determine our best options.

Too often, the benefits that accrue from networking are obscured by the blur of our overcommitted schedules. If, however, we make a more conscious effort to create relationships and stay in contact with others in our field and beyond, we may find these relationships of significant importance in helping to create balance in our lives.

Financial Resources

More than a few women in our study identified adequate financial resources as an essential to creating a more balanced life.

"One of the few times in life when having money can really buy some peace of mind is when you have young children"—or at least that is how one of my patients saw it recently. Although the young mother sharing this insight would not, by her own admission, qualify as a model of emotional tranquillity, she did have a point. In her case, she was trying to extricate herself from a very unhappy marriage. Being fully capable of supporting herself and her three children in a very comfortable lifestyle made that process a whole lot easier.

As the owner of a successful business, she was in the position of being able to afford excellent child care and household help. As her own boss, she answered to no one but the marketplace, and she had whatever flexibility she needed regarding her children's needs. She was able to arrange her schedule so she was home for dinner each evening, and she spent most weekends exclusively with her family. She had even set up a playroom in her executive suite where her children could come to play in the afternoons. She took her children and their nanny on business trips and spent very little time attending to household chores. All of this was possible because she was successful, and with her success came significant financial resources.

Of course, it would be utter foolishness to equate money with happiness, but things can be easier when family resources allow a financial buffer to ameliorate some of the stress of the workplace.

Many of the stay-at-home mothers in our Stanford survey group acknowledged how grateful they were to have husbands whose incomes allowed them to be home while their children were young. One stay-at-home mom wrote:

> I couldn't do what I'm doing now if my husband did not earn a good living. I'm thankful that he does, because it provides an opportunity I wouldn't have otherwise. We both want this for our children, and I am happy to be able to be the one at home with them.

Because staying at home with young children is obviously not an option for all working mothers, having sufficient financial resources to employ quality child care and household help is not an insignificant consideration. Having some measure of discretionary resources can also make the difference between remaining in an untenable work situation and looking for an opportunity that improves one's work life. Similarly, as in the example above, financial resources can be an important part of an exit strategy from a bad relationship. They can provide options for a working mother that might not otherwise be available.

One closing note about finances and women: *Time and again, I have been struck by how hard it is for many of us (and our employers) to assess our worth in the workplace.* Although perhaps this is so because for some of us, financial rewards are not our primary motivators, we often seem to have difficulty coming to terms with our financial worth. For example, it is not uncommon for my female residents upon graduation to express concern about charging the going rate for their services. They often indicate that they do not feel they know enough to command the fees charged in private practice. This may be a genuine (but is often an inaccurate and overly modest) assessment of their skill set on leaving their residency program; however, I have never had a male resident express a similar reservation. One could posit that perhaps this problem is unique to women in the helping professions, but our research suggests otherwise.

When we asked our Stanford women to identify the rewards of work that were most important to them, financial remuneration was not high on their list; in fact, it was near the bottom, with power and authority. Instead, respect, recognition, autonomy, and flexibility were far more valued attributes among the women we studied.

Many indicated, however, that despite the fact that money was not of central importance to them, too little money could certainly make life difficult. In thinking about balance issues, then, it is important to not underestimate the benign effect that a financial buffer can have in helping us to attain some measure of balance in our lives.

Courage

Ninth on our list of essentials is a concept that could best be identified as courage. By way of example:

> After owning this restaurant for a year, I'm having the first scary cash flow crunch. My AmEx card just got suspended! But even with all this happening, it's still less stressful for me than corporate life. I love owning this restaurant. I could write pages on why it's perfect for me at this point in my life. Money is a scramble at this point, but loving what one does is how I measure success. I am exceedingly grateful for the experience I've had along the way and where I've landed.

For this 1980s Settler, courage meant being able to exit corporate America in favor of following her dream to open her own business.

For other women in our sample, courage took many forms. Some, like the Pioneers who applied to business school in the 1920s and 1930s, courage meant taking jobs that were unheard of for their generation of women. For them, courage was a willingness to defy tradition and accept challenges never before undertaken by women.

For others, courage meant being tougher than came naturally. Several women recounted the indignity of being called "a bitch" when they stood up for what was right. And others, like one 1980s Settler, recalled the difficulty of "fighting back tears in tough negotiations" but never backing down. Others had the courage to accept defeat with grace and keep a positive attitude despite the trauma of divorce, job loss, financial adversity, or personal tragedies.

For most of us, courage comes in both small and large packages. It can be the courage to speak up at work when it might be easier to avoid an issue and let someone else take the hit. Or might be the courage to try to do what others won't even attempt—only to fail but keep right on trying.

As professional women, each of us had to face some formidable challenges to get to where we are today. Because there were so few women ahead of us, we could not rely on what had come before but rather had to create our own opportunities for growth and change. As mothers and professionals, we have sought to redefine work, and we have clearly paid a price for that effort. By and large, it has been our willingness to accept such challenges and to persevere in the face of adversity that has enabled us to succeed in life. It is our courage that enables us to make the extra effort, to set our own course, and to live with the consequences of the paths that we have chosen.

Luck

> Luck is what you have left over after you've given 100 percent.
> —Langston Coleman

When all is said and done, the final outcome of any situation involves some measure of that illusive quality called luck. Why and how it happens, and who luck chooses to smile on, is anyone's guess. It is part of the great unknown that some people attribute to the work of a higher power and others view as the randomness of the universe.

I have included luck here in the list of essentials for professional women with children for two reasons: first, because so many of the women in our study referred to luck as a partial explanation for their success in balancing their lives, and second, because luck serves as a reminder that there are some things that we simply cannot control.

As women, and as professionals, we tend to be fairly compulsive about life. We tend to prepare and overprepare for the things that are important to us, and we dedicate a lot of energy to ensuring a positive outcome. Because we are used to succeeding in the things we do, we tend to believe that we make our own luck. When things do not go according to plan, we blame ourselves.

Even though it may be true that some part of luck is really the result of hard work and determination, it is equally important to remember that *despite our best efforts, despite all of our diligence, we cannot control everything that happens in life. The only thing we can control is how we respond to the challenges that life lays out for us.*

Summing It Up

Just as we found in our earlier discussion of partners and personality positives, none of us is going to score a perfect 10 on the essentials for a balanced life. As writer Josh Billings reminds us "Life consists not in holding good cards but in playing those you do hold well." We can only do the best we can with what we have at any given moment. In fact, on the issue of balancing our personal and professional lives, we must consider that a truly balanced life may be an elusive, and perhaps even unattainable, concept. Life is always a work in progress, and as such, perfect balance is not a realistic goal. What we can hope for instead is a good approximation of the kind of life we want for our families and ourselves. As professionals and mothers we can and must focus our considerable energies on what matters most to us, recognizing that the importance of some issues may change over the course of our lives, while others, like our families and loved ones, will remain at the core.

◆　◆　◆

ACTION PLAN: ASSESSING THE ESSENTIALS

The Assessing the Essentials Worksheet is designed to stimulate thought and reflection on ways of claiming the balance we want in our lives.

ASSESSING THE ESSENTIALS WORKSHEET

	What I Have Little　　Much	What Change Is Needed?/ What Do I Need to Do?
1. **Love and support**	1 . . . 5 . . . 10	_____
		_____

	What I Have Little Much	What Change Is Needed?/ What Do I Need to Do?
		_____
		_____
		_____
2. Determination/drive	1...5...10	_____
		_____
		_____
		_____
		_____
3. Spirituality	1...5...10	_____
		_____
		_____
		_____
4. Open perspective	1...5...10	_____
		_____
		_____
		_____
5. Good genes/good sense	1...5...10	_____
		_____
		_____
		_____
		_____
6. Right preparation	1...5...10	_____
		_____
		_____
		_____
7. Right work situation	1...5...10	_____
		_____
		_____

	What I Have Little Much	What Change Is Needed?/ What Do I Need to Do?
		_____ _____
8. Financial resources	1 ... 5 ... 10	_____ _____ _____ _____ _____
9. Courage	1 ... 5 ... 10	_____ _____ _____ _____ _____
10. Luck	1 ... 5 ... 10	_____ _____ _____ _____ _____

CHAPTER 12

Balancing the Equation

EXPERIENCE: PUTTING IT ALL TOGETHER

The young woman sitting in front of me, casually dressed in an olive polo shirt and khaki shorts, smiled broadly as she recounted her experiences of the past year. She was relaxed and joked about the fact that although she had changed quite a bit since our last appointment, my office was exactly the same, except for the plant that I had managed to drown in the interim. The intervening time had been good for her, and for the first time since I had known her, she actually seemed happy.

REBECCA'S STORY

You may remember this young woman. Rebecca was the woman we met at the very beginning of this book. She had come to my office in crisis, despairing at ever regaining a sense of control over the chaos of her life. She had three young children, a caring but often absent husband, and a highly demanding job. Judging from her current appearance, a lot had changed for her since her last visit.

Our work together, although brief and crisis-oriented, had led to her concluding that having extended family around while one was trying to accomplish great things was important. In her case, that meant considering a move back east. After much soul searching, deliberation, and negotiation with both her husband and her employer, she decided to relocate. From what she described, the move had paid off.

"I negotiated a lateral transfer to our New York office, and while the content of my work changed somewhat, I didn't lose any seniority, and I managed to acquire work with a less demanding travel schedule." Rebecca reported. "Not coincidentally, our office is located in a suburb not far from my parents' home, so I now have willing grandparents to provide back up baby-sitting and emergency support. That's something I never had on the West Coast."

With her commute time cut in half and the guilt of not being around for some of her children's activities mitigated by the availability of an ever-present grandparent, Rebecca was feeling more relaxed in handling her significant work responsibilities. Although her situation with her husband, who had always been supportive, if unavailable because of his own work commitments, had not changed much—he went from working at a start-up on the West Coast to one on the East Coast with the same excessive time demands—Rebecca reported that he, too, was much happier on the East Coast. He enjoyed being closer to family and friends, and was pleased to "have his wife back," as Rebecca described it.

Clearly, not all was perfect. A snapshot summary of Rebecca's experience runs the risk of contributing to the "happily ever after" myth. Getting to a place where Rebecca found some semblance of balance in her life, or rather, as she described it, "Some light at the end of the tunnel that didn't happen to be an oncoming train" had been hard. Both Rebecca and her husband had had to make trade-offs and difficult decisions—decisions that at the time did not leave them feeling all that secure. "Would I find meaningful work back east, or would I be doing irrevocable harm to my career? Jim's career was an even bigger concern. He wasn't just transferring to another office, he was starting from scratch and saying good-bye to a big investment in sweat equity.

"There were discussions, heated discussions, arguments, and all-out shouting matches as we tried to resolve the situation that we were in. The thing that kept us focused on finding a solution was the extent to which we were both miserable in the life we were leading. Therapy was a big help because it encouraged us to slog through the issues and not just throw up our hands."

There are still days when Rebecca describes "pulling her hair out" because of some crisis at work, an unanticipated problem with the children, or the interminable quest to make order out of chaos on both fronts. The difference now was that these "impending disasters" were not the norm. They were things that needed to be worked around, and the needed supports were in place. Rebecca and her husband could accommodate the unexpected because there were people and services they could rely on.

Even though money was a touchy subject between them, given that Jim's earnings were seriously reduced in his new position, both agreed to invest more money up front on daily cleaning and household help. "I love it and I don't know how I ever managed before. It was crazy. It was a short-term economy that nearly destroyed our marriage," Rebecca said.

Rebecca and Jim are still working through the issues that brought them into therapy in the first place, but for the most part, they are on their way. Their story brings to mind the question of just what it takes to make things work for professionals with children. For this couple, balancing the equation meant securing desperately needed external support and making some difficult decisions in the process. For other couples, the needs may be different. In fact, Rebecca and Jim's experience suggests the variety of solutions that need to be considered when attempting to put it all together. In this our final chapter, we will focus on how the necessary resources, both external and personal, fit together to balance the work/life equation.

◆　◆　◆

LESSONS LEARNED

Balancing the Work–Life Equation Means Finding the Right Pieces of the Puzzle

From our research we have identified certain essential resources that must be in place for some measure of personal and professional balance to exist. These essential resources can be grouped into four categories:

- Work resources
- Family resources
- Support resources
- Personal resources

Before defining each of these four categories, let's get an overview of how the balance equation works.

Doing the Math

Our research suggests that trying to achieve personal and professional balance in our lives as professional women requires some approximation of the following formula:

THE BALANCE EQUATION
Work Resources + Family Resources + Support Resources + Personal Resources = Balance Score

Of course, not all things that affect how we experience our lives both personally and professionally can be entered neatly into a formula such as this one. The equation suggested here is designed to serve as a model for understanding what is not working in our lives and to help us to identify what we must do differently to accomplish our goal of a more balanced life.

As we shall see in the Action Plan exercise that follows, the outcome of the Balance Equation depends on the resources that exist within each of the four categories outlined above. To do the math, simply assess the adequacy of your work, family, support, and personal resources according to the guidelines outlined below and plug the results into the Balance Equation.

Most of us know, without the assistance of an equation, when our life is not in balance, but this particular model is helpful in identifying the following:

- Why our life feels the way it does
- What areas are out of kilter in our lives
- What changes need to occur for a more balanced perspective to exist

How this formula operates will be clearer once we have a chance to understand the resources needed for the equation to work. Included in the Action Plan section of this chapter is a Balancing the Equation Worksheet that will allow you to use this equation to identify areas of imbalance in your life and to formulate strategies for addressing those concerns.

Let's begin by looking at the four categories of resources that enter into the Balance Equation.

The Balance Equation Consists of Four Categories of Resources

As you will recall, the four categories of resources identified by our research as critical to achieving a sense of balance between personal life and professional life were work resources, family resources, support resources, and personal resources.

Here's how each resource category is defined:

Work Resources

Work resources include the positive aspects of one's work that contribute to a sense of personal and professional balance—essentially the extent to which one's work is consonant with having a healthy family life.

Work traits like autonomy and flexibility would weigh significantly in the positive balance direction, as would having a boss or coworkers who are working parents themselves, or at least cognizant of and empathetic to the vicissitudes of life for working parents. Having a job that does not require extensive travel and/or excessive hours, as well as work that does not typically extend into nonwork hours (evenings and weekends) would also be viewed as a positive work resource in our model.

To get a sense of how work resources enter the equation, let's look at the situation of Ellen, an attorney who worked as an employment law specialist for a prominent law firm.

ELLEN'S STORY

Ellen was one of the rising stars at her law firm. She had graduated from a top law school, had been recruited heavily by law firms on both coasts, and had chosen to stay in the San Francisco Bay Area to be near her family. On the basis of her keen intellect, engaging personality, and outstanding performance during her time with the firm, Ellen was clearly labeled "partner material."

Ellen was married to a successful physician, and shortly after the start of her fifth year as a law associate, Ellen became pregnant with their first child. Although delighted to be pregnant, Ellen worried about how the pregnancy would affect her career. Ellen took heart from the fact that there were several female partners at the firm who had children, and she hoped that somehow it would work out.

What Ellen never anticipated was the extent to which her husband was not on board for the changes that were taking place in their lives.

Their marriage had been "difficult" at times, but Ellen was stunned by her husband's decision to leave her during the sixth month of her pregnancy. It had never occurred to Ellen that her husband was capable of such emotional cruelty. He left her for another woman, because he couldn't tolerate "the neglect and indifference she had shown him during their marriage," a neglect that he perceived "would only get worse once the baby arrived." Ellen was astounded by his complaint, and even more so by his actions, but she struggled to soldier on.

Ellen relied on family support, particularly her parents, to see her through this difficult time. She stayed at their home during the latter part of her pregnancy and gave birth by cesarean section to a beautiful and healthy baby girl. Ellen's delight in her child eased her pain over her errant, soon-to-be-ex-husband, who was vacationing in Europe during the birth of their first child.

Tragically for Ellen, her husband's callousness was only the start of a series of misfortunes. Within three months of her daughter's birth, Ellen's father suffered a fatal heart attack. Ellen's mother, who had been an enormous help to Ellen throughout her life, was overwhelmed at the loss of her husband and withdrew into a serious depression. Her mother's emotional state not only left Ellen bereft of family support but added to the significant emotional losses Ellen herself had sustained in a very short time.

Throughout this ordeal, however, Ellen's daughter was a great joy to her, and somehow, despite all the tragedy she had endured, Ellen managed to keep her spirits up. Her younger brother and several good friends helped her emotionally and provided much needed interim support. Ellen sought and found comfort in her religious faith and steadfastly refused to give up hope that things would turn around.

During her maternity leave, Ellen employed a full-time nanny and weekly household help in preparation for her return to her law firm. Once she got there, however, Ellen discovered that unpredictability on both the home and the work fronts wreaked havoc with her carefully planned return to work. Unanticipated client meetings, unscheduled deadlines, last-minute travel, and so on, all created tensions with her nanny, who resented the expanding scope of her responsibilities.

Ellen's law firm was notorious for its demanding pace. Her immediate boss, although sympathetic to Ellen's losses, subscribed to a variant of the "you had the child—you figure it out" school of management. Ellen tried valiantly to keep everyone happy but found herself coming up short on all fronts. After several child-care and child health-related crises necessitated Ellen's absence from work, the partners at her firm let her know in no uncertain terms that her unavailability on-site for meetings was unacceptable, regardless of the fact that her work product had been consistently excellent.

Going to work with "a buzz in my head" from significant sleep deprivation left Ellen "grouchy, exhausted, and completely unenthusiastic about work." She often felt like she was a zombie going through the motions and unable to be really present in anything she did. She worried that she, too, would become depressed like her mother, and she sought counseling to avert that possibility.

Even though money was not an overriding concern, as her now ex-husband was required to provide some child support, Ellen worried about losing her job. She was uncertain as to what other job options existed, and she desperately did not want to lose her hard-earned position at a top-flight law firm.

For Ellen, the demands of being a single parent, coupled with the expectations of her highly demanding career, were conspiring to undo much of her previous successes. The equilibrium she hoped to establish between her personal and professional life had failed to materialize.

Enter a friend, in this case quite unexpectedly, and not a moment too soon. After a particularly arduous stretch of work, Ellen received a call from a friend who had previously worked with her at her firm. He called to sound her out about the possibility of her coming to work as an in-house attorney for a local university. Several attorneys, all of whom had previously worked at elite law firms, and all of whom had quit those firms to establish some balance in their lives, were already on board. They were looking for an employment law specialist.

"Balance—he actually said balance," Ellen exclaimed in a session we had shortly after his phone call. She couldn't believe this fellow, whom she deeply admired, had actually had the guts to quit his job to "find balance in his life." She said, "If he can do it, maybe I can, too."

Ellen pursued discussions with the university's general counsel, who was pleased to consider her for a position on his staff. Accepting the university's offer would mean a clear compromise in Ellen's earning potential, and her detour off the partnership track would foreclose certain career options in the future. But these difficulties were more than offset by the positive advantages of university employment: regular and manageable working hours, supportive coworkers who had "been there and done that," and an atmosphere of collegial congeniality.

After much soul searching, Ellen decided to leave the security of her prestigious white-shoe law firm for the less tony waters of an in-house position. She traded the social and economic perks of a major law firm for the benefits of a less pressured environment, one in which "people leave work at a decent hour, where they cover for each other when a crisis erupts, and no one thinks of children as liability to be worked around." Additionally, Ellen would get to do challenging work with bright and interesting peers—people who, by Ellen's description, seemed to care about their work as "a part of their life, not as a substitute for one."

For Ellen, making the hard call and choosing an alternative, uncharted path worked out really well. Having positive resources from her work—a job that was viable in its scope and coworkers and managers who respected her needs as a single mother—allowed Ellen to find the right balance between the competing demands in her life.

Family Resources
Like positive work resources, positive family resources form an integral part of the Balance Equation. From the balance perspective, positive family resources would include:

- Fewer children
- Fewer young children
- Fewer special needs for the children in the family

The equation posited above reflects the fact that if a professional woman has many children or young children, and/or children with special needs, these circumstances add to the overall stress on the system. Under those conditions, one has to compensate with additional resources from other areas in one's life to reach some semblance of personal–professional balance. To understand how family resources fit in the Balance Equation, let's look at the example of a patient of mine, the CEO of a small but highly successful Internet firm in Silicon Valley.

JEN'S STORY
Although highly successful in a fast-paced field, Jen was also a very devoted mother of two school children, a 10-year-old son and an 8-year-old daughter. The demands of Jen's career placed her in the upper limits of hours devoted to work. On average, she spent upward of 70 hours a week working but managed to eat dinner with her family most days and spend time with her children before bedtime. She employed a full complement of very good help at home and managed the competing demands of work and family quite well.

Jen had things under control until her children reached school age and each began to demonstrate special educational needs. Her son was identified as a highly gifted child who was clearly bored with his schoolwork and whose intellectual talents far outstripped the resources of the local public school. He clearly needed more challenge in his schoolwork if he was to avoid becoming a behavior problem in the classroom.

At the other end of the spectrum, Jen's daughter was diagnosed with relatively severe learning disabilities that necessitated more individualized therapeutic attention than she had been receiving. A bright child in her own right, Jen's daughter additionally struggled with self-image problems that stemmed from her awareness of her brother's gifts and her own challenges.

Each child required immediate educational and emotional intervention. After innumerable visits to speech pathologists, educational specialists, and child psychologists, appropriate school settings for each child were identified. That accomplished, there began endless rounds of interviews with administrators and teachers, followed by nightly family discussions. After much discussion, new and more labor-intensive plans for each child were hammered out.

Adding these demands to the schedule of a highly leveraged businesswoman with a husband whose work demands rivaled her own meant something had to give. In this case, Jen came to the conclusion that the needs of her children were more immediately pressing than those of her career. Both she and her husband decided that it was her turn to step off the career path for a bit. Contrary to what is the case for most couples, he had made similar sacrifices in the past for the sake of her business. By their reckoning, it was his turn to amp up his career and taking time out at this point would be very disadvantageous to him. Additionally, Jen felt she really welcomed the opportunity to be home for a while and wanted to be more involved in the day-to-day life of her family.

Jen negotiated a year-long "sabbatical" for herself. During that time, the COO took over many of her day-to-day responsibilities. Jen was available for consultation on the more dynamic issues facing her company but left the details to the COO. What this translated into was that Jen was "on sabbatical" for nonemergencies but put in about 4 to 6 hours a day on pressing business. Although nearly a full day for many employees, a 6-hour workday was truly part time for Jen. The board of her company, while reserving the right to reconsider, accepted this arrangement because they knew that she was the best at what she did and that they would rather have her part time than not at all.

It was far from easy for Jen to wean herself from her involvement in all aspects of her company's business. She often caught herself agreeing to attend meetings she could, and should, avoid if she were to work "part time." And even with her more limited involvement with work, she often found herself bereft of "breathing space" in her busy days. She, like so many professional women, managed to fill the time available with activities. In Jen's case, she became the coach of her daughter's soccer team and chaired the parents' association at her son's school.

For Jen, having children with special needs meant that the family resources were taxed at the very same time that work demands were their highest. For her, balancing the equation meant replenishing family resources by dedicating more of herself to family needs for a period of time. Had she and her husband decided otherwise, he might have been the one to dedicate more personal resources to family needs. In the greater scheme of things, it probably was unimportant who balanced out the depleted family resources, just as long as the needed resources materialized.

Support Resources

A third component of the Balance Equation is that of support resources. Under this category would fall such features as:

- Supportive (available) partner
- Supportive (available) extended family
- Supportive (available) friends
- Adequate household help
- Good and sufficient child care
- Adequate financial resources

Even though one might alternatively consider the presence or absence of a supportive partner or extended family as family resources, support resources actually reflect the extent to which a professional woman has it within her power to call on others to assist her in her attempts to achieve balance in her life.

It is important to note that support resources are defined broadly to mean not just psychological support but also *actual support*—the availability to help out. Psychological support is tremendously important in creating a sense of balance in life, but psychological support without actual physical availability does little to directly address balance issues. As was often the case among the married professional couples in our research, if a woman with young children did not have a partner who could be present to provide the necessary backup in terms of child care and/or household responsibilities, serious family and personal distress might emerge. In those instances, the presence of an extended family member, a competent and willing friend, or child-care provider could compensate for the absent partner, allowing for some measure of balance.

Similarly, the presence of adequate financial resources allows working parents to purchase services that could provide the support needed to promote the well-being of the family. Obviously, throwing money at the problem is not the answer; however, what I am suggesting is that some measure of financial security can, and often does, provide the support so needed by working parents—quality child care, adequate household help, and so forth. Such necessary support would not be possible if financial resources did not exist.

Take, for example, the situation of another patient, Lisa, a clinical psychologist and the married mother of one young daughter, with another child on the way.

LISA AND GREG'S STORY

One of the most persistent features of Lisa's life was her long-standing commitment to public service. Coming from a relatively affluent background, Lisa decided early on that her life's work would be devoted to caring for others less fortunate than herself. As a psychology major in college, Lisa's dream had been to dedicate her abundant energies to the area of social welfare.

Shortly after graduating from college, Lisa applied for and was accepted into a prestigious East Coast program in clinical psychology. On completing her degree, Lisa returned to the West Coast for an internship and shortly afterward accepted a position as a psychologist in a community mental health clinic. Lisa loved her work but soon discovered the significant stresses involved in the long hours and low pay typical of a community mental health practice. Despite this concern, Lisa enjoyed the challenge of her work and the camaraderie of a dedicated group of people.

During her internship, Lisa met and subsequently married a young physician, Greg. He was a psychiatrist who also worked in community mental health, specializing in violence prevention. Her husband's expertise kept him in great demand on public commissions and policy boards. Both Lisa and her husband worked long hours—often with weekend call—but both were quite satisfied with their highly engaging careers.

Three years after their marriage, Lisa and Greg had their first child, a daughter. Although the maternity benefits provided by the county health system were generous—up to one year off with half pay—the addition of an infant to their highly leveraged work–home equation tipped the balance for Lisa and Greg.

Having a child meant serious changes for both of them. Given that they both worked somewhat erratic hours, they needed full-time child care and then some. Because a nanny who kept very specific hours would not work with their schedules, a live-in nanny had definite appeal. Additionally, live-in help was a lot cheaper than an hourly worker. Such help, however, required that they turn over one of their two bedrooms to the nanny, a move that left them both bereft of an office. Neither of them was pleased with the prospect of adding another person to the household. They needed more room, but their public-sector incomes did not permit such expansion.

To further complicate matters, in the wake of increased attention to issues of violence, Greg's work began to take on national prominence. Now he was not just sought out by local agencies but was also summoned to Washington, D.C. to share his expertise with national authorities on the subject. His frequent absence from the home at the time when Lisa was returning to her job made their situation even more difficult.

When the nanny who had helped raise their daughter quit abruptly in the middle of her second year of employment, the situation deteriorated to one of desperation. Previously, Lisa and her husband had enjoyed a relatively happy and noncontentious marriage, but they soon found themselves constantly arguing.

"We waste more energy—energy we don't have—arguing over the stupidest stuff," Lisa complained when she came to see me. "Who did the dishes more, who picked up Stephie last . . . dumb stuff like that. We're into a total martyr thing." Each resented the other's inability to truly provide support for their difficult and demanding schedules. Additionally, although Lisa and Greg loved their daughter and enjoyed being parents, they were both seriously troubled by the intrusive presence of a nanny in their small home. Worst of all, they found themselves in shouting matches over the slightest thing, and neither Lisa nor Greg was able to short-circuit the repetitive arguments once they got started.

With all this arguing and stress going on, one might wonder how they ever managed to conceive a second child. The answer came down to a bit of unplanned luck, along with a willingness to compromise on some hard issues. Lisa and Greg agreed that they wanted to have a second child within Lisa's "biological window," which they realized was closing rapidly. Knowing that they had to act quickly or risk not being able to conceive, the question of what to do about their situation was of immediate concern to them. To address that question, both had to be willing to make significant compromises. Lisa decided to use some money she had in trust to employ more adequate help. Even though Lisa was strenuously opposed to using family money that she had earmarked for the children's education, she realized the necessity of drawing on financial resources to address the current problem.

The sticking point for them as a couple, however, was the fact that they both loved their work and both felt unwilling to leave behind their current careers in favor of more financially lucrative alternatives. Greg could have easily decided to join a forensic practice, which would pay well and demand far less of his time and energy, but he was very reluctant to do so. Similarly, although open to exploring other possibilities, Lisa was reluctant to be the one who "caved" on this issue.

Both agreed, however, that having a second child was the most important issue, and they decided to go ahead and try to conceive. As luck would have it, Lisa and Greg got pregnant on their first attempt, and they are ecstatic at the prospect of welcoming their second child. Both Lisa and Greg are realistic enough to know that agreeing to the kinds of compromises that they will each need to make will be difficult. Giving up work that one loves is easier said than done, and old resentment often flares when time and energy are short. As a couple, however, they feel confident that their happiness at the newest addition to their family will guide them well in the decisions that will inevitably follow.

Personal Resources

Within the category of personal resources fall particular characteristics of personality that, from our research, appear to be instrumental in helping professional women achieve some measure of balance in their personal and professional lives. Obviously, these characteristics by themselves offer no solutions, because some, like drive and determination, can clearly lead to overcommitment and imbalance in life. The personal characteristics that helped on this issue, however, were identified as the following:

- The ability to love and enjoy being a parent
- Good health, energy, and spirits
- Attention to the spiritual side of life
- Determination and a can-do spirit
- The courage to embrace innovation/resourcefulness
- A healthy perspective on life

Our findings were filled with examples of professional women who exemplify many of these attributes in the course of their daily lives. Many of the women described in this book demonstrate the kinds of personal resources essential to successfully balancing the work–home life equation. In fact, in many instances, it is the very significant personal resources that these women possess that allows them to compensate for absent resources in other areas of their lives—occasionally to their own physical and psychological detriment.

The experience of Elizabeth, one of my patients, is illustrative of how personal resources can sway the tide in a difficult situation.

ELIZABETH'S STORY

For as long as she could remember, Elizabeth had wanted to run her own business. She was the kid with the proverbial lemonade stand who learned early in life to diversify—she offered cookies and iced tea, as well as the standard lemonade. She also had an instinctive appreciation of the three basic rules of real estate—location, location, and location—so she set up her stand in front of the local soccer field during practices and games. Needless to say, her stand was a hit.

Although she majored in history in college, Elizabeth never outgrew her desire to run her own business. While working as a research analyst after college, Elizabeth ran into a high school friend who had started a small but rapidly expanding sports marketing business. This friend invited Elizabeth to join her venture. Setting aside her acceptance to business school, Elizabeth plunged into a new career in sports marketing.

Four months into this enterprise, ill health forced Elizabeth's partner to leave the business, and Elizabeth soon found herself struggling to stay ahead of the curve with the demands of her new venture. Shortly after she went solo, Elizabeth, who had married during college, became pregnant after several years of infertility. Although she was delighted to be pregnant, her marriage had been teetering on the brink of dissolution at the time. Within two months, she and her partner split up, and Elizabeth was confronting the reality of single parenthood. With no family nearby, she had to rely on a close circle of friends to provide much-needed support during her pregnancy. As fate would have it, her son was born two months premature and required extensive neonatal attention. During the long, anxious hours of not knowing how her son would respond to the invasive medical procedures needed to keep him alive, Elizabeth called on her friends to sustain her.

All of these life struggles occurred within the context of escalating business demands, which failed to take account of Elizabeth's difficult circumstances. Most others might have been tempted to relinquish control of the business at that point, but Elizabeth was determined to make it all work. Although the competing demands of a growing business and a newborn child clearly took their toll on Elizabeth's energy and normally high spirits, she managed to soldier on despite the significant obstacles in her path.

"I wasn't fully there for the first six months of Chris's life," she recounted one day in my office. "I was exhausted all the time, and I was so worried about him. I couldn't focus on the business. I didn't have anyone to run it, and although my brother tried to help, he had his own job. Pretty soon the business started to lose ground. It went into a spiral from which it couldn't recover. It needed attention that I couldn't provide. Deciding to close the business and sell off what I could was the hardest decision I ever made. It was really sad, and I felt like a tremendous failure for doing it."

Elizabeth felt pretty depressed for some time after she sold her business. She sought counseling and worked hard at coming to terms with her loss and repairing her sense of efficacy.

"Things are better now, especially because Chris is healthy. I know I'll start a new business someday. It just wasn't the right time in my life. But still it's hard to accept that I couldn't make it all work. The most important thing is that I have my son, and he's healthy. That's all that really matters."

For Elizabeth, having the personal resources of determination, physical and psychological energy, and the courage to attempt the difficult, if not the impossible, helped to preserve her dream longer than most dreams. She has had to make some hard choices recently, and at this point her professional ambitions are on hold, but the same qualities and personal resources that served her so well in crisis will enable her to ultimately create the life she wants for her son and herself.

◆ ◆ ◆

ACTION PLAN: BALANCING THE PERSONAL–PROFESSIONAL EQUATION

The Balancing the Equation Worksheet is designed to help you identify what issues need to be addressed so you can seek a better balance in your professional and personal life. For each of the four categories of resources, simply estimate the extent to which each of the resources is present in your life: estimate whether you feel your present life has or doesn't have a specific resource. The "some(what)" category may be a good compromise at times, but too many of these "sort of" responses may obscure your results.

BALANCING THE EQUATION WORKSHEET

Instructions: Circle the answer that best reflects your circumstances.

Work Resources

Yes	Some	No	
2	1	0	Boss who is supportive of my desire to balance work and personal life
2	1	0	Coworkers who are supportive of my desire to balance my work and personal life
2	1	0	Flexible work schedule
2	1	0	Autonomy in my work
2	1	0	Manageable hours
2	1	0	Few weekends or evenings/little travel

_____ Score for Work Resources (sum of the above)

Family Resources

Yes	Some	No	
4	N/A	0	Fewer than three children
4	N/A	0	No children under 5 years old
4	N/A	0	No children with special needs

_____ Score for Family Resources (sum of the above)

Support Resources

Yes	Some	No	
2	1	0	Supportive/available partner
2	1	0	Supportive/available extended family
2	1	0	Supportive/available friends
2	1	0	Adequate household help
2	1	0	Good and adequate child care
2	1	0	Adequate financial resources

_____ Score for Support Resources (sum of the above)

Personal Resources

Yes	Some	No	
2	1	0	Love and an enjoyment of family
2	1	0	Good health, energy, and spirits
2	1	0	A spiritual compass
2	1	0	Determination/can-do spirit
2	1	0	An open perspective/ability to take the long view
2	1	0	Courage/resourcefulness

_____ Score for Personal Resources (sum of the above)

Balance Your Work–Life Equation

Insert your scores for each of the following four categories and sum:

_____ **Work Resources** + _____ **Family Resources** + _____ **Support Resources** + _____ **Personal Resources** = _____ **Balance Score**

How to Understand Your Balance Scores

Balancing Pretty Well: Balance Scores of 34 and Above
If your balance score is in the high range, it is a good bet that overall your life feels fairly well balanced. A score of 34 and above reflects the fact that you possess a fair measure of the resources needed to balance an engaged professional life with an active personal one.

If there is a sense of imbalance in your life, it may show up because of a specific deficit in certain resources. For example, you may have scored higher in personal and work resources but lower in support and family resources. It may be that your personal and work resources are compensating for the lack of resources in other areas. In this case, it would be important to focus some attention on identifying and addressing the deficits that exist in the support and family arena—for example: Do you need extra support in the form of better or more available child care or household help? Do you need to consider improving your family's financial picture? Do you need to encourage more active participation on the part of your partner in shouldering family responsibilities?

In general, lower scores in specific categories suggest places where resources might need to be shored up in order to improve, or just maintain, an overall sense of balance in your life.

Hanging in the Balance: Balance Scores Between 17 and 33
A balance score in the middle range (between 17 and 33) suggests that your personal and professional life reflects some measure of balance, albeit somewhat tenuously. How closely you approach the limits of this middle range suggests how often your work–life equation can feel in or out of kilter.

For example, if your balance score hovers around the high teens, chances are you often experience unresolved conflicts between the demands of your personal and professional life. This is particularly true during times of stress, when the resources available to address accelerating demands may be absent or inadequate.

On the other hand, if your balance score is in the high twenties or low thirties, the competing demands of your work and home life are more likely to be offset by the resources available to you. Stress here does not throw the whole system out of whack, although individual days or weeks can be disrupted by unusual circumstances, like a sick child or an absent child-care provider.

Carefully examining the individual areas in which deficits may exist will help you to identify the resources that are in need of increased attention and concern.

So That's Why I Feel Like I Do: Balance Scores Lower Than 16

If your score is 16 or lower, you do not need this worksheet to tell you that your personal–professional equation is seriously out of kilter. A score of 16 or lower indicates that the resources you have available to address concerns of balancing your work and family obligations are clearly insufficient. Deficits most probably exist in several resource categories, and it is unlikely that anyone experiencing such deficits would be content with the current state of affairs.

For the sake of your health and well-being, a systematic examination of the absent resources is in order. Although addressing these deficits may require some hard choices, they will surely be no harder than struggling along in your present state.

A Final Note

In the course of writing this book, I have often been struck by the thought that the need for a book of this sort should no longer exist. Surely by now a growing awareness and appreciation of how hard it is to do all the things we do as women, as professionals, and as mothers must have allowed us to find the right solution to making it work. Yet no sooner does that thought occur to me than I meet yet another professional woman who is seriously struggling to find the way to a healthier and more balanced life. Each woman teaches me something new about the challenges we confront and the lengths to which we go to take care of our families and ourselves.

Although the stresses in our lives may be multiple, I am continually amazed at the resources we find within ourselves for dealing with these challenges. It is important for us to remember how many women in our research struggled with the same kinds of imbalance we all have experienced at some point in our lives. It is equally important to remember that those who "have been there" declare assuredly that life gets better as time goes on: From those women came the wisdom that things get a lot easier as children get older, and that, with time, the needs of our families become more consonant with our professional aspirations.

No matter how we choose to deal with our professional lives once we have children, the fact remains that we did the hard work up front. We chose a professional avenue as a way of ensuring our future well-being, and that decision was perhaps the most important career choice that we could ever have made. Like deciding on children, it is an irrevocable key to the wealth of options that we have created for ourselves.

I am deeply convinced that we each know within our hearts what is right for ourselves and our families. Doubts may sometimes arise, but there is no better barometer of how well we are doing than what our families tell us. As one friend, a recently "retired" district attorney, said, "there's nothing like having your child brag about your accomplishments. I couldn't believe my ears when I heard my son (5) telling his friends that his mom 'put bad guys away' and that if they weren't good, he'd tell his mom."

Another friend described her teenage daughter telling her that "it was cool" to have "a mom who knew her way around the world, who could do anything—like travel and give speeches." In inimitable teenage patois, the daughter told my friend how "totally dope" it was that she had a mom whom she could talk to about things that other parents "don't have a clue about," because they'd never been out there "doing stuff."

We all live for the day when our children will let us know that it has all been worthwhile, and with a little luck, during an occasional unguarded moment, that is exactly what they will do.